PHOTOGRAPHERS ON PHOTOGRAPHY

PHOTOGRAPHERS ON PHOTOGRAPHY

A CRITICAL ANTHOLOGY EDITED BY NATHAN LYONS

PRENTICE-HALL, INC., ENGLEWOOD CLIFFS, NEW JERSEY IN COLLABORATION WITH

THE GEORGE EASTMAN HOUSE, ROCHESTER, NEW YORK

Designed by Nathan Lyons

Library of Congress Catalog Card No.: 66-22343
Printed in the United States of America—C
P-66475, C-66476
Current Printing (Last Digit):
10   9   8

PRENTICE-HALL INTERNATIONAL, INC., *London*
PRENTICE-HALL OF AUSTRALIA, PTY. LTD., *Sydney*
PRENTICE-HALL OF CANADA, LTD., *Toronto*
PRENTICE-HALL OF INDIA (PRIVATE) LTD., *New Delhi*
PRENTICE-HALL OF JAPAN, INC., *Tokyo*

This anthology has been prepared to afford a closer study of critical source material by photographers from the turn of the century to the present. Surveying approximately one hundred years of the literature of photography, it presents points of view which have contributed to the development of contemporary photographic expression.

The book is arranged alphabetically by photographer. The reader may, by consulting the Table of Contents, follow a chronological development of the material presented. Each photographer is introduced by a brief quotation which is central to his concern; beyond this introductory statement all articles are quoted in full. An index of biographical notes and a selected bibliography have been prepared on each contributor for additional reference. A short entry form has been adopted in citing the bibliographies (unless otherwise stated, place of publication is New York City).

I wish to extend my appreciation to the photographers represented for permission to reproduce copyrighted material; without their cooperation this anthology would not have been possible. And to Rosalinde Fuller for consent to publish material by Francis Bruguière; Georgia O'Keeffe and Doris Bry for permission to publish articles by Alfred Stieglitz; Dorothy Norman for release of "Four Happenings," by Alfred Stieglitz, originally published in *Twice-a-Year;* Sybil Moholy-Nagy for articles by Moholy-Nagy; Cole Weston for release of material by Edward Weston; Paul Taylor for release of material by Dorothea Lange.

To the George Eastman House and its Director, Beaumont Newhall, I wish to express my gratitude for an environment which encouraged and enabled me to complete the necessary research for this anthology. For their invaluable assistance, I wish to thank Alice Andrews and Thomas Barrow of the George Eastman House Staff and Robert Bretz, Elizabeth Kimbrough, and Maureen Sweeney for their aid in proofing the bibliographic entries.

CONTENTS

CONTENTS

For centuries man has striven to re-create and extend his concept of the world through pictures. Prior to the invention of photography, mechanical and optical devices, (camera obscura, camera lucida, pantograph, etc.) were quite often employed to heighten the illusion and reality of events portrayed on the picture plane. The development of a stable method for recording and making permanent an image of external objects by means of a lens or other image-forming devices developed as a natural extension of this concern for representation, which of necessity would produce the invention of photography. Out of a physio-chemical order, an implosion of scientific inquiry in the nineteenth century created its own biographer with an unprecedented facility for making pictures. Three factors appear to condition the early development of this new picture making medium. The first is its ability to render a picture with exceptional delineation, and the second, the authority that this kind of picture suggested to those who viewed it. Natural truth and photography became synonymous; a quality of truth that would have made the wart of Boswell's attention envious.

We enter into the twentieth century minimizing only slightly an earlier stigma of photography as an indiscriminate all-seeing eye, the myopic salvation of a machine age transforming itself into a machine art. It is here that we can begin to trace the third major development in photographic picture making. In *Technics and Civilization* (1934), Lewis Mumford observed that, "The history of the camera, and of its product, the photograph, illustrates the typical dilemmas that have arisen in the development of the machine process and its application to objects of esthetic value. Both the special feats of the machine and its possible perversions are equally manifest." The chief perversion to be cited was that of an almost total adoption of an art-consciously conceived picture statement that emulated the classical conception of nineteenth century painters.

The presence of pictorial considerations in photography can be traced from 1844. William Henry Fox Talbot in *The Pencil of Nature* suggested the "beginnings of a new art" when he included in this discussion of the practical applications of photography the photograph entitled "The Open Door," presented solely for its "picturesque" quality. In 1845, J. J. E. Mayall illustrated, in a series of ten daguerreotypes, the Lord's Prayer. Later he composed a series of six daguerreotypes in the manner of Campbell's "Soldier's Dream." This allegorical tradition develops into the mid-1860's where an established pictorial tradition is generally evident and championed by O. G. Rejlander and Henry Peach Robinson. Much of the work, however, was contrived, and sought for its justification the authority of a seeing developed from Burnet's *A Treatise on Painting*, originally a popular instructional work written for painters, but in later editions adapted for use by photographers. These classical considerations of thematic content, geometric perspective, and composition were to be attacked openly and repeatedly by P. H. Emerson, the leader of the Naturalistic School of Photography. Concerning Mr. Burnet's treatise, Emerson concluded that, "In short, the whole work is illogical, unscientific, and inartistic, and has not a leg to stand on. It is very specious to say that all compositions are made according to geometrical forms, nothing can be easier than to take arbitrary points in a picture and draw geometrical figures adjoining them."

Emerson felt that pictorial work should become more naturalistic and that the allegorical and doctrinal did not, ". . . lie within the scope of art." Naturalistic photography, to Emerson was ". . . an *impersonal* method of expression, a more or less correct reflection of nature, wherein (1) truth of sentiment, (2) illusion of truth of appearance (so far as is possible), and (3) decoration are of first and supreme importance."

A basic contradiction appears to exist in Emerson's thesis. While he felt that the photograph was a "mechanically recorded reflection of Nature" and therefore it could not be a work of art, he also stated that ". . . there is no absolute truth to Nature from the visual standpoint, for as each man's sight is different, the only absolute truth to

Nature for each man is his own view of her (though certain broad features remain true to all)." This acknowledgement of a personal point of view and yet the limitation of its significance because it was expressed by what appeared to be an "impersonal method" might indicate that ground was giving way to a psychological standpoint based on vision, but in general photography's significance was not yet clearly understood.

One aspect began to be acknowledged; the importance of the environment of pictures produced by photography was noted by the critic, Sadakichi Hartmann, in 1910, "The results of photography permeate all intellectual phases of our life. Through the illustrations of newspapers, books, magazines, business circulars, advertisements, objects that previous to Daguerre's invention were not represented pictorially have become common property."

To overcome the unfortunate confusion of its early beginnings, the photographic picture maker at the turn of the century was to find himself in a position which necessitated the rediscovery of his own medium. In attempting this the tone at times has been exceedingly defensive, but is generally underscored by a concern for this much needed clarification of identity. ". . . as the language or vocabulary of photography has been extended, the emphasis of meaning has shifted —shifted from what the world looks like to what we feel about the world and what we want the world to mean." This statement by Aaron Siskind in 1958 suggests a critical distinction which should resolve Emerson's dilemma by placing the authorship of picture on the photographer and not the machine.

The anthology traces this development of concern from 1889 to the present. The articles, many of which have been relatively inaccessible, have been selected to best represent each photographer's individual philosophy and contribution to the development of contemporary photographic expression.

N. L., 1966, Curator of Photography, The George Eastman House

BERENICE ABBOTT (1898-) *The photographer's punctilio is his recognition of the now—to see it so clearly that he looks through it to the past and senses the future. This is a big order and demands wisdom as well as understanding of one's time. Thus the photographer is the contemporary being par excellence; through his eyes the now becomes past.* THE WORLD OF ATGET, *New York, Horizon Press, 1964, p. xxvi.*

IT HAS TO WALK ALONE   1951
Infinity, Vol. 7, No. 11, pp. 6-7, 14.

The greatest influence obscuring the entire field of photography has, in my opinion, been pictorialism. But first let me define it: pictorialism means chiefly the making of pleasant, pretty, artificial pictures in the superficial spirit of certain minor painters. What is more, the imitators of these superficial qualities are not aware of the true values for which painting strives. Photography can never grow up if it imitates some other medium. It has to walk alone; it has to be itself.

If a medium is representational by nature of the realistic image formed by a lens, I see no reason why we should stand on our heads to distort that function. On the contrary, we should take hold of that very quality, make use of it, and explore it to the fullest. It is possible that the subject matter best suited to that characteristic quality be the one dictated by it.

After the early pioneer days of photography, which were very creative and healthy, a wave of rank pictorialism set in and flourished. This type of work was usually very sentimental. Its settings were staged; and the system was to flatter everything. These limitations of painting, catering to the worst Victorian standards, are familiar to most of us. The man most responsible for the whole movement was Henry Peach Robinson, an Englishman who was very successful financially and who exported the mania to this country where it was gobbled up by Americans. The word "salon" descended from Robinson, and the "salon" print is still rampant in American clubs.

But there are always two sides to the question, and perhaps there always will be. In those days there was, fortunately, another side of the picture. Men like Mathew Brady, William H. Jackson, Sullivan, Gardner, and others, were making magnificent realistic pictures of their world and of their time.

At the beginning of the century serious photographers were rightfully disdainful of Robinson and his followers. They graduated to a more refined or elevated grade; they became the fellow travelers of the more modern painters. They were interested in proving that photography was art with a capital "A," and they were quite touchy about it. Their work was spiked with mystical and subjective overtones. Terms like "equivalents," "hand of God," etc., were used to bewilder the layman. Art was by the few, for the few, and cultural America was represented by the back end of a horse to people who did not know that they were being insulted.

These photographers raised the craft, as such, to a higher technical level with their reverence for glorified technique. The United States was wedded to technology and was favorably inclined toward a technological art. In the case of Stieglitz, who was an institution within himself, and who was God to many, and to many others not at all, he did make, when he ventured outside himself, a few great pictures. In Stieglitz' time what was unquestionably an advance in pictorialism, is not an advance in 1950.

These latter-day pictorialists did not know that they were pictorialists. They were what I can only call, for lack of a better word, the advanced or super-pictorial school. The individual picture, like a painting, was the thing. Above all, the perfect print. Subjectivity predominated.

About this same period another man was working quietly unknown, unappreciated, but with a profound love of life. With concentrated energy and mature discernment, this man came to photography in the second half of his life. His name was Eugene Atget. He gave the world hundreds of great photographs. He was very busy and excited in discovering photography and what it meant. He didn't talk much; his time was spent penetrating and recording his immediate and wonderful world. His work is purely and entirely photographic, and it is still comparatively little known today.

While not of the same stature or range, another photographer on this side of the ocean showed remarkable photographic acumen in the early half of this century. I believe the true photographer is a curiously odd type of species, not easy to define, but his photographic gift is a highly charged and trained vision. This vision is focused, by the nature of the medium, on the here and now. Realist *par excellence,* inescapably contemporary, Lewis Hine had this photographic gift. He responded to the world around him, armed with a camera and his penetrating eagle-like, agile, but disciplined eye. Stieglitz and his disciples looked down their noses at Lewis Hine and fell in line with the coterie of Katherine Dreier's gallery. It was about that time (1918) that the abstractions of cracked paint began.

At the risk of over-simplification I propose that there is a third fling of pictorialism—the abstract school—the imitators of abstract painting, the photographers of the pure design, the cracked window pane, or the cracked paint. I think this represents the end.

Now they would be like the great painter Mondrian. Recently I have even seen would-be Jackson Pollocks. But instead of spattering paint at a canvas, in desperation they might yet resort to ripping the emulsion off the paper or spattering a print with hypo. Anything goes.

Why do I concern myself with these problems? Because it affects me, and other photographers, if, due to a preponderant amount of this type of work, it holds back sorely needed improvements of the instruments we need to work with. This is why I must take issue with the pictorialists. They are the ones who choose the subjects which are so easily expressed within the primitive limitations of present-day, backward equipment.

This brings me to the vast amateur field, and finally to the serious photographer. On the positive side, the amateur market presents the possibility for the development of a great democratic medium—photography by the many and for the many. It is also a potential source for the development of professional photographers. This vast potential is rich, uncultivated soil, but it can erode away if it is flooded by pictorialism. The amateurs imitate the pictorialists because this is the line of least resistance, and they delight the manufacturers with their prodigal use of film, paper, and cheap cameras. The result is a mass production type of photography, limited in subject material, hackneyed in approach.

But the serious photographer is a forgotten man. He is sorely in need of far reaching improvements in all directions and over the entire field. He is living in a dynamic time and place, working with Model T cameras and outmoded sensitive materials. Photography does not stand by itself in a vacuum; it is linked on the one side to manufacturers of materials and on the other side to the distributors of the product, that is, to publishers, editors, business leaders, museum directors, and to the public. Unless they do their share of growing up to their responsibilities the photographer can languish or take up knitting. What we need of equipment is this: let it possess as good a structure as the real-life content that surrounds us. We need more simplifications to free us for seeing. And we need editors and publishers who will try to understand photography and who will live up to their responsibility to raise the general cultural level of our country which we, who love America, believe in for its great potential. We need a creative attitude on the part of the manufacturer, the distributor, and the consumer.

I should like to give a quotation from Goethe who was discussing a poet. Said Goethe: "He was a decided talent, without doubt, but he has the general sickness of the present day—subjectivity—and of that I would fain heal him." Does not the very word "creative" mean to build, to initiate, to give out, to act—rather than to be acted upon, to be subjective? Living photography builds up, does not tear down. It proclaims the dignity of man. Living photography is positive in its approach; it sings a song of life—not death.

PHOTOGRAPHY AT THE CROSSROADS   1951
Universal Photo Almanac, pp. 42-47.

The world today has been conditioned, overwhelmingly, to visualize. The *picture* has almost replaced the *word* as a means of communication. Tabloids, educational and documentary films, popular movies, magazines, and television surround us. It almost seems that the existence of the word is threatened. The picture is one of the principal mediums of interpretation, and its importance is thus growing ever vaster.

Today the challenge to photographers is great because we are living in a momentous period. History is pushing us to the brink of a realistic age as never before. I believe there is no more creative medium than photography to recreate the living world of our time.

Photography gladly accepts the challenge because it is at home and in its element: namely, realism—real life—the *now*. In fact, the photographic medium is standing at its own crossroads of history, possibly at the end of its first major cycle. A decision as to which direction it shall take is necessary, and a new chapter in photography is being made—as indeed many new chapters are now taking the place of many older ones.

The time comes when we progress, must go forward, must grow. Else we wither, decay, die. This is as true for photography as for every other human activity in this atom age. It is more important than ever to assess and value photography in the contemporary world. To understand the *now* with which photography is essentially concerned, it is necessary to look at its roots, to measure its past achievements, to learn the lessons of its tradition. Let us briefly span its beginnings —they were truly spectacular.

The people who were interested in photography and who contributed to its childhood success were most serious and capable. In the early years of the nineteenth century, a tremendous amount of creativeness and intelligence was invested in the new invention. Enthusiasm among artists, scientists, intellectuals of all kinds, and the lay public, was at a high pitch. Because of the interest in and demand for a new picture-making medium, technical development was astonishingly rapid.

The aesthetic counterpart of such rapid growth is to be seen in photographers like Brady, Jackson, O'Sullivan, Nadar, and their contemporaries. There was such a boom in technical progress, as has not been surpassed even today. The recently published *History of Photography* by J. M. Eder, translated by Edward Epstean, documents this acceleration in detail.

America played a healthy and vital part in the rise of photography. American genius took to the new medium like the proverbial duck to water. An extremely interesting study of photography in the United States—an important book for everyone—is Robert Taft's *Photography and the American Scene*. Here the material and significant growth of the medium is integrated with the social and economic growth of our country.

In photography, America neither lagged nor slavishly imitated, and we can boast of a sound American tradition. Portraits flourished as in no other country. The Civil War created a demand for millions

of "likenesses" of the young men marching off to the front. The new-
ness of our country was of course another stimulus to growth, with
many people sending pictures of themselves to relatives left behind
in the westward movement, or to prospective brides and husbands in
the "Old Country." The migratory, restless population of the United
States flowed west, over the Alleghenies from Pennsylvania into Ohio
and other states of the Western Reserve, past the Mississippi and into
the west; and wherever they went, they left little hoards, little treasures of old photographs—invaluable archives for the historian today.
In the winning of the frontier, photographers also played their part,
going with U. S. Geologic Survey expeditions after the Civil War.
Among these, William H. Jackson stands as a shining example.

This organic use for photography produced thousands of straightforward, competent operators, whereas in England there were comparatively few; apparently because a monopoly of all patents tied
up the photographic process and prevented the spread of interest in
and use of the new invention. Here in the United States, it was
virtually impossible to make such a monopoly stick.

This ferment and enthusiasm produced fine results. Our daguerreotypes were superb. They were acclaimed all over Europe and
systematically won all the first prizes at the international exhibitions.
People were wild with enthusiasm for these realistic "speaking likenesses," and everybody was doing it. In fact, anyone could afford the
photograph, whereas before only the wealthy could pay the price to
have their portraits painted. As a result, the photographic business
flourished.

After a whole-hearted start with Yankee ingenuity, money got into
photography along with pseudo-artists; commercialism developed
with a bang. And as with any business which, as it grows, serves the
greatest common denominator, so with photography. Cash took over.
Instead of the honest, realistic likeness, artificial props with phony
settings began to be used. A period of imitating the unreal set in.
Supply houses sprang up, with elaborate Grecian urns and columns
and fancy backdrops—all for the greatest possible show and ostenta-
tion. Retouching and brush work also set in. What was thought to be
imitation or emulation of painting became rampant.

It need not be added that the imitation was of bad painting, because
it had to be bad, dealing largely or wholly with the sentimental, the
trite and pretty, the picturesque. Thus photography was torn from
its moorings, the whole essence of which is realism.

Much of this was due to a terrible plague, imported from England
in the form of Henry Peach Robinson. He became the shining light
of photography, charged large prices, took ribbon after ribbon. He
lifted composition bodily from painting, but the ones he chose were
probably some of the worst examples in history. Greatest disaster of
all, he wrote a book in 1869 entitled *Pictorial Photography*. His system

was to flatter everything. He sought to correct what the camera saw. The inherent genius and dignity of the human subject was denied.

Typical of his sentimental pictures were his titles, and titles of other photographers of the period: "Poor Joe," "Hard Times," "Fading Away," "Here Comes Father," "Intimate Friends," "Romantic Landscape," "By the Stream," "End of a Winter's Day," "Kiss of Dew," "Fingers of Morning." If some of the subject matter and titles are not too far removed from some of today's crop of pictorialists, then obviously the coincidence of similar thinking has the same sentimental unrealistic fundation in common. This Robinsonian school had an influence second to none—it stuck, simply, because it made the practice and theory of photography *easy*. In other words, flattery pays off. Thus today there are still many photographers of the Pictorial School who continue to emulate the "master" of 1869.

As a popular art form, photography has expanded and intensified its activity in recent years. The most noticeable trend has been the widespread publication of articles and books on *How-To-Do-It*. Yet what is more important now is *What-To-Do-With-It*. That very widespread distribution which gives photography much of its strength and power, demands that there be a greater sense of awareness on the part of photographers and editors alike.

Unfortunately, along with growth and the strength it signifies, goes the possibility of a decline in our photographic sensibilities and output. Actually, the progress of photography is frequently delayed by inadequate equipment, which needs fundamental, far-reaching improvement. This is not to condemn the industry as a whole, but rather certain segments of it, for their stationary outlook and lack of proper perspective. Photography gains much of its strength from the vast participation of the amateur, and of course this is the market where mass production thrives.

But—it is high time industry paid attention to the serious and expert opinion of experienced photographers, and to the needs of the professional worker as well. This is important because a good photographer cannot fulfill the potential of contemporary photography if he is handicapped with equipment and materials made for amateurs only, or simply for a quick turnover. The camera, the tripod, and other picture-taking necessities, too often designed by draftsmen who never took a serious picture in their lives, must be vastly better machines if they are to free the photographer creatively, instead of dominating his thinking.

Many photographers spend too much time in the darkroom, with the result that creative camera work is seriously interfered with. The stale vogue of drowning in technique and ignoring content adds to the pestilence and has become, for many, part of today's general hysteria. "... *and craftsmanship I set up as a pedestal for art; Became the merest craftsman; to my fingers I lent a docile, cold agility, And sureness to my ear. I stifled sounds, And then dissected music like a corpse, Checked harmony by algebraic rules."*

Apart from the foregoing gripes, what then makes a picture a creative piece of work? We know it cannot be just technique. Is it content —and if so, what is content? These are basic questions that enlightened photographers must answer for themselves.

Let us first say what photography is *not*. A photograph is not a painting, a poem, a symphony, a dance. It is not just a pretty picture, not an exercise in contortionist techniques and sheer print quality. It is or should be a significant document, a penetrating statement, which can be described in a very simple term—selectivity.

To define selection, one may say that it should be focused on the kind of subject matter which hits you hard with its impact and excites your imagination to the extent that you are forced to take it. Pictures are wasted unless the motive power which impelled you to action is strong and stirring. The motives or points of view are bound to differ with each photographer, and herein lies the important difference which separates one approach from another. Selection of proper picture content comes from a fine union of trained eye and imaginative mind.

To chart a course, one must have a direction. In reality, the eye is no better than the philosophy behind it. The photographer creates, evolves a better, more selective, more acute seeing eye by looking ever more sharply at what is going on in the world. Like every other means of expression, photography, if it is to be utterly honest and direct, should be related to the life of the times—the pulse of today. The photograph may be presented as finely and artistically as you will; but to merit serious consideration, must be directly connected with the world we live in.

What we need is a return, on a mounting spiral of historic understanding, to the great tradition of realism. Since ultimately the photograph is a statement, a document of the *now,* a greater responsibility is put on us. Today, we are confronted with reality on the vastest scale mankind has known. Some people are still unaware that reality contains unparalleled beauties. The fantastic and unexpected, the ever-changing and renewing is nowhere so exemplified as in real life itself. Once we understand this, it exercises a dynamic compulsion on us, and a photo-document is born.

The term "documentary" is sometimes applied in a rather derogatory sense to the type of photography which to me seems logical. To connect the term "documentary" with only the "ash-can school" is so much sheer nonsense, and probably stems from the bad habit of pigeon-holing and labelling everything like the well-known 57 varieties. Actually, documentary pictures include every subject in the world—good, bad, indifferent. I have yet to see a fine photograph which is not a good document. Those that survive from the past invariably are, and can be recognized in the work of Brady, Jackson, Nadar, Atget, and many others. Great photographs have "magic"— a revealing word that comes from Steichen. I believe the "magic" photographers are documentarians only in the broadest sense of the word.

According to Webster, anything "documentary" is: "that which is taught, evidence, truth, conveying information, authentic judgment." Add to that a dash of imagination, take for granted adequate technique to realize the intention, and a photographer's grasp will eventually equal his reach—as he turns in the right direction at the crossroads.

ANSEL ADAMS (1902-) *Photography is but one phase of the potential of human expression; all art is the expression of one and the same thing—the relation of the spirit of man to the spirit of other men and to the world.* DANGER SIGNALS, *PSA Journal, Vol. 14, November* 1948; *p.* 575.

WHAT IS GOOD PHOTOGRAPHY?   1940
Camera Craft, Vol. 47, pp. 43-44.

Dear Sirs:

The tranquil Autumn air of the mountains is a good counter-irritant to the steaming mood of the section of Correspondence of the December *Camera Craft.* Nobody seems to be accomplishing anything, but the incubation of hard feelings—and nobody seems to have made any attempt to get down to unemotional facts in his protestations. Far be it for me to pose as an arbitrator, or an oracle, or a catalyst—but I cannot evade adding a few words with the hope— however forlorn—that they will serve as oil upon the foaming waves.

In the first place, no less an authority in art than Arthur Pope once said to me, "the artist should never write about his art"—and he is entirely right. The artist speaks in terms of his medium; transcription of his ideas in words are almost always inadequate and misleading in the most precise sense. We all write too much, speak too much, preach too much. It would be better if we just said what we have to say in photography. After all, we are photographers; if our work has "what it takes" it will not need the embalming of words to perpetuate it. Let the critics—the professional critics—fuss with the winding sheets.

All of us, perhaps, know this, but we will keep right on writing and lecturing, and giving our colleagues soul-shattering Bronx cheers via the "letters" column.

What I am really getting at is this: Weston writes something, Partridge writes something, I write something. So what? We can all make better photographs than we can write about them. If we can't express our principles of photography in our photographs, we certainly cannot express them in our writings on photography. I believe that we do not need any·justification in type for our adventures in silver. Presumably we are all afraid of something. I am probably

afraid that some spectator will not understand my photography—
therefore I proceed to make it really less understandable by writing
defensibly about it. All I can do in my writings is to stimulate a
certain amount of thought, clarify some technical facts and "date"
my work. But when I preach "sharpness," "brilliancy," "scale," etc.,
I am just mouthing words, because no words can really describe
those terms and qualities—it takes the actual print to say, "here it is."
If I want to get into an argument with Mr. Mortensen, and vice versa,
we can do it best by jousting with our photography, rather than with
our pens. I am sure Mr. Mortensen would agree with me in this. But
we both do a lot of writing!!

Weston is one of my closest friends, but I must say in all frankness
that one of his photographs says more about him and his photography
than fifty pages of text he might produce. What he writes about photography in the Encyclopedia Britannica—an objective treatise on the
art—is something else.

I refer to writing about one's own work, or jousting for one's own
"school." Partridge is an excellent artist—a superb etcher, and exceedingly well versed in the principles of all the arts. He has taken up
photography apparently to say something he was unable to say in the
other media. He has done some very good things. He would be the
last one to call himself a great photographer, and there is nothing
about his writings to indicate conceit. He is enthusiastic about the
art, and he is giving us an expert opinion. I do not agree with all he
says, but I certainly admire his discussion-provoking statements. But,
you see, his writing serves to make some people think Partridge is
posing as an ultimate authority—which is not so.

I have certainly laid myself wide open many times, in speech and
writing, to all sorts of tomatoes, orchids and good solid bricks. Probably I deserved all of them—especially the last. I gave a little talk
before a camera group the other evening, and the sum total of my
accomplishment seems to me to have been: 1. I inadequately re-stated
what I have already said in my pictures. 2. I did not give any real
constructive technical ideas. 3. I irritated a lot of people, and added
one more degree of confusion to an already hopelessly involved subject. I feel that there should be a Society for the Perpetuation of Plain
Simple Facts—and let it go at that. But I will probably continue to
give talks and produce pages of text; the itch to preach exists as an
all-consuming fire in practically everyone.

The name "F64" has certainly been misinterpreted, maligned,
glorified, abused, and most generally misunderstood. The "Group
F64" was loosely formed of several photographers—mostly professionals—to act together towards the strengthening of clean photographic thought and production. "F64" was never intended as a strict
literal descriptive term. How many people who write and talk about
"F64" really know about it—what the Group was—who were the art-

ists comprising it—what they actually did? Believe me, a diamond-sharp glossy print does NOT represent "F64" unless there is that most-important-something-else in it—the quality of art in perception and execution. This statement is totally without meaning to those who do not know what "the quality of Art in perception and execution" is. And they never will know, in spite of Mr. Weston, Mr. Partridge, and Mr. Adams, and all their writings, unless they truly *want* to know—to venture forth from the safe ritualistic shelter of the commonplace and look for themselves.

If "F64" means a pedagogic inflexible system of thought and action, then I am through with it completely. But if it signifies an *attitude* towards a clean, straightforward approach to photography, I am all for it. The latter is what it was supposed to be; but a lot of people are trying to break it down into a mere technical aspect-habit.

The beauty of a photograph by Weston does not lie in the assortment of facts about negative, material, papers, developers—it lies in the realization of his *vision*. And I believe his vision is in perfect relation to the medium of straight photography.

What we have to say is infinitely more important than our mechanical means of saying it. On the other hand, if we cloud our message with poor techniques, shallow taste, and inflexible method we are not going to get very far. We have to inquire within ourselves and forget taboos along with ivory towers.

Mr. Douglas is wrong in saying that the "Group F64" school is related to the "1890 school." It bears a much closer relationship to the 1860's and the 1870's and what those decades produced in straightforward photography. He forgets one terribly important thing—the *style* of the early days is one thing, and the aesthetic intentions (or lack of them) of the early photographers, another thing.

I humbly refer you all to Alfred Stieglitz. Mr. Stieglitz' spectrum of accomplishment is greater than that of all of us put together. Stieglitz would never say that certain objects of the world were more or less beautiful than others—telegraph poles, for instance, compared with oak-trees. He would accept them for what they are, and use the most appropriate object to express his thoughts and convey his vision. I think Mr. Loeber is right in his denouncement of "exalted rubbish." But he does not state that it is only "exalted rubbish" when the photographer considers it so. Factual rubbish is considered vile because of connotations and convention. It is very dangerous to start off with hazy definitions. No photograph of Stieglitz' is *ugly*—every subject employed is transmuted into an expression of beauty—but true beauty does *not* mean mere *prettiness*.

Mr. Partridge's prophecy of the future of photography frankly irritates me, simply because no one can possibly tell which way human expression is going—except to be reasonably sure that the pendulum will continue to swing. But I believe many people, Mr. Loeber in-

cluded, misinterpret *discussion* as *final dictum*. I know Mr. Partridge
has no intention of Hitlerizing photography; but I am not so sure
that some of the "Old Guard" would not "liquidate" a lot of contemporary work if it had the opportunity to do so. Even photographers are protected by the Bill of Rights!

Believe me, the Purist (awful term) is really trying to get photography out of pigeon-holes, rather than in them, as Mr. Forrester
believes they are trying to do. Well, "Ye who are without sin . . . ."

A PERSONAL CREDO   1944
American Annual of Photography, Vol. 58, pp. 7-16.

It is difficult to evaluate the status of contemporary photography
apart from the fields of war activity. The war, of course, utilizes practically all available materials, leaving little for the amateur or professional—to say nothing of the most important ingredients, time and
inclination. Yet, within the war effort, apart from the enormous
amount of purely technical application, there exists a vast opportunity for important documentation, ~~and for~~ propaganda, reportage,
and the purely expressive aspects of the art. The sheer practical
urgency of the times will probably inhibit much of the personal forms
of photography, but it will be a matter of lasting regret if the greatest
moments of the tremendous human upheaval are not recorded as only
the camera is capable of doing. As an organized approach to this inclu-
sive documentation is probably impossible now, it will be necessary
to rely on high editorial ability to selectively collate the myriads of
photographs which will be produced by the armed forces, by industry,
and by the social service organizations.

The world of commercial photography must carry on as best it can.
In the advertising fields there seems to be less emphasis on immediate
selling and more on institutional good-will, the latter bearing a sharp
eye on the post-war world. I feel there will be, however, a decided
difference between the pre-war and the post-war world, and those
who are patiently awaiting a resumption of the old ways will be
rudely disillusioned. I know that professional photography will survive and tremendously expand, but many of its present aspects will
change.

The salons will carry on, too. In this, and other fields as well, the
restrictions will probably be healthy, as reduced output seems complementary to intense expression. As for "the independents"—their
situation is unpredictable, but I am confident that any man having
something to say will find a way to say it.

Documentation—in the present social interpretation of the term—
will burst into full flower at the moment of peace. Herein lies the
magnificent opportunity of all photographic history. Here is where
the camera can be related to a vast constructive function: the revelation of a new world as it is born and grows into maturity. I believe

that the highest function of post-war photography will be to relate
the world of nature to the world of man, and man to men in the fullest
meaning of the terms.

It is easy to rest upon the vague security of words; the terms
"beauty," "dignity," "spirituality," and "function" are but symbols
of qualities, and are vulnerable to connotations. Let us hope that
categories will be less rigid in the future; there has been too much of
placing photography in little niches—commercial, pictorial, documentary, and creative (a dismal term). Definitions of this kind are
inessential and stupid; good photography remains good photography
no matter what we name it. I would like to think of just "photography"; of each and every photograph containing the best qualities
in proper degree to achieve its purpose. We have been slaves to categories, and each has served as a kind of concentration camp for the
spirit. The function of a photograph may be of the simplest practical
nature, or it may relate to a most personal and abstract emotion; the
sincerity of intention and the honesty of spirit of the photographer
can make any expression, no matter how "practical," valid and beautiful. What is required is an underlying *ethic* and sensitivity to the
important and true qualities of the world in which we live. No man
has the right to dictate what other men should perceive, create or
produce, but all should be encouraged to reveal themselves, their perceptions and emotions, and to build confidence in the creative spirit.

The frantic concentration on volume and on the spectacular in the
modern commercial world has most certainly inhibited simple and
direct personal expression. The forces of demand are powerful, and
it is seldom that the creative person has the opportunity to contribute his own qualities of perception and emotion in the face of
accepted patterns of thought and interpretation. The advertising
photographer "adjusts" himself to his client; the competitive salon
photographer often thinks more of acceptances and awards than of
his own inner creative convictions; people are given what they want
(which may mean that they continue to get only what they already
have). I believe the people want, and can appreciate, far more than
they have been given. The style of the popular publications is apparently profitable—hence it must be "right." I dispute this—not in fact,
but in principle. I have faith in people and believe it is our fault if
we have not touched them with the best we have to give. The agents
who *presume,* and the readers who *accept* will be influenced to the
greatest extent by consistently superior work on our part. If all photographers could but realize the ultimate importance of a high *ethic*
and would join in a collective determination to maintain clean standards, a vast change for the better would obtain. Unfortunately some
who have achieved leadership in the profession often dictate from
a confused throne of success—a success which may be more financial
than otherwise.

With a few exceptions, publications of the photographic world are founded on the desire to stimulate the photographic trade; materials, equipment, gadgets have been in high flood of production and sales and the advertising of these countless items have been the backbone of this publishing. The dangerous suggestion that you can hire someone to do the drudgery, plus the encouragement of superficial thought and methods, has robbed photography of much dignity, clarity and effectiveness. If photography were to become a difficult mechanical medium, and if it were possible to explain the actual lack of need for most materials and gadgets, many publications would have no reason to exist, and I believe pictures, on the whole, would be better. Photographers have been led to make a fetish of equipment, and are falsely encouraged in superficial concepts and methods, resulting in unfortunate misconceptions of the basic potentialities of photography. I believe the ideal photographic journal should be simple and rather dignified—but not austere—and contain good reproductions of good photographs of every description, and accurate, definitive texts. It should also contain legitimate advertising of *proven equipment and materials*. Unfortunately, most of the photographic magazines are conspicuous for their lack of policy, being mere trade-journals in the expanded meaning of the term.

There is an unfortunate blind spot in the manufacturer-consumer relationship. The former is obligated to *exact* procedures of research and manufacture, and consistent standards of production. The latter, except in a few specialist fields, is limited to a *precise* method of use of equipment and materials; there is no reason why he should be versed in the complexities of research and manufacture any more than an architect would need to know the complexities of steel manufacture—knowledge of what steel *will do* and confidence that it will do it, is all he requires. It is my observation that the manufacturers lean towards defining photography in terms of equipment and materials, when they should really define their products in terms of *photography*. The manufacturer should not dictate the progress of applied photography; he should anticipate and follow it. On the other hand, the photographers should be in close contact with the manufacturers in other than commercial dealings; they should mutually work towards continued improvement of the craft, and the perfection of equipment and materials. I do not know of a creative photographer who would not welcome such an association and gladly co-operate in every possible way. Through practical knowledge and experience, empirical as it may be, the photographers know more about the art and craft of their medium than do the manufacturers. It is ridiculous for them to presume adequate knowledge of the advanced chemical and physical methods of the research technician, or the involved and exquisite controls of production, but they are rightfully the planners and arbiters of their own craft.

Underlying the whole fabric of art and creative work is the contemporary world-ethic. The conflict of a few who are intent upon pursuit of the ideal, and the many who exploit brains and imagination, is age-old; but in our time a sinister development of this condition is all too apparent. The momentum derived from mechanical facility carries truly unworthy work far beyond its natural height. In many phases of the professional photographic fields there is a marked inadequacy of taste and technique, and, above all, a lack of respect and understanding in regard to the possibilities and limitations of the medium. There are men working for big money in the profession who are but charlatans of the most flagrant type; they possess an adequate mechanical ability which only serves to accent their presumptuous lack of taste and sensitivity. Yet even these deserve tolerant appraisal; they are encouraged in their approach by the vast commercial clientele, which is but partially aware of its destructive influence. People are being trained in thoroughly superficial ways for what should be serious and profound professions. Our civilization protects our health, our safety, and our pocketbooks, by controlled professional standards and legal supervision. But nothing much is done for our spirit, which is of much greater importance. We are defenseless against gross impositions on our emotions, our aesthetic sense, and our ethics. Hence, I believe in the absolute necessity of a strong and severe licensing control of professional photography, and of a firm guild organization among the creative artists and professionals. Medicine, the law, architecture, engineering, and other professions, are strengthened by such procedures of control, and I see no reason why photography should not be among them. Assuming that it requires five to eight years of serious training to be proficient in the major professions, why should photographers be turned loose on the world with only a superficial knowledge of their craft, and little or no experience in application?

However, the picture is not entirely dark; there are many unknowns who are working daily miracles in routine photography. And there are increasing numbers of men and women in many fields who are advancing photography through the sheer quality and sincerity of their work and of their belief in what the medium can accomplish. Many of these are amateurs in the best sense of the term. In the future our age will be remembered (as all other ages are remembered) by the productions of our creative people; photography is secure in such names as Stieglitz, Weston, Lange, and many others—not in the names of successful opportunists who may happen to hold contemporary popularity. Millions of men have lived to fight, build palaces and boundaries, shape destinies and societies; but the compelling force of all times has been the force of originality and creation profoundly affecting the roots of the human spirit.

I have often thought that if photography were *difficult* in the true sense of the term—meaning that the creation of a simple photograph would entail as much time and effort as the production of a good watercolor or etching—there would be a vast improvement in total output. The sheer ease with which we can produce a superficial image often leads to creative disaster. We must remember that a photograph can hold just as much as we put into it, and no one has ever approached the full possibilities of the medium. Without desire for self-flagellation, I often wish we were limited to processes as difficult as the old wet-plate and sun-print methods. We would then be efficient, and would not have time or energy to make photographs of casual quality or content. The requirements of care and precision would result inevitably in a superior and more intense expression. I have seen many of the old photographs of Hill, Cameron, Brady, O'Sullivan, Emerson, Atget, and others of earlier days, and I always marvel at their intensity, economy, and basic emotional quality. I am aware of the fact that most of these early photographs were made for *factual* purposes; there is little evidence of self-conscious art intention. I believe a great statement in any medium remains a great statement for all time; and, while I do not favor the imitation of other men or of other times, I feel we should recognize the spirit of the earlier photographers, through the best examples of their work, and strengthen our own thereby. For more than one hundred years photography, through the work of relatively few men, has maintained a magnificent spiritual resonance, as moving and profound as great music. Of course, great photographs are being made today, and it is our hope that the creative work of the future will achieve heights undreamed of heretofore. It is up to us—the photographers of today—to make this hope a reality.

I have been asked many times, "What is a great photograph?" I can answer best by showing a great photograph, not by talking or writing about one. However, as word definitions are required more often than not, I would say this: A great photograph is a full expression of what one feels about what is being photographed in the deepest sense, and is, thereby, a true expression of what one feels about life in its entirety. And the expression of what one feels should be set forth in terms of simple devotion to the medium—a statement of the utmost clarity and perfection possible under the conditions of creation and production. That will explain why I have no patience with unnecessary complications of technique or presentation. I prefer a fine lens because it gives me the best possible optical image, a fine camera because it complements the function of the lens, fine materials because they convey the qualities of the image to the highest degree. I use smooth papers because I know they reveal the utmost of image clarity and brilliance, and I mount my prints on simple cards because I believe any "fussiness" only distracts from and weakens the print. I do not retouch or manipulate my prints because I believe in the

importance of the direct optical and chemical image. I use the legitimate controls of the medium only to augment the *photographic* effect.
Purism, in the sense of rigid abstention from any control, is ridiculous; the logical controls of exposure, development and printing are
essential in the revelation of photographic qualities. The correction
of tonal deficiencies by dodging, and the elimination of obvious de-
fects by spotting, are perfectly legitimate elements of the craft. As
long as the final result of the procedure is *photographic,* it is entirely
justified. But when a photograph has the "feel" of an etching or a
lithograph, or any other graphic medium, it is questionable—just as
questionable as a painting that is photographic in character. The
incredibly beautiful revelation of the lens is worthy of the most
sympathic treatment in every respect.

Simplicity is a prime requisite. The equipment of Alfred Stieglitz
or Edward Weston represents less in cost and variety than many an
amateur "can barely get along with." Their magnificent photographs were made with intelligence and sympathy—not with merely
the machines. Many fields of photography demand specific equipment of a high order of complexity and precision; yet economy and
simplicity are relative, and the more complex a man's work becomes,
the more efficient his equipment and methods must be.

Precision and patience, and devotion to the capacities of the craft,
are of supreme importance. The sheer perfection of the lens-image
implies an attitude of perfection in every phase of the process and
every aspect of the result. The relative importance of the craft and
its expressive aspects must be clarified; we would not go to a concert
to hear scales performed—even with consummate skill—nor would
we enjoy the sloppy rendition of great music. In photography, technique is frequently exalted for its own sake; the unfortunate com-
plement of this is when a serious and potentially important statement
is rendered impotent by inferior mechanics of production. Of course,
"seeing," or visualization, is the fundamentally important element.
A photograph is not an accident—it is a concept. It exists at, or before,
the moment of exposure of the negative. From that moment on to the
final print, the process is chiefly one of *craft;* the pre-visualized photograph is rendered in terms of the final print by a series of processes
peculiar to the medium. True, changes and augmentations can be
effected during these processes, but the fundamental thing which was
"seen" is not altered in basic concept.

The "machine-gun" approach to photography—by which many
negatives are made with the hope that one will be good—is fatal to
serious results. However, it should be realized that the element of
"seeing" is not limited to the classic stand-camera technique. The
phases of photography which are concerned with immediate and
rapid perception of the world—news, reportage, forms of documentary
work (which may not admit contemplation of *each* picture made)

are, nevertheless, dependent upon a basic attitude and experience. The instant awareness of what is significant in a rapidly changing elusive subject presupposes an adequate visualization more general in type than that required for carefully considered static subjects such as landscape and architecture. The accidental contact with the subject and the required immediacy of exposure in no way refutes the principles of the basic photographic concept. Truly "accidental" photography is practically non-existent; with preconditioned attitudes we *recognize* and are arrested by the significant moment. The awareness of the *right moment* is as vital as the perception of values, form, and other qualities. There is no fundamental difference in the great landscapes and quiet portraits of Edward Weston and the profoundly revealing pictures of children by Helen Levitt. Both are photographic perceptions of the highest order, expressed through different, but entirely appropriate, techniques.

Not only does the making of a photograph imply an acute perception of detail in the subject, but a fine print deserves far more than superficial scrutiny. A photograph is usually looked *at*—seldom looked *into*. The experience of a truly fine print may be related to the experience of a symphony—appreciation of the broad melodic line, while important, is by no means all. The wealth of detail, forms, values—the minute but vital significances revealed so exquisitely by the lens—deserve exploration and appreciation. It takes *time* to really see a fine print, to feel the almost endless revelation of poignant reality which, in our preoccupied haste, we have sadly neglected. Hence, the "look-through-a-stack-of-prints-while-you're-waiting" attitude has some painful connotations.

Sympathetic interpretation seldom evolves from a predatory attitude; the common term *"taking* a picture" is more than just an idiom; it is a symbol of exploitation. *"Making* a picture" implies a creative resonance which is essential to profound expression.

My approach to photography is based on my belief in the vigor and values of the world of nature—in the aspects of grandeur and of the minutiæ all about us. I believe in growing things, and in the things which have grown and died magnificently. I believe in people and in the simple aspects of human life, and in the relation of man to nature. I believe man must be free, both in spirit and society, that he must build strength into himself, affirming the "enormous beauty of the world" and acquiring the confidence to see and to express his vision. And I believe in photography as one means of expressing this affirmation, and of achieving an ultimate happiness and faith.

INTRODUCTION   1948
Portfolio One, San Francisco.

To photograph truthfully and effectively is to see beneath the surfaces and record the qualities of nature and humanity which live or are latent in all things. Impression is not enough. Design, style, technique,—these, too, are not enough. Art must reach further than impression or self-revelation. Art, said Alfred Stieglitz, is the affirmation of life. And life, or its eternal evidence, is everywhere.

Some photographers take reality as the sculptors take wood and stone and upon it impose the dominations of their own thought and spirit. Others come before reality more tenderly and a photograph to them is an instrument of love and revelation. A true photograph need not be explained, nor can be contained in words.

Expressions without doctrine, my photographs are presented here as ends in themselves, images of the endless moments of the world. I dedicate them to the memory and to the spirit of Alfred Stieglitz.

FRANCIS BRUGUIÈRE (1880-1945) *What lives in pictures is very difficult to define ... it finally becomes a thing beyond the thing portrayed ... some sort of section of the soul of the artist that gets detached and comes out to one from the picture. ... I do think that the idea of "that living thing" must be in the heart before it can be brought to life by an artist. (From a letter to a young artist, n.d.)*

CREATIVE PHOTOGRAPHY   1935-36
Modern Photography Annual, pp. 9-14.

In the closing years of the nineteenth century there were many signs to show that a maximum of exact representativeness in art had passed.

Now again, in the first and second decades of the twentieth century we find art turning away, as if glutted from reality, disregarding outer form for the traces of motion, becoming once more analytical and symbolical. The drift seems likely to continue. It is also helped now by the increasing efficiency of photography for merely circumstantial precision. The world wearies of undigested fact.

THE OUTLINE OF HISTORY: H. G. WELLS

1

The above general statement of the position of art in our time, though it refers in general to painting, sculpture and architecture, may also be said to apply to their handmaiden, photography. Considering that photography is a scientific, chemical development of the nineteenth century and is scarcely a hundred years old, it is no wonder that it has been looked on askance. This questioning attitude is easily understood, as it is the general state of mind in which most people indulge when confronted by anything that does not fit into their preconceived ideas of what a thing should be.

Mr. Wells speaks of the "merely circumstantial precision" of photography, and this is the general concept of what photography should be. If that were so it would mean the end of all efforts towards experimental creation in the medium. In the last few years, through the perfecting of the enlarging process, photographs have become

adaptable to mural decorations. This would seem to offer hope that
the photographer may become a decorative artist. In New York large
surfaces of wall are covered by photographs that quite hold their
own in interest in relation to paintings on a similar scale. It is possible, by the application of some of the principles I have indicated, to
transform the "circumstantial precision" of the photograph into
something quite as creative in mass, line and tone as decorative
mural painting.

Up to the present, large-scale colour photography is not possible,
so the decorative photograph is in masses of black and white. But
photographic colour of quality seems to be on the way. The colour
photographs of Curtis Moffat show that colour is capable of individual treatment, realistically as well as abstractly.

The application of design to the photograph is entirely in the
hands of the photographer. It means that he must be equipped both
technically and aesthetically. The photographer ultimately will have
to be trained with as much care as those who practice the other arts.
It will not be a haphazard pursuit as it is now, but will depend on
the creative capabilities of the individual. Photography is not easily
mastered. One's attitude to it should be one of continual questioning
and dissatisfaction. Its progress depends on striving to preserve it
from easy pitfalls.

2

The photographer can interest himself in numerous technical
devices in order to keep his interest alive.

There is that aim of all photographers—"the perfect negative."
This, in itself, is an ideal which is rarely if ever obtained. I do not
know what a "perfect negative" is; but I suppose it must be one from
which an absolutely satisfactory print can be made without any
dodging or manipulation. Then the tones of the print are in perfect
relationship, the detail of the lightest parts being in absolute balance
with the detail of the deepest shadows, and the subordinate tones
holding their relationship to the highest lights and deepest darks in
a way that is above criticism. Such a state of affairs exists in nature,
and it is one of the problems of the photographer to record approximately this ideal balance with his camera.

A photograph has been said to look "just like nature," but no one
has ever agreed just how nature looks; it may, therefore, be questioned
whether a photograph really looks anything like nature. The photograph is a species of graph, representing nature, that may more or
less resemble it. It can never have the luminous texture of light in
nature, nor the quality of nature's colour, any more than a painting
can. It is a compromise! At times it seems to be more than nature,
at other times less!

Even in a photograph nature can "look up"! A photograph can be
something in itself—it can exist independently as a photograph apart

from the subject; it can take on a life of its own, aside from its documentary value.

3

The documentary value of a photograph is immense, as is universally acknowledged: about such a self-evident value it is unnecessary to speak, seeing that there already exists so much underlining of the obvious.

The majority of photographers are interested only in the documentary side of photography: that means pointing the camera at a subject which exists in nature, and trying to render the subject clearly as far as the limits of the materials of photography will permit. There are any number of variants to this rendering of the subject, such as the type of film, lens, or plate used. A large number of special materials can be employed, and their use is best determined by consulting a speed card, such as is published by Watkins, for plate speed numbers, or by consulting the advertisements in the *British Journal of Photography*.

Some of the emulsions on plates and films are very rapid, some very slow, some sensitive to all the colours of the spectrum, some rendering only a few in their supposed relative shades. So what is actually rendered on the negative is a variable quantity of nature based on the material used.

Again, there are colour screens which allow the light to pass through the lens to the sensitive plate at different degrees of speed; these, in turn, govern the quality of the resultant image.

Then the development of the latent image into a negative is governed by the time, temperature and chemical formula of the developer, which greatly affects the quality of the negative produced.

All this is what might be termed the fundamental base of photography. It has primarily to do with visible light, and as it is this quality that the ordinary, non-scientific photograph is concerned with, our remarks are confined to this branch of photography.

Parenthetically, it may be observed that the infra-red photo is a subject that might well hold the attention of some photographers, for it deserves painstaking experiment.

Now, all this seems to point to the fact that photography is a medium that expresses the action of light reflected from objects. This light is precipitated chemically, having been caught by the lens on sensitive material: the result is a photograph. Light acts on photographic material, producing a result that is called photographic, and is brought to a final result chemically.

The photographer has the choice of either dealing with the things that can be seen (landscapes, portraits, still-lifes), or of creating his own world. Portraits and still-life studies are capable of being arranged in an infinite number of ways, and of being lit in an infinite number of ways. In landscape photography it means waiting for what the photographer considers the right moment: he must use his judgment accordingly.

4

It is possible for photographers to make or design objects that can be treated with light, thereby creating a world of their own which is in many ways as interesting as the visible, external world. The same laws of composition of light and shade and line govern this personal world, only it has not the so-called aspect of nature that is termed documentary.

By many practitioners of photography it is not considered "legitimate" to create a personal world: they limit the photograph to the documentary, and seem to be satisfied that it shall remain a document for ever. Human beings like to think of things in secure and proper places, to which they alone hold the key; if anyone tampers with the lock, he is a pariah! I have seen it stated by well-known photographers, and heard it from their own lips, that the photograph must be exactly the document they have defined, and that nothing else must exist in the medium!

Some of these photographers were, at one time, ardent advocates of the gum bichromate, and the gum platinum print; to say nothing of using uncorrected or "fuzzy" lenses. The gum and oil prints perhaps took too much hand work: some were not good, but some were! It is the result which counts! A good gum or oil print is just as interesting as the most meticulous, microscopically detailed documentary photograph, which depends for its quality on the most exact lens corrections. In fact there is something human in the gum prints' faults and strivings, something which machine accuracy misses. However, these are mediums little practised today; perhaps the processes were too indirect, although interesting.

The process, which was observed from the beginning of photography, termed "solarization," has been technically perfected by Man Ray. It is accomplished by exposing a fully developed negative or print to the light for a few seconds, and then continuing development and fixing. It is, as far as I know, the most promising process in the hands of the modern photographer. Here there is no hand work, the results being controlled by light and chemicals: there is what might be termed "legitimate" manipulation of the light, similar to that used in "dodging"—and what photographer does not "dodge" his prints? The possibilities of the resultant image range from a slight to a complete transformation of the photographic image.

In making subjects of my own, I have used paper-cut designs brought into low relief, and lit, generally, by one small spot lamp of 250 watts: the same lamp has been placed in different positions through a series of exposures. The field is not limited to paper; any plastic material will answer the purpose. Then you can have the pleasure of making your own "unnatural" world, to which it is not unpleasant to return if you are a photographer, and have been working daily with fashions, portraits, or advertising!

5

There are other methods of making "unnatural" photos. There is the photogram, from which photography originated. It is accomplished by placing objects on sensitive paper or film and exposing a light above them or from different angles. The shadow of the objects is cast and remains light; or, if transparent or semi-transparent objects are used, beautiful designs of multiple tones are built up.

There is the use of a piece of paper in place of the lens. In this paper a design is cut, and through it the light from a filament of an electric light bulb is projected. Quite beautiful patterns of light may be thus obtained, that can only be seen under a condition of this kind. Silver paper, highly mirrored, allows most interesting patterns to be formed, which are photographic.

Then there is multiple exposure through which compositions can be made in endless variety to suit individual taste.

Such processes involve a certain amount of patience on the part of the photographer. They are none of them commercial, unless some advertiser may fall for "the novelty of an idea."

By referring to patience, I do not mean that it takes anything like 20 or 30 hours to produce a photograph: most of the photographs I have made have not taken me as many minutes.

A critic once said to me: "It must take you many hours to do one of those photographs; is it worth the expenditure of time?" He might well ask the question, for he considered that all steps in the direction of making the photograph a medium of expression are doomed to failure by the fact that the photograph is believed to be impermanent, that anyone who wants to can easily do something of a similar nature. In fact, he echoed the general opinion held by those who know little about the medium. It would appear from this that photography is considered a kind of journalism: not a thing of beauty and a joy for ever, but something quickly to be discarded.

But however that may be, for many who practise it, it is a fascinating medium, capable of expansion in the right hands. One looks to the amateur for whatever advance may be accomplished in the future; for he alone has the leisure and money, and is not beset by the practical problems of a commercial photographer. Photography may be considered an expensive medium in which to experiment.

The camera will develop into the perfect instrument for the artist. It reacts instantly to his sensitiveness and creative imagination. But it is a foreign tool to the artist. Not much technique has been developed for it as yet. The pencil or brush is a simple thing to master. The camera is intricate.

HORIZONS: NORMAN BEL GEDDES

WYNN BULLOCK (1902-) *There is nothing mysterious about space-time. Every speck of matter, every idea, is a space-time event. We cannot experience anything or conceive of anything that exists outside of space-time. Just as experience precedes all awareness and creative expression, the visual language of our photographs should ever more strongly express the fourth dimensional structure of the real world.* PHOTOGRAPHIC EDUCATION. (*From an unpublished manuscript, 1965.*)

SPACE AND TIME   1962
Photography, Vol. 17, No. 9, pp. 42-49.

For a number of years I have felt the need for being consciously aware that nature is not alone a three dimensional world of external appearances that our physical senses perceive as objects, but equally a world in which all things have a fourth dimension. This added dimension is perceived by still undefined senses that make up the mind. This has led me to search for the meaning of the fourth dimension.

I am convinced that for the creative painter or photographer to interpret an object in terms of its external surface dimensions is to see' the object superficially. Searching deeper into the nature of things, I ask myself what makes one person more interesting visually than another person or one tree different or more meaningful than another tree.

Ordinarily, objects are seen and felt most easily and strongly in the ever-recurring *now* of time. Seen in this way the meaning of a particular tree is imprisoned in an attitude of mind that tends to limit its reality to its surface appearance. The five senses on a physical level can only react by outside stimulation in the ever-recurring *now*. They cannot bring back the past or respond to the future reality of anything because three-dimensionality is the function of the senses. So reality to the physical senses always remains only a tiny fraction of the reality of the tree.

This level of reality is a static experience which only the mind can make dynamic by blending past, present and future into a greater measure of reality. The present is only an intersection in the time of every event in the universe. It is like the single frame of a motion picture film. When the single frame is seen the motion stops. It is a function of the creative mind to overcome the inertia of the (now) perceived reality.

When Cartier-Bresson referred to *the decisive moment* of taking a picture he meant, I feel, the mirrored moment that expresses the object so as to evoke in the mind of the viewer significant and inner qualities.

Once the mind is aware of the profound difference between seeing an object for its three-dimensionality only, and seeing it fourth-dimensionally as an event in time and space, only then does the mind search for and find symbols to express this added dimension.

This is a desired goal in all mediums of art expression. The greatness of music in large part is related to the fact that it is not basically a three dimensional medium of expression. It seeks its meaning in the infinite and invisible world of sound, which in itself is a fourth-dimensional event. It differs from the object world as a source of material for the creative mind, in that the object on the visual level is limited by its own meaning as an event. As such this acts as a limitation in terms of creative expression. Sound, on the other hand, is an event of far greater magnitude related in fact to all objects and all space, thereby offering unlimited creative possibilities in terms of source material.

Visual expressions of all kinds in terms of fourth-dimensional meanings have been held back, relative to music, because of the many utilitarian and practical reasons for expressing objects literally. However, in the last hundred years painting has advanced rapidly in freeing itself from this practical emphasis to one of abstract expression that relates it more, in terms of freedom of expression, to music.

As a result, its meaning has become more profound and subtle by making the painting or picture itself, through the basic visual elements it employs, expressive of higher dimensional meanings found in nature. More specifically, visual elements such as dots, lines, planes and forms, when used abstractly or non-objectively, can be used as an expression of their own basic meaning in nature itself.

The use of these elements can in fact be related almost directly to music in terms of meaning. A dot can be used, as Kandinsky has pointed out, as an equivalent to a sound effect but on the visual level. For example a dot in the center of a circle is a silent sound. Dots arranged within the frame of a picture can express an order of staccato sounds as well as creating inner tensions related to space and time dimensions.

If so simple a means can produce such a profound difference, think of the unlimited possibilities inherent in dots and lines to picture frame. These possibilities are directly related to the qualities of movement, rest, grace, awkwardness, order, space and time, etc., which define the meaning of the dot and linear character of objects in the physical world. It should be understood that dots and lines and the three-dimensional forms together with all the means required to express them within the picture frame are the true inhabitants of this world. Used other than for their own qualities diminishes their meaning.

Proof of this, not on a theoretical, but on a purely practical level is evidenced by the fact that varying degrees of abstraction or even complete non-objectivity have become the dominant style of painting today.

But what about photography? Until very recently any attempt to bridge the gap between the literal object world and the world of abstract images has been spoken of as experimental. This adjective was applied by no less an authority than Beaumont Newhall to the work of our great name photographers Man Ray and Moholy-Nagy. It is true that techniques used, such as solarization and photograms, were experimental in the sense that the exact final result could not be determined at the time of taking a picture. Many of the methods popularly used today, such as moving the camera during exposure, photographing fast moving objects, recording light patterns on moving water also have this limiting control factor, and I believe that this is a weakening of the creative process.

It is most interesting to note, however, that during the past few years there has been a vital new interest in abstract photography. This can be seen in the work of a small but select group of photographers in America. Minor White and some of his advanced students, Walter Chappell, and the pioneer in the field, Aaron Siskind, are representative. One of the largest and most important exhibits in New York City at the Museum of Modern Art, called "The Sense of Abstraction," was an important recognition of the trend.

The favorite techniques used today include solarization, photograms, close-up photography of objects that destroys their literal meaning but employ abstract qualities of the image, and equivalents. I find many of the pictures made by these methods visually provocative but I am led in a different direction for the following reasons. The element of chance inevitable at the time of taking these pictures is one. Another is the lack of plasticity inherent in creating images of objects. This is less a factor in closeup photography than it is in conventional distances, but it still has a degree of weakness. And such weaknesses are not found in either music or painting.

In my own work I feel that I have found a way of overcoming some of the weaknesses previously mentioned. It is the technique of producing light pictures. Amazing the way light and sound are found to have equivalent virtues for creative expression. Sound is everywhere. It is completely plastic, it has psychological and physiological impact. Its levels of meaning and dimensional qualities are so great it need not be subservient to practical uses. It has great time and space dimensions. All of these things make it great as subject matter in its own right.

Let us examine light. Light is everywhere. It is completely plastic and lends itself freely and instantly to all dimensional levels of expression. It has psychological and physiological impact, like sound, —both being vibrations. It need not depend on imitation. It has all the visible colors and, in itself, far greater time and space dimensions than sound. I think, without a question of a doubt, that in the future light pictures viewed as transparencies and backed with a luminous glass (that is now being developed here in America) will hang on the walls of homes, offices, and public buildings just as abstract and non-objective paintings do today. Such pictures will have a scale of color values not possible by any pictures seen by reflected light and in actuality will be in a sense a live picture. I find it gratifying that my interest in these pictures is shared by a large number of people connected with colleges and professional photographic associations. Recently I was given the highest award of the Northern California Professional Photographers Association for contributions to professional photography as a fine art. My light pictures were an important factor in deciding the award.

These are made with a 35mm Exakta with extension bellows for close-up work. Many people who do close-up work wish to preserve the physical identity of the objects used. I do just the opposite. I wish to destroy the object reality and create the reality of the world of light. All the dimensions of the physical world, plus the full spectrum of colors together with time and space dimensions combine to make up this world. I use a light source (sunlight or tungsten) and direct it on any objects that have an affinity for light, such as water, cellophane, and glass. I use the ground glass of my camera as the painter uses canvas. I know how light reacts to my materials and arrange them roughly in front of the camera's lens. With this done I begin to move them slowly one way or another, controlling the action of light so as to create the picture desired. I use only straight photographic methods and so have control of the medium at all times.

HARRY CALLAHAN (1912-) *It's the subject matter that counts. I'm interested in revealing the subject in a new way to intensify it.* PHOTOGRAPHS: HARRY CALLAHAN, *Santa Barbara, Van Riper & Thompson,* 1964.

AN ADVENTURE IN PHOTOGRAPHY
1946
Minicam Photography, Vol. 9, No. 6, pp. 28-29.

These pictures of weeds in the snow are desired to express feeling more than anything else and if they convey feeling to you, I'll be ever so pleased.

Taking them was a standard photographic problem. There was no sun and I was not interested in the snow textures, but in the lines that the weeds made. So, I doubled the normal exposure on the snow and over developed the negative. The photographs showing light on the water were a combination of simple imagination plus an interest in the moving highlights that the sun on the water makes. This was an experiment, not new probably, but new to me which was the exciting part of it. In looking into the ground glass I could see the shapes that the moving water made with the sun reflecting upon them. I was anxious to see what these shapes would be on the film. They were made at one second exposure. All photographs are contact prints from 9 x 12 cm. negatives made with 9½" lens.

Photography is an adventure just as life is an adventure. If man wishes to express himself photographically, he must understand, surely to a certain extent, his relationship to life. I am interested in relating the problems that affect me to some set of values that I am trying to discover and establish as being my life. I want to discover and establish them through photography. This is strictly my affair and does not explain these pictures by any means. Anyone else not having the desire to take them would realize that I must have felt this was purely personal. This reason, whether it be good or bad, is the only reason I can give for these photographs.

The photographs that excite me are photographs that say something in a new manner; *not* for the sake of being different, but ones that are different because the individual is different and the individual expresses himself. I realize that we all do express ourselves, but those who express that which is always being done are those whose thinking is almost in every way in accord with everyone else. Expression on this basis has become dull to those who wish to think for themselves.

I wish more people felt that photography was an adventure the same as life itself and felt that their individual feelings were worth expressing. To me, that makes photography more exciting.

HENRI CARTIER-BRESSON (1908-) *Thinking should be done beforehand and afterwards—never while actually taking a photograph. Success depends on the extent of one's general culture, on one's set of values, one's clarity of mind and vivacity. The thing to be feared most is the artificially contrived, the contrary to life.* HENRI CARTIER-BRESSON ON THE ART OF PHOTOGRAPHY, (*an interview by Yvonne Baby*), *Harper's Magazine*, November 1961, p. 74.

INTRODUCTION   1952
The Decisive Moment, New York, Simon & Schuster.

I, like many another boy, burst into the world of photography with a Box Brownie, which I used for taking holiday snapshots. Even as a child, I had a passion for painting, which I "did" on Thursdays and Sundays, the days when French school children don't have school. Gradually, I set myself to try to discover the various ways in which I could play with a camera. From the moment that I began to use the camera and to think about it, however, there was an end to holiday snaps and silly pictures of my friends. I became serious. I was on the scent of something, and I was busy smelling it out.

Then there were the movies. From some of the great films, I learned to look, and to see. "Mysteries of New York," with Pearl White; the great films of D. W. Griffith—"Broken Blossoms"; the first films of Stroheim; "Greed"; Eisenstein's "Potemkin"; and Dreyer's "Jeanne d'Arc"—these were some of the things that impressed me deeply.

Later I met photographers who had some of Atget's prints. These I considered remarkable and, accordingly, I bought myself a tripod, a black cloth, and a polished walnut camera three by four inches. The camera was fitted with—instead of a shutter—a lenscap, which one took off and then put on to make the exposure. This last detail, of course, confined my challenge to the static world. Other photographic subjects seemed to me to be too complicated, or else to be "amateur stuff." And by this time I fancied that by disregarding them, I was dedicating myself to Art with a capital "A."

Next I took to developing this Art of mine in my washbasin. I found the business of being a photographic Jack-of-All-Trades quite entertaining. I knew nothing about printing, and had no inkling that certain kinds of paper produced soft prints and certain other highly contrasted ones. I didn't bother much about such things, though I invariably got mad when the images didn't come out right on the paper.

In 1931, when I was twenty-two, I went to Africa. On the Ivory Coast I bought a miniature camera of a kind I have never seen before or since, made by the French firm Krauss. It used film of a size that 35mm would be without the sprocket holes. For a year I took pictures with it. On my return to France I had my pictures developed—it was not possible before, for I lived in the bush, isolated, during most of that year—and I discovered that the damp had got into the camera and that all my photographs were embellished with the superimposed patterns of giant ferns.

I had had blackwater fever in Africa, and was now obliged to convalesce. I went to Marseille. A small allowance enabled me to get along, and I worked with enjoyment. I had just discovered the Leica. It became the extension of my eye, and I have never been separated from it since I found it. I prowled the streets all day, feeling very strung-up and ready to pounce, determined to "trap" life— to preserve life in the act of living. Above all, I craved to seize the whole essence, in the confines of one single photograph, of some situation that was in the process of unrolling itself before my eyes.

The idea of making a photographic reportage, that is to say, of telling a story in a sequence of pictures, was something which never entered my head at that time. I began to understand more about it later, as a result of looking at the work of my colleagues and at the illustrated magazines. In fact, it was only in the process of working for them that I eventually learned—bit by bit—how to make a reportage with a camera, how to make a picture-story.

I have travelled a good deal, though I don't really know how to travel. I like to take my time about it, leaving between one country and the next an interval in which to digest what I've seen. Once I have arrived in a new country, I feel almost like settling down there, so as to live on proper terms with the country. I could never be a globe-trotter.

In 1947, five free-lance photographers, of whom I was one, founded our co-operative enterprise called "Magnum Photos."

This co-operative enterprise distributes our picture-stories to magazines in various countries.

Twenty-five years have passed since I started to look through my view-finder. But I regard myself still as an amateur, though I am no longer a dilettante.

THE PICTURE-STORY

What actually *is* a photographic reportage, a picture-story? Sometimes there is one unique picture whose composition possesses such vigor and richness, and whose content so radiates outward from it, that this single picture is a whole story in itself. But this rarely happens. The elements which, together, can strike sparks out of a subject, are often scattered—either in terms of space or time—and bringing them together by force is "stage management," and, I feel, cheating. But if it is possible to make pictures of the "core" as well as the struck-off sparks of the subject, this is a picture-story; and the page serves to reunite the complementary elements which are dispersed throughout several photographs.

The picture-story involves a joint operation of the brain, the eye, and the heart. The objective of this joint operation is to depict the content of some event which is in the process of unfolding, and to communicate impressions. Sometimes a single event can be so rich in itself and its facets that it is necessary to move all around it in your search for the solution to the problems it poses—for the world is movement, and you cannot be stationary in your attitude toward something that is moving. Sometimes you light upon the picture in seconds; it might also require hours or days. But there is no standard plan, no pattern from which to work. You must be on the alert with the brain, the eye, the heart; and have a suppleness of body.

Things-As-They-Are offer such an abundance of material that a photographer must guard against the temptation of trying to do everything. It is essential to cut from the raw material of life—to cut and cut, but to cut with discrimination. While he is actually working, a photographer must reach a precise awareness of what he is trying to do. Sometimes you have the feeling that you have already taken the strongest possible picture of a particular situation or scene; nevertheless, you find yourself compulsively shooting, because you cannot be sure in advance exactly how the situation, the scene, is going to unfold. You must stay with the scene, just in case the elements of the situation shoot off from the core again. At the same time, it's essential to avoid shooting like a machine-gunner and burdening yourself with useless recordings which clutter your memory and spoil the exactness of the reportage as a whole.

Memory is very important, particularly in respect to the recollection of every picture you've taken while you've been galloping at the speed of the scene itself. The photographer must make sure, while he is still in the presence of the unfolding scene, that he hasn't left any gaps, that he has really given expression to the meaning of the scene in its entirety, for afterward it is too late. He is never able to wind the scene backward in order to photograph it all over again.

For photographers, there are two kinds of selection to be made, and either of them can lead to eventual regrets. There is the selection we make when we look through the view-finder at the subject; and there is the one we make after the films have been developed and printed. After developing and printing, you must go about separating the pictures which, though they are all right, aren't the strongest. When it's too late, then you know with a terrible clarity exactly where you failed; and at this point you often recall the telltale feeling you had while you were actually making the pictures. Was it a feeling of hesitation due to uncertainty? Was it because of some physical gulf between yourself and the unfolding event? Was it simply that you did not take into account a certain detail in relation to the whole setup? Or was it (and this is more frequent) that your glance became vague, your eye wandered off?

In the case of each of us it is from our own eye that space begins and slants off, enlarging itself progressively toward infinity. Space, in the present, strikes us with greater or lesser intensity, and then leaves us, visually, to be closed in our memory and to modify itself there. Of all the means of expression, photography is the only one that fixes forever the precise and transitory instant. We photographers deal in things which are continually vanishing, and when they have vanished, there is no contrivance on earth which can make them come back again. We cannot develop and print a memory. The writer has time to reflect. He can accept and reject, accept again; and before committing his thoughts to paper he is able to tie the several relevant elements together. There is also a period when his brain "forgets," and his subconscious works on classifying his thoughts. But for photographers, what has gone, has gone forever. From that fact stem the anxieties and strength of our profession. We cannot do our story over again once we've got back to the hotel. Our task is to perceive reality, almost simultaneously recording it in the sketchbook which is our camera. We must neither try to manipulate reality while we are shooting, nor must we manipulate the results in a darkroom. These tricks are patently discernible to those who have eyes to see.

In shooting a picture-story we must count the points and the rounds, rather like a boxing referee. In whatever picture-story we try to do, we are bound to arrive as intruders. It is essential, therefore, to approach the subject on tiptoe—even if the subject is still-life. A velvet hand, a hawk's eye—these we should all have. It's no good jostling or elbowing. And no photographs taken with the aid of flashlight either, if only out of respect for the actual light—even when there isn't any of it. Unless a photographer observes such conditions as these, he may become an intolerably aggressive character.

The profession depends so much upon the relations the photographer establishes with the people he's photographing, that a false relationship, a wrong word or attitude, can ruin everything. When

the subject is in any way uneasy, the personality goes away where
the camera can't reach it. There are no systems, for each case is
individual and demands that we be unobtrusive, though we must
be at close range. Reactions of people differ much from country to
country, and from one social group to another. Throughout the
whole of the Orient, for example, an impatient photographer—or
one who is simply pressed for time—is subject to ridicule. If you
have made yourself obvious, even just by getting your light-meter
out, the only thing to do is to forget about photography for the
moment, and accommodatingly allow the children who come rushing
at you to cling to your knees like burrs.

THE SUBJECT

✓ There is subject in all that takes place in the world, as well as in
our personal universe. We cannot negate subject. It is everywhere.
So we must be lucid toward what is going on in the world, and
honest about what we feel.

✓ Subject does not consist of a collection of facts, for facts in themselves offer little interest. Through facts, however, we can reach an
understanding of the laws that govern them, and be better able to
select the essential ones which communicate reality.

✓ In photography, the smallest thing can be a great subject. The
little, human detail can become a leitmotiv. We see and show the
world around us, but it is an event itself which provokes the organic
rhythm of forms.

✓ There are thousands of ways to distill the essence of something
that captivates us, let's not catalogue them. We will, instead, leave
it in all its freshness. . . .

There is a whole territory which is no longer exploited by painting.
Some say it is because of the discovery of photography. However it
came about, photography has taken over a part of this territory in
the form of illustration.

One kind of subject matter greatly derided by present-day painters
is the portrait. The frock coat, the soldier's cap, the horse—now repel
even the most academic of painters. They feel suffocated by all the
gaiter buttons of the Victorian portrait makers. For photographers—
perhaps because we are reaching for something much less lasting in
value than the painters—this is not so much irritating as amusing,
because we accept life in all its reality.

People have an urge to perpetuate themselves by means of a portrait, and they put their best profiles forward for posterity. Mingled
with this urge, though, is a certain fear of black magic; a feeling
that by sitting for a camera portrait they are exposing themselves to
the workings of witchcraft of a sort.

One of the fascinating things about portraits is the way they enable
us to trace the sameness of man. Man's continuity somehow comes
through all the external things which constitute him—even if it is

only to the extent of someone's mistaking Uncle for Little Nephew in the family album. If the photographer is to have a chance of achieving a true reflection of a person's world—which is as much outside him as inside him—it is necessary that the subject of the portrait should be in a situation normal to him. We must respect the atmosphere whch surrounds the human being, and integrate into the portrait the individual's habitat—for man, no less than animals, has his habitat. Above all, the sitter must be made to forget about the camera and the man who is handling it. Complicated equipment and light reflectors and various other items of hardware are enough, to my mind, to prevent the birdie from coming out.

What is there more fugitive and transitory than the expression on a human face? The first impression given by a particular face is often the right one; but the photographer should try always to substantiate the first impression by "living" with the person concerned. The decisive moment and psychology, no less than camera position, are the principal factors in the making of a good portrait. It seems to me it would be pretty difficult to be a portrait photographer for customers who order and pay since, apart from a Maecenas or two, they want to be flattered, and the result is no longer real. The sitter is suspicious of the objectivity of the camera, while what the photographer is after is an acute psychological study of the sitter.

It is true, too, that a certain identity is manifest in all the portraits taken by one photographer. The photographer is searching for identity of his sitter, and also trying to fulfill an expression of himself. The true portrait emphasizes neither the suave nor the grotesque, but reflects the personality.

I infinitely prefer, to contrived portraits, those little identity-card photos which are pasted side by side, row after row, in the windows of passport photographers. At least there is on these faces something that raises a question, a simple factual testimony—this in place of the poetic identification we look for.

COMPOSITION

If a photograph is to communicate its subject in all its intensity, the relationship of form must be rigorously established. Photography implies the recognition of a rhythm in the world of real things. What the eye does is to find and focus on the particular subject within the mass of reality; what the camera does is simply to register upon film the decision made by the eye. We look at and perceive a photograph, as a painting, in its entirety and all in one glance. In a photograph, composition is the result of a simultaneous coalition, the organic co-ordination of elements seen by the eye. One does not add composition as though it were an afterthought superimposed on the basic subject material, since it is impossible to separate content from form. Composition must have its own inevitability about it.

In photography there is a new kind of plasticity, product of the instantaneous lines made by movements of the subject. We work in unison with movement as though it were a presentiment of the way in which life itself unfolds. But inside movement there is one moment at which the elements in motion are in balance. Photography must seize upon this moment and hold immobile the equilibrium of it.

The photographer's eye is perpetually evaluating. A photographer can bring coincidence of line simply by moving his head a fraction of a millimeter. He can modify perspectives by a slight bending of the knees. By placing the camera closer to or farther from the subject, he draws a detail—and it can be subordinated, or he can by tyrannized by it. But he composes a picture in very nearly the same amount of time it takes to click the shutter, at the speed of a reflex action.

Sometimes it happens that you stall, delay, wait for something to happen. Sometimes you have the feeling that here are all the makings of a picture—except for just one thing that seems to be missing. But what one thing? Perhaps someone suddenly walks into your range of view. You follow his progress through the view-finder. You wait and wait, and then finally you press the button—and you depart with the feeling (though you don't know why) that you've really got something. Later, to substantiate this, you can take a print of this picture, trace on it the geometric figures which come up under analysis, and you'll observe that, if the shutter was released at the decisive moment, you have instinctively fixed a geometric pattern without which the photograph would have been both formless and lifeless.

Composition must be one of our constant preoccupations, but at the moment of shooting it can stem only from our intuition, for we are out to capture the fugitive moment, and all the interrelationships involved are on the move. In applying the Golden Rule, the only pair of compasses at the photographer's disposal is his own pair of eyes. Any geometrical analysis, any reducing of the picture to a schema, can be done only (because of its very nature) after the photograph has been taken, developed, and printed—and then it can be used only for a post-mortem examination of the picture. I hope we will never see the day when photoshops sell little schema grills to clamp onto our viewfinders; and the Golden Rule will never be found etched on our ground glass.

If you start cutting or cropping a good photograph, it means death to the geometrically correct interplay of proportions. Besides, it very rarely happens that a photograph which was feebly composed can be saved by reconstruction of its composition under the darkroom's enlarger; the integrity of vision is no longer there. There is a lot of talk about camera angles; but the only valid angles in existence are the angles of the geometry of composition and not the ones fabricated by the photographer who falls flat on his stomach or performs other antics to procure his effects.

COLOR

In talking about composition we have been so far thinking only in terms of that symbolic color called black. Black and white photography is a deformation, that is to say, an abstraction. In it, all the values are transposed; and this leaves the possibility of choice.

Color photography brings with it a number of problems which are hard to resolve today, and some of which are difficult even to foresee, owing to its complexity and its relative immaturity. At present, color film emulsions are still very slow. Consequently, photographers using color have a tendency to confine themselves to static subjects; or else to use ferociously strong artificial lights. The slow speed of color film reduces the depth of focus in the field of vision in relatively close shots; and this cramping often makes for dull composition. On top of that, blurred backgrounds in color photographs are distinctly displeasing.

Color photographs in the form of transparencies seem quite pleasing sometimes. But then the engraver takes over; and a complete understanding with the engraver would appear to be as desirable in this business as it is in lithography. Finally, there are the inks and the paper, both of which are capable of acting capriciously. A color photograph reproduced in a magazine or semi-luxury edition sometimes gives the impression of an anatomical dissection which has been badly bungled.

It is true that color reproductions of pictures and documents have already achieved a certain fidelity to the original; but when the color proceeds to take on real life, it's another matter. We are only in the infancy of color photography. But all this is not to say we should take no further interest in the question, or sit by waiting for the perfect color film—packaged with the talent necessary to use it—to drop into our laps. We must continue to try to feel our way.

Though it is difficult to foresee exactly how color photography is going to grow in photo-reporting, it seems certain that it requires a new attitude of mind, an approach different than that which is appropriate for black and white. Personally, I am half afraid that this complex new element may tend to prejudice the achievement of the life and movement which is often caught by black and white.

To really be able to create in the field of color photography, we should transform and modulate colors, and thus achieve liberty of expression within the framework of the laws which were codified by the Impressionists and from which even a photographer cannot shy away. (The law, for instance, of simultaneous contrast: the law that every color tends to tinge the space next to it with its complementary color; that if two tones contain a color which is common to them both, that common color is attenuated by placing the two tones side by side; that two complementary colors placed side by side emphasize both, but mixed together they annihilate each other; and so on.)

The operation of bringing the color of nature in space to a printed surface poses a series of problems extremely complex. To the eye, certain colors advance, others recede. So we would have to be able to adjust the relations of the colors one to the other, for colors which place themselves in nature in the depth of space, claim a different placing on a plane surface—whether it is the flat surface of a painting or a photograph.

The difficulties involved in snapshooting are precisely that we cannot control the movement of the subject; and in color-photography reporting, the real difficulty is that we are unable to control the inter-relation of colors within the subject. It wouldn't be hard to add to the list of difficulties involved, but it is quite certain that the developmen of photography is tied up with the development of its technique.

TECHNIQUE

Constant new discoveries in chemistry and optics are widening considerably our field of action. It is up to us to apply them to our technique, to improve ourselves, but there is a whole group of fetishes which have developed on the subject of technique.

Technique is important only insofar as you must master it in order to communicate what you see. Your own personal technique has to be created and adapted.solely in order to make your vision effective on film. But only the results count, and the conclusive evidence is the finished photographic print; otherwise there would be no end to the number of tales photographers would tell about pictures which they ever-so-nearly got—but which are merely a memory in the eye of the nostalgia.

Our trade of photo-reporting has been in existence only about thirty years. It came to maturity due to the development of easily handled cameras, faster lenses, and fast fine-grain films produced for the movie industry. The camera is for us a tool, not a pretty mechanical toy. In the precise functioning of the mechanical object perhaps there is an unconscious compensation for the anxieties and uncertainties of daily endeavor. In any case, people think far too much about techniques and not enough about seeing.

It is enough if a photographer feels at ease with his camera, and if it is appropriate to the job which he wants it to do. The actual handling of the camera, its stops, its exposure-speeds and all the rest of it, are things which should be as automatic as the changing of gears in an automobile. It is no part of my business to go into the details or refinements of any of these operations, even the most complicated ones, for they are all set forth with military precision in the manuals which the manufacturers provide along with the camera and the nice, orange calf-skin case. If the camera is a beautiful gadget, we should progress beyond that stage at least in conversation. The same applies to the hows and whys of making pretty prints in the darkroom.

During the process of enlarging, it is essential to re-create the values and mood of the time the picture was taken; or even to modify the print so as to bring it into line with the intentions of the photographer at the moment he shot it. It is necessary also to re-establish the balance which the eye is continually establishing between light and shadow. And it is for these reasons that the final act of creating in photography takes place in the darkroom.

I am constantly amused by the notion that some people have about photographic technique—a notion which reveals itself in an insatiable craving for sharpness of images. Is this the passion of an obsession? Or do these people hope, by this "trompe l'œil" technique, to get to closer grips with reality? In either case, they are just as far away from the real problem as those of that other generation which used to endow all its photographic anecdotes with an intentional unsharpness such as was deemed to be "artistic."

THE CUSTOMERS

The camera enables us to keep a sort of visual chronicle. For me, it is my diary. We photo-reporters are people who supply information to a world in a hurry, a world weighted down with preoccupations, prone to cacophony, and full of beings with a hunger for information, and needing the companionship of images. We photographers, in the course of taking pictures, inevitably make a judgment on what we see, and that implies a great responsibility. We are, however, dependent on printing, since it is to the illustrated magazines that we, as artisans, deliver raw material.

It was indeed an emotional experience for me when I sold my first photograph (to the French magazine *Vu*). That was the start of a long alliance with magazines. It is the magazines that produce for us a public, and introduce us to that public; and they know how to get picture-stories across in the way the photographer intended. But sometimes, unhappily, they distort them. The magazine can publish exactly what the photographer wanted to show; but the photographer runs the risk of letting himself be molded by the taste or the requirements of the magazine.

In a picture-story, the captions should invest the pictures with a verbal context, and should illuminate whatever relevant thing it may have been beyond the power of camera to reach. Unfortunately, in the sub-editor's room, mistakes sometimes slip in which are not just simple misspellings or malapropisms. For these mistakes the reader often holds the photographer responsible. Such things do happen.

The pictures pass through the hands of the editor and the layout man. The editor has to make his choice from the thirty or so pictures of which the average picture-story consists. (It is rather as though he had to cut a text article to pieces in order to end up with a series of quotations!) For a picture-story, as for a novel, there are certain set forms. The pictures of the editor's choice have to be laid out within the space of two, three, or four pages, according to the amount of interest he thinks they are likely to arouse, or according to the current state of paper shortage.

The great art of the layout man lies in his knowing how to pick from this pile of pictures the particular one which deserves a full-page or a double-page spread; in his knowing where to insert the small picture which must serve as an indispensable link in the story. (The photographer, when he is actually taking the pictures for his story, should give a thought to the ways in which it will be possible to lay out those pictures to the most advantage.) The layout man will often have to crop one picture so as to leave only the most important section of it—since, for him, it is the unity of the whole page or of the whole spread that counts above all else. A photographer can scarcely be too appreciative of the layout man who gives his work a beautiful presentation of a kind which keeps the full import of the story; a display in which the pictures have spatially correct margins and stand out as they should; and in which each page possesses its own architecture and rhythm.

There is a third anguish for a photographer—when he looks for his story in a magazine.

There are other ways of communicating our photographs than through publication in magazines. Exhibitions, for instance; and the book form, which is almost a form of permanent exhibition.

I have talked at some length, but of only one kind of photography. There are many kinds. Certainly the fading snapshot carried in the back of a wallet, the glossy advertising catalogue, and the great range of things in between—are photography. I don't attempt to define it for everyone. I only attempt to define it to myself:

To me, photography is the simultaneous recognition, in a fraction of a second, of the significance of an event as well as of a precise organization of forms which give that event its proper expression.

I believe that, through the act of living, the discovery of oneself is made concurrently with the discovery of the world around us which can mold us, but which can also be affected by us. A balance must be established between these two worlds—the one inside us and the one outside us. As the result of a constant reciprocal process, both these worlds come to form a single one. And it is this world that we must communicate.

But this takes care only of the content of the picture. For me, content cannot be separated from form. By form, I mean a rigorous organization of the interplay of surfaces, lines, and values. It is in this organization alone that our conceptions and emotions become concrete and communicable. In photography, visual organization can stem only from a developed instinct.

ALVIN LANGDON COBURN (1882-1966) *I believe that most creative artists worthy of the name, of whatever school or medium be it pen or brush, marble or scale of tones, have an inner world of inspiration which interpenetrates this world of action, and into this sanctuary they may, yea must, at times retire for meditation and refreshment. Some say in sleep this state is reached, and dreams the bringing back of some vague glimmerings to the waking life; but the way is more firm than this, and happy is he who finds the central way.* MORE MEN OF MARK, *London, Duckworth & Co., 1922, p. 19.*

THE RELATION OF TIME TO ART   1911
Camera Work, No. 36, pp. 72-73.

After living constantly for two years in the quiet and seclusion of a London suburb, and then suddenly being plunged into the rush and turmoil of New York, where time and space are of more value than in any other part of our world, this consideration of the relation of time to art has been forced upon me.

As photography has, up to the present time, been my sole means of expression, I can best understand and attempt to explain my meaning by consideration of the part time plays in the art of the camera.

Photography is the most modern of the arts, its development and practical usefulness extends back only into the memory of living men; in fact, it is more suited to the art requirements of this age of scientific achievement than any other. It is, however, only by comparing it with the older art of painting that we will get the full value of our argument plainly before us; and in doing so we shall find that the essential difference is not so much a mechanical one of brushes and pigments as compared with a lens and dry plates, but rather a mental one of a slow, gradual, usual building up, as compared with an instantaneous, concentrated mental impulse, followed by a longer period of fruition. Photography born of this age of steel seems to have naturally adapted itself to the necessarily unusual requirements of an art that must live in skyscrapers, and it is because it has become so much at home in these gigantic structures that the Americans undoubtedly are the recognized leaders in the world movement of pictorial photography.

Just imagine any one trying to paint at the corner of Thirty-fourth street, where Broadway and Sixth Avenue cross! The camera has recorded an impression in the flashing fragment of a second. But what about the training, you will say, that has made this seizing of the momentary vision possible? It is, let me tell you, no easy thing to acquire, and necessitates years of practice and something of the instinctive quality that makes a good marksman. Just think of the combination of knowledge and sureness of vision that was required to make possible Stieglitz's "Winter on Fifth Avenue." If you call it a "glorified snapshot" you must remember that life has much of this same quality. We are comets across the sky of eternity.

It has been said of me, to come to the personal aspect of this problem, that I work too quickly, and that I attempt to photograph all

New York in a week. Now to me New York is a vision that rises out of the sea as I come up the harbor on my Atlantic liner, and which glimmers for a while in the sun for the first of my stay amidst its pinnacles; but which vanishes, but for fragmentary glimpses, as I become one of the grey creatures that crawl about like ants, at the bottom of its gloomy caverns. My apparently unseemly hurry has for its object my burning desire to record, translate, create, if you like, these visions of mine before they fade. I can do only the creative part of photography, the making of the negative, with the fire of enthusiasm burning at the white heat; but the final stage, the print, requires quiet contemplation, time, in fact, for its fullest expression. That is why my best work is from American negatives printed in England.

Think for a moment of the limitations of photography. You are confined to what a friend of mine sums up in the high-sounding words, "contemporary actuality," and now I find that my vision of New York has gradually taken upon itself a still narrower range, for it is only at twilight that the city reveals itself to me in the fullness of its beauty, when the arc lights on the Avenue click into being. Many an evening I have watched them and studied carefully just which ones appeared first and why. They begin somewhere about Twenty-sixth street, where it is darkest, and then gradually the great white globes glow one by one, up past the Waldorf and the new Library, like the stringing of pearls, until they burst out into a diamond pendant at the group of hotels at Fifty-ninth street.

Probably there is a man at a switchboard somewhere, but the effect is like destiny, and regularly each night, like the stars, we have this lighting up of the Avenue.

THE FUTURE OF PICTORIAL PHOTOGRAPHY   1916
Photograms of the Year 1916, pp. 23-24.

An artist is a man who tries to express the inexpressible. He struggles and suffers knowing that he can never realise his most perfect ideal. Occasional moments of ecstasy lure him on, but nothing is final in art; it is always progressing and advancing, as man's intelligence expands in the light of more perfect knowledge of himself and the universe.

It is this progress of the arts that has interested me. Where is it leading us? There are the "moderns" in Painting, in Music, and in Literature. What would our grandfathers have said of the work of Matisse, Stravinsky, and Gertrude Stein? What *do* our grandfathers say? They hold up their hand in horror, they show their bad manners by scoffing and jeering at something they are too antiquated to understand. It is the revolutionary of today, however, who is the "classic" of tomorrow; there is no escaping the ruthless forward march of time.

Yes, if we are alive to the spirit of our time it is these moderns who interest us. They are striving, reaching out towards the future, analysing the mossy structure of the past, and building afresh, in colour and sound and grammatical construction, the scintillating vision of their minds; and being interested particularly in photography, it has occurred to me, why should not the camera also throw off the shackles of conventional representation and attempt something fresh and untried? Why should not its subtle rapidity be utilised to study movement? Why not repeated successive exposures of an object in motion on the same plate? Why should not perspective be studied from angles hitherto neglected or unobserved? Why, I ask you earnestly, need we go on making commonplace little exposures of subjects that may be sorted into groups of landscapes, portraits, and figure studies? Think of the joy of doing something which it would be impossible to classify, or to tell which was the top and which the bottom!

In last year's exhibition of the Royal Photographic Society there was a little group of prints by American workers, mostly entitled "Design"—many of my readers will remember them. They were groups of various objects photographed because of their shape and colour value, and with no thought of their sentimental associations. There were, I believe, tables, golf clubs, portfolios, etc, etc. The idea was to be as abstract as it is possible to be with the camera. Max Weber, the Cubist painter-poet, was responsible for the idea of these designs, and Weber is one of the most sincere artists that it has ever been my good fortune to meet; but of course these experiments in a new direction only met with sneers and laughter—it is always the same with an innovation in any direction. In his new book, "Essays on Art," Weber says: "To express moods that stir the emotion from within, as does music, the plastic artist, when he conceives of energetic rhythmic interlaced forms or units, should be much more moved than even by music. It is like cementing a thought, or arresting a perfect moment of time, or like giving body to space, or solidity to air, or coloured light to darkness."

How many of us are moved like this in photography? We think of the camera as a rather material means of self-expression—if we think about it at all; but is it really so? Pause for a moment and consider the mysterious quality of light registering itself in sensitized gelatine —all the scientific poetry in the words "latent image." In the days when men were burned at the stake for practising "black magic" the photographer would have been an undoubted victim if it had been invented in those dark times; but now every "nipper" has a "Brownie," and a photograph is as common as a box of matches— perhaps even more so, this being war time! Photography is too easy in a superficial way, and in consequence is treated slightingly by people who ought to know better. One does not consider Music an inferior art simply because little Mary can play a scale. What we need in photography is more sincerity, more respect for our medium and less respect for its decayed conventions.

All the summer I have been painting, and so I can come back to photography with a more or less fresh viewpoint, and it makes me want to shout, "Wake up!" to many of my photographic colleagues. "Do something outrageously bad if you like, but let it be freshly seen." If we go on fishing out our old negatives and making a few feeble prints of them, just as we have been doing for the past ten years, photography will stagnate. I have the very greatest respect for photography as a means of personal expression, and I want to see it alive to the spirit of progress; if it is not possible to be "modern" with the newest of all the arts, we had better bury our black boxes, and go back to scratching with a sharp bone in the manner of our remote Darwinian ancestors. I do not think that we have begun to even realize the possibilities of the camera. The beauty of design displayed by the microscope seems to me a wonderful field to explore from the purely pictorial point of view, the use of prisms for the splitting of images into segments has been very slightly experimented with, and multiple exposures on the same plate—outside of the childish fakes of the so-called "spirit photographs"—have been neglected almost entirely.

As a start I suggest that an exhibition be organised of "Abstract Photography"; that in the entry form it be distinctly stated that no work will be admitted in which the interest of the subject matter is greater than the appreciation of the extraordinary. A sense of design is, of course, all important, and an opportunity for the expression of suppressed or unsuspected originality should prove very beneficial.

You may think what you like about the modern movement in the arts, but the world will never be the same place again. We may disapprove of modernity in art, but we can never go back to Academicism with the smug complacency of yore. The hollowness, the unthinkable dullness of it all, is now only too clearly apparent. And it is my hope that photography may fall in line with all the other arts, and with her infinite possibilities, do things stranger and more fascinating than the most fantastic dreams.

ROBERT DEMACHY (1859-1938) . . . *a consensus of feeling which appears to be coming universal amongst people who write tends to confine us henceforth within what they call, without further explanation—and Heaven knows we should be grateful for one—the Limits of Photography; so that a print purely artistic in its nature can not be admirable unless it distinctly offers us the photographic character and the qualities of the medium carried to their highest degree of perfection.* MONSIEUR DEMACHY AND ENGLISH PHOTOGRAPHIC ART, *Camera Work, No. 18, 1907, p. 42.*

ON THE STRAIGHT PRINT   761661   1907
Camera Work, No. 19, pp. 21-24.

The old war between straight photography and the other one—

call it as you like—has begun over again. It is not, as it ought to be, a question of principle. No, it has become a personal question amongst a good many photographers, because most of them, and especially those who take purely documentary photographs, look to being recognized as artists. It follows that any definition of art that does not fit in with their methods will be violently attacked because the recognition of such a definition would limit pictorial photography to a certain number of men instead of throwing open the doors of the temple to the vast horde of camera carriers.

It is not without certain misgivings that I am attempting to give a clear résumé of this ever debated question, for I know that the above paragraph will be used against me and I shall be accused of "pleading for my saint" as we say. As a fact I am doing nothing of the sort, for though I believe firmly that a work of art can only be evolved under certain circumstances, I am equally convinced that these same circumstances will not perforce engender a work of art. Meddling with a gum print may or may not add the vital spark, though without the meddling there will surely be no spark whatever.

My meaning I hope has been made clear. Still there is a second point to be elucidated, and that is the precise signification of a term that we shall be using presently, "straight print." According to the sense that is given to this term the whole structure of our arguments may be radically changed and the subsequent verdict falsified. For here is *par avance* my opinion in a few words. A straight print may be beautiful, and it may prove super-abundantly that its author is an artist; but it can not be a work of art. You see now that it is necessary before entering into details to give a clear definition of the nature of the straight print as I understand it, and also a definition of the work of art. A straight print, to be worthy of its name, must first of all be taken from a straight negative. There must be no playing upon words in a serious controversy of this nature. One must not call "straight" a bromide mechanically printed, but from a negative reduced locally and painted on the glass side with all the colors of the rainbow. This leads us to describe the straight negative. It will be a negative produced by normal development, or better still by tank development, during which no control is possible; and of course it will not be submitted to any subsequent retouching either on the film or on the glass. From this negative a print will be taken with a normal exposure without local shading. If the paper used for printing has to be developed, it will not be developed locally nor interfered with in any way during development. It will be mounted or framed without its surface being touched by a finger or a brush.

This is my idea of the sense of the term "straight print." If any readers consider that it is a false idea they had better leave the next pages unread. Now, speaking of graphic methods only, what are the distinctive qualities of a work of art? A work of art must be a transcription, not a copy, of nature. The beauty of the motive in nature has nothing to do with the quality that makes a work of art. This special quality is given by the artist's way of expressing himself. In other words, there is not a particle of art in the most beautiful scene of nature. The art is man's alone, it is subjective not objective. If a man slavishly copies nature, no matter if it is with hand and pencil or through a photographic lens, he may be a supreme artist all the while, but that particular work of his can not be called a work of art.

I have so often heard the terms "artistic" and "beautiful" employed as if they were synonymous that I believe it is necessary to insist on the radical difference between their meanings. Quite lately I have read in the course of an interesting article on American pictorial photography the following paragraph: "In nature there is the beautiful, the commonplace and the ugly, and he who has the insight to recognize the one from the other and the cunning to separate and transfix only the beautiful, is the artist." This would induce us to believe that when Rembrandt painted the "Lesson in Anatomy" he proved himself no artist. Is there anything uglier in nature than a greenish, half-disemboweled corpse; or anything more commonplace than a score of men dressed in black standing round a table? Nevertheless, the result of this combination of the ugly and the commonplace is one of the greatest masterpieces in painting. Because the artist intervened.

If Rembrandt had painted that scene exactly as he saw it in nature he would have given us exactly the same impression that he would have felt in front of the actual scene, a sensation of disgust—mingled perhaps with a vivid admiration for the manual and visual skill of the copyist, but without a shadow of any art sensation.

Let us change the circumstances and take as example a beautiful motive such as a sunset. Do you think that Turner's sunsets existed in nature such as he painted them? Do you think that if he had painted them as they were, and not as he felt them, he would have left a name as an artist? Why, if the choice of a beautiful motive was sufficient to make a work of art ninety percent of the graphic works in the world, paintings, drawings, photographs and chromos would be works of art, a few of them only, distinctly ugly and not as many commonplace.

Choose the man whom you consider the very first landscape artist photographer in the world; suppose he has, thanks to his artistic nature and visual training, chosen the hour and spot, of all others. Imagine him shadowed by some atrocious photographic bounder furnished with the same plates and lens as the master. Imagine this plagiarist setting his tripod in the actual dents left by the artist's machine and taking the same picture with the same exposure. Now, suppose that both are straight printers? Who will be able later on to tell which is the artist's and which is the other one's picture? But figure to yourself the artist printing his negative, selectively, by the gum bichromate or the oil process, or developing his platinotype print with glycerine. Even if the other man used the same printing method, one print will have the artist's signature all over it from the sky to the ground, the other will be a meaningless muddle. For *the man* has intervened in both cases. One has made a work of art out of a simply beautiful picture, the other has probably spoiled its beauty and certainly has introduced no art. The moral of this fable is two-fold. It shows that a beautiful straight print may be made by a man incapable of producing a work of art, and that a straight print can not possibly be a work of art even when its author is an artist, since it may be identical to that taken by a man who is no artist.

You will answer that a gum or an oil print from a master can be copied by a patient and painstaking worker, just as the above beautiful motive was stolen from the artist—well, you may try. I know of a man who has been copying Steichen to the extent of having canvas background painted exactly like the brush-developed background of one of his gum portraits. I prefer not to speak of the result. That it was all to the credit of Steichen you may believe.

Not once but many times have I heard it said that the choice of the motive is sufficient to turn an otherwise mechanically produced positive into a work of art. This is not true; what is true is that a carefully chosen motive (beautiful, ugly, or commonplace, but well composed and properly lighted) is necessary in the subsequent evolution towards art. It is not the same thing. No, you can not escape the consequences of the mere copying of nature. A copyist may be an artist but his copy is not a work of art; the more accurate it is, the worse art it will be. Please do not unearth the old story about Zeuxis and Apelles, when the bird and then the painter were taken in. I have no faith in sparrows as art critics and I think the mistake of the painter was an insult to his brother artist.

The result of all this argument will be that I shall be taxed with having said that all unmodified prints are detestable productions, fit for the wastepaper basket, and that before locally developed platinotype, gum bichromate, ozotype and oils, there were no artists to be found amongst photographers. I deny all this. I have seen many straight prints that were beautiful and that gave evidence of the artistic nature of their authors, without being, in my private opinion, works of art. For a work of art is a big thing. I have also seen so-called straight prints that struck me as works of art, so much so that I immediately asked for some technical details about their genesis, and found to my intimate satisfaction that they were not straight prints at all. I have seen brush-developed, multi-modified gum prints that were worse—immeasurably worse—than the vilest tintype in exist-ence, and I have seen and have in my possession straight prints by

Miss Cameron and by Salomon, one of our first professionals, just after Daguerre's time, that are undoubtedly the work of artists. All is not artistically bad in a straight print. Some values are often well rendered; some "passages" from light to shade are excellent, and the drawing can be good if proper lenses are used at a proper distance from the motive; but there is something wanting, something all important, extremely difficult to express in words. If you can see it there is no use trying to describe it; if you do not, it is useless also, for you would not understand. But apart from the absence of this mysterious something, this thumb-mark of the living, thinking, and feeling artist, are there not other things wrong in all straight photographs—faults due not only to the inevitable human errors in exposure and development, but to photography itself, photographic faults in the rendering of values (that no orthochromatic plates are capable of correcting without creating other exaggerations just as bad), faults in the equal translation of important and useless detail, in the monotonous registering of different textures, in the exaggeration of brilliant spots, and in other things, too? What will the pure photographer do when he has detected these faults? If he allows them to remain out of respect for the laws of the pure goddess photography, he may prove himself a high priest photographic, but will he still be a true artist, faithful to the gospel of art? I believe that, unless he has had his fingers amputated according to the dictates of Bernard Shaw, he will feel them itching to tone down or to lighten this spot or that, and to do other things also. But he *may not* do these things, the Law of the Straight Print forbids it. The conclusion is simple enough, for there is no middle course between the mechanical copy of nature and the personal transcription of nature. The law is there; but there is no sanction to it, and the buttonpressers will continue to extol the purity of their intentions and to make a virtue of their incapacity to correct and modify their mechanical copies. And too many pictorialists will meddle with their prints in the fond belief that any alteration, however bungling, is the touchstone of art. Later on perhaps a sane, ·moderate school of pictorial photography will evolve. *La vérité est en marche, mais elle marche lentement.*

Before ending I can not but confess my astonishment at the necessity of such a profession of faith as the one I have been making. Pictorial photography owes its birth to the universal dissatisfaction of artist photographers in front of the photographic errors of the straight print. Its false values, its lack of accents, its equal delineation of things important and useless, were universally recognized and deplored by a host of malcontents. There was a general cry toward liberty of treatment and liberty of correction. Glycerine-developed platinotype and gum bichromate were soon after hailed with enthusiasm as liberators; today the oil process opens outer and inner doors to personal treatment. And yet, after all this outcry against old-

fashioned and narrow-minded methods, after this thankful acceptance of new ones, the men who fought for new ideas are now fighting
for old errors. That documentary photographers should hold up the
straight print as a model is but natural, they will continue doing so
in aeternum for various personal reasons; but that men like A and B
should extol the virtues of mechanical photography *as an art process,*
I can not understand.

I consider that, from an art point of view, the straight print of
today is not a whit better than the straight print of fifteen years ago.
If it was faulty then it is still faulty now. If it was all that can be
desired, pictorial photographers, the Links and the various secessionists of the new and the old world have been wasting their time,
to say the least, during the last decade.

PETER H. EMERSON (1856-1936) *The opticians were right from the mathematical standpoint, and I was right from the physiological and psychological
standpoints, and so it was evident there were two truths to nature—the perspective or mathematical truth and the psychological or visual truth.* NATURAL-
ISTIC PHOTOGRAPHY, 3rd ed., New York, Scoville & Adams, 1899, p. 170.

SCIENCE AND ART 1899
Naturalistic Photography, 3d ed. rev., New York, Scovill & Adams,
Appendix A, pp. 67-79. (Paper read at the Camera Club Conference
held in the rooms of the Society of Arts, London, March 26, 1889.)

MR. PRESIDENT, LADIES, AND FELLOW-PHOTOGRAPHERS:—Before beginning this paper I would fain ask of you two things—your attention
and your charity, but especially your charity. The reception which
you accord me, ladies and gentlemen, assures me you will give both,
and I thank you beforehand.

Since all mental progress consists, as Mr. Herbert Spencer has
shown, for the most part in differentiation—that is in the analysis of
an unknown complex into known components—surely it were a folly
to confuse any longer the aims of Science and Art. Rather should we
endeavor to draw an indelible line of demarcation between them, for
in this way we make mental progress, and Science and Art at the same
time begin to gather together their scattered forces, each one taking
under its standard those powers that belong to it, and thus becoming
integrated, and necessarily stronger and more permanent; for evolution is integration and differentiation passing into a coherent hetero-
geneity. Now I do not mean to premise that this confusion between
Science and Art exists everywhere—it does not. But I feel sure that it
exists largely in the ever-increasing body of persons who practise
photography. The majority of them have not thoroughly, nay, not
even adequately, thought the matter out. It is obvious, according
to the teachings of evolution, that, if we are to make progress, this
differentiation must be made, thoroughly understood and rigidly
adhered to by every practitioner of photography. Each one must have
his aim clearly stamped upon his mind, whether it be the advance-

ment of science or the creation of works whose aim and end is to give
aesthetic pleasure. Proceed we now to analyze the difference between
the aims and ends of Science and Art. Let us first approach the
subject from the scientific standpoint.

Assuming that we have before us a living man, let us proceed
together to study him scientifically, for the nonce imagining our
minds to be virginal tablets, without score or scratch. Let us proceed
first to record the color of his skin, his hair and eyes, the texture of
his skin, the relative positions of the various orifices in his face, the
number of his limbs, the various measurements of all these members.
So we go on integrating and differentiating until we find that we
have actually built up a science—ethnology. If we pursue the study,
and begin to compare different races of men with each other, we find
our ethnology extends to a more complex anthropology.

We next observe that the eyelids open and close, the lips open,
sounds issue from the mouth, and our curiosity leads us to dissect a
dead subject, and we find that beneath the skin, fat, and superficial
fasciae there are muscles, each supplied with vessels and nerves to
their common origins, and are led to the heart and brain. In short,
we find the science of anatomy grows up under our hands, and if we
go on with our studies we are led into microscopy. Then we begin to
ponder on the reasons why the blood flows, on the reasons why the
corrugator supercilii and *depressores anguli oris* act in weeping, the
musculus superbus in practical arrogance, and the *levator anguli oris*
in snarling or sneering. So we go on studying the functions of all the
organs we find in our man, and lo! we are deep in physiology; and
if we go deeply enough we find the thread lost in the most complex
problems of organic chemistry and molecular physics. And so we
might go on studying this man; and if our lives were long enough,
and if we had capacity enough, we should be led through a study of
this man to a knowledge of all physical phenomena, so wonderful
and beautiful is the all-pervading principle of the conservation of
energy, and so indestructible is matter. As we proceeded with our
studies we should have been observing, recording, positing hypothe-
ses, and either proving or disproving them. In all these ways we
should have been adding to the sum of knowledge. And in the greatest steps we made in our advancement we should have made use of
our *constructive imagination*—the highest *intellectual* power, according to recent psychologists.

The results of these investigations, if we were wise, would have
been recorded in the simplest and tersest language possible, for such
is the language of Science. It is needless to point out that in these
records of our studies, as in the records of all scientific studies, *too
many* facts could not possibly be registered. Every little fact is welcome in scientific study, so long as it is true. And thus the humblest
scientific worker may help in the great work; his mite is always

acceptable. Such is, alas, not the case with that jealous goddess, Art; she will have nothing to do with mediocrity. A bad work of art has no *raison d'etre;* it is worse than useless—it is harmful.

To sum up, then, "Science," as Professor Huxley says, "is the knowledge of the laws of Nature obtained by observation, experiment, and reasoning. No line can be drawn between common knowledge of things and scientific knowledge; nor between common reasoning and scientific reasoning. In strictness, all accurate knowledge is Science, and all exact reasoning is scientific reasoning. The method of *observation* and *experiment* by which such great results are obtained in Science is identically the same as that which is employed by every one, every day of his life, but refined and rendered precise."

Now let us turn to Art, and look at our imaginary man from the artistic standpoint. Assuming that we have learned the technique of some method of artistic expression, and that is part of the science we require, we will proceed with our work.

Let us look at the figure before us from the sculptor's point of view. Now what is our mental attitude? We no longer care for many of the facts that vitally interested us when we were studying the man scientifically; we care little about his anatomy, less about his physiology, and nothing at all about organic chemistry and molecular physics. We care nothing for his morality, his thoughts, his habits and customs—his sociological history, in fact; neither do we care about his ethnological characters. If he be a good model, it matters little whether he be *Greek, Italian,* or *Circassian.* But we do care, above all, for his type, his build, and the grace with which he comports himself; for our aim is to make a statue like him, a statue possessing qualities that shall give aesthetic pleasure. For the *raison d'etre* of a work of art ends with itself; there should be no ulterior motive beyond the giving of aesthetic pleasure to the most cultivated and sensitively refined natures.

The first thing, then, we must do is to sit in judgment on our model. Will he do for the purpose? Are his features suitable? Is *he* well modelled in all parts? Does he move easily and with grace? If he fulfils all these conditions we take him. Then we watch his movements and seize on a beautiful pose. Now with our clay we begin to model him. As we go on with our work we begin to see that it is utterly impossible to record all the facts about him with our material, and we soon find it is undesirable to do so—nay, pernicious. We cannot model those hundreds of fine wrinkles, those thousands of hairs, those myriads of pores in the skin that we see before us. What, then, must we do? We obviously *select* some—the most salient, if we are wise—and *leave out* the rest.

All at once the fundamental distinction between Science and Art draws upon us. We *cannot* record too many facts in Science; the fewer facts we record in Art, and yet express the subject so that it cannot be better expressed, the better. All the greatest artists have *left out* as much as possible. They have endeavored to give a fine *analysis* of the model, and the Greeks succeeded.

It is beside the question to show how Science has exercised an injurious influence upon certain schools in art; but that would be very easy to do. At the same time, the best Art has been founded on scientific principles—that is, the big physical facts have been true to nature.

To sum up, then, Art is the selection, arrangement, and recording of certain facts, with the aim of giving aesthetic pleasure; and it differs from Science fundamentally, in that as few facts as are compatible with complete expression are chosen, and these are arranged so as to appeal to the emotional side of man's nature, whereas the scientific facts appeal to his intellectual side.

But, as in many erroneous ideas that have had currency for long, there lurks a germ of truth, so there lurks still a leaven of Art in Science and a leaven of Science in Art; but in each these leavenings are subordinate, and not at the first blush appreciable. For example, in Science the facts can be recorded or demonstrated with selection, arrangement, and lucidity; that is the leaven of Art in Science. Whilst in Art the big physical facts of nature must be truthfully rendered; that is the leaven of Science in Art.

And so we see there is a relationship between science and art, and yet they are as the poles asunder.

2

We shall now endeavor to discuss briefly how our remarks apply to photography. Any student of photographic literature is well aware that numerous papers are constantly being published by persons who evidently are not aware of this radical distinction between science and art.

The student will see it constantly advocated that every detail of a picture should be impartially rendered with a biting accuracy, and this *in all cases.* This biting sharpness being, as landscape painters say, *"Quite fatal from the artistic standpoint."* If the rendering were always given sharply, the work would belong to the category of topography or the *knowledge* of places, that is *Science.* To continue, the student will find directions for producing an *unvarying* quality in his negative. He will be told how negatives of low-toned effects may be made to give prints like negatives taken in bright sunshine; in short, he will find that these writers have a *scientific ideal,* a sort of *standard negative* by which to gauge all others. And if these writers are questioned, the student will find the *standard negative* is one in which all detail is rendered with microscopic sharpness, and one taken evidently in the brightest sunshine. We once heard it seriously proposed that there should be some sort of *standard lantern-slide.* My allotted time is too brief to give further examples. Suffice it to say, that this unvarying *standard negative* would be admirable if *Nature* were unvarying in her moods; until that comes to pass there must be as much variety in negatives as there are in different moods in Nature.

It is, we think, because of the confusion of the aims of Science and Art that the majority of photographs fail either as scientific records or pictures. It would be easy to point out how the majority are false scientifically, and easier still to show how they are simply devoid of all artistic qualities. They serve, however, as many have served, as topographical records of faces, buildings, and landscapes, but often incorrect records at that. It is curious and interesting to observe that such work always requires a *name*. It is a photograph of *Mr. Jones,* of *Mont Blanc,* or of the *Houses of Parliament.* On the other hand, a work of Art really requires *no name*—it speaks for itself. It has no burning desire to be named, for its aim is to give the beholder aesthetic pleasure, and *not* to add to his knowledge or the *Science* of places, *i.e.,* topography. The work of Art, it cannot too often be repeated, appeals to man's emotional side; it has no wish to add to his knowledge—to his *Science*. On the other hand, topographical works appeal to his intellectual side; they refresh his *memory* of absent persons or landscapes, or they add to his *knowledge*. To anticipate criticism, I should like to say that of course in all mental processes the intellectual, and emotional factors are inseparable, yet the one is always subordinated to the other. The emotional is subordinate when we are solving a mathematical problem, the intellectual is decidedly subordinate when we are making love. Psychologists have analyzed to a remarkable extent the intellectual phenomena but the knowledge of the components of the sentiments or the emotional phenomena is, as Mr. Herbert Spencer says, "altogether vague in its outlines, and has a structure which continues indistinct even under the most patient introspection. Dim traces of different components may be discerned; but the limitations both of the whole and of its parts are so faintly marked, and at the same time so entangled, that none but very general results can be reached."

The chief thing, then, that I would impress upon all beginners is the necessity for beginning work with a clear distinction between the aims and ends of Science and Art. When the Art student has acquired enough knowledge—that is, *Science*—to express what he wishes, let him, with jealous care, keep the scientific mental attitude, if I may so express it, far away. On the other hand, if the student's aim is scientific, let him cultivate rigidly scientific methods, and not weaken himself by attempting a compromise with Art. We in the photographic world should be either scientists or pictorial photographers; we should be aiming either to increase knowledge—that is, science—or to produce works whose aim and end is to give aesthetic pleasure. I do not imply any comparison between Science and Art to the advantage of either one. They are both of the highest worth, and I

admire all sincere, honest, and capable workers in either branch
with impartiality. But I do not wish to see the aims and ends of the
two confused, the workers weakened thereby, and above all, the
progress of Science hindered and delayed.

3

Next I shall discuss briefly the ill-effects of a too sedulous study of
Science upon an Art student.

The first and, perhaps, the greatest of these ill-effects is the *positive*
mental attitude that Science fosters. A scientific student is only concerned with stating a fact clearly and simply; he must tell the truth,
and the *whole truth*. Now, a scientific study of photography if
pushed too far, leads, as a rule to that state of mind which delights
in a wealth of clearly-cut detail. The scientific photographer wishes
to see the veins in a lily-leaf and the scales on a butterfly's wing. He
looks, in fact, so closely, so microscopically, at the butterfly's wing
that he never sees the poetry of the life of the butterfly itself, as with
buoyant wheelings it disappears in marriage flight over the lush grass
and pink cuckooflowers of May.

I feel sure that this general delight in detail, brilliant sunshiny
effects, glossy prints, etc., is chiefly due to the evolution of photography: these tastes have been developed with the art, from the silver
plate of *Daguerre* to the double-albumenized paper of today. But,
as the art develops, we find the love for gloss and detail giving way
before platinotype prints and photo-etchings.

The second great artistic evil engendered by Science is the careless
manner in which things are expressed. The scientist seeks for truth,
and is often indifferent to its method of expression. To him, "Can
you not wait upon the lunatic?" is, as the late Matthew Arnold said,
as good as "Canst thou not minister to a mind diseased?" To the
literary artist, on the other hand, these sentences are as the poles
asunder—the one in bald truth, the other literature. They both
suggest the same thing; yet what aesthetic pleasure we get from the
one, and what a dull fact is, "Can you not wait upon the lunatic?"
There are photographs and photographs; the one giving as much
pleasure as the literary sentence, the other being as dull as the matter-
of-fact question. The student with understanding will see the fundamental and vital distinction between Science and Art as shown even
in these two short sentences.

And now, ladies and gentlemen, I do not think I can do better
than finish this section by quoting another passage from the writings
of the late Matthew Arnold.

"*Deficit una mihi symmetria prisca.*—'The antique symmetry was
the one thing wanting to me,' said Leonardo da Vinci, and he was
an Italian. I will not presume to speak for the American, but I am
sure that in the Englishman, the want of this admirable symmetry
of the Greeks is a thousand times more great and crying than in any

Italian. The results of the want show themselves most glaringly, perhaps, in our architecture, but they show themselves also in our art. *Fit details strictly combined, in view of a large general result nobly conceived:* that is just the beautiful *symmetria prisca* of the Greeks, and it is just where we English fail, where all our art fails. Striking ideas we have, and well executed details we have; but that high symmetry which, with satisfying delightful effect, contains them, we seldom or never have. The glorious beauty of the Acropolis at Athens did not arise from single fine things stuck about on that hill, a statue here, a gateway there. No, it arose from all things being perfectly combined for a supreme total effect."

CONCLUSION.

And now I must finish my remarks. I have not perhaps told you very much, but if I have succeeded in impressing upon beginners and some others the vital and fundamental distinction between Science and Art, something will have been achieved. And if those students who find anything suggestive in my paper are by it led to look upon photography in future from a new mental attitude, something more important still will have been attained. For, in my humble opinion, though it is apparently but a little thing I have to tell, still its effect may be vital and far-reaching for many an honest worker, and if I have helped a few such, my labor will have been richly rewarded indeed.

ROBERT FRANK (1924-) *Black and white are the colors of photography. To me, they symbolize the alternatives of hope and despair to which mankind is forever subjected. Most of my photographs are of people; they are seen simply, as through the eyes of the man in the street. There is one thing the photograph must contain, the humanity of the moment. This kind of photography is realism. But realism is not enough—there has to be vision, and the two together can make a good photograph. It is difficult to describe this thin line where matter ends and mind begins.* BLACK AND WHITE ARE THE COLORS OF ROBERT FRANK, *quoted by Edna Bennett, Aperture, Vol. 9, No. 1, 1961, p. 22.*

A STATEMENT   1958
U. S. Camera Annual, p. 115.

I am grateful to the Guggenheim Foundation for their confidence and the provisions they made for me to work freely in my medium over a protracted period. When I applied for the Guggenheim Fellowship, I wrote: ". . . To produce an authentic contemporary document, the visual impact should be such as will nullify explanation...."

With these photographs, I have attempted to show a cross-section of the American population. My effort was to express it simply and without confusion. The view is personal and, therefore, various facets of American life and society have been ignored. The photographs were taken during 1955 and 1956; for the most part in large cities such as Detroit, Chicago, Los Angeles, New York and in many other places during my journey across the country. My book, containing these photographs, will be published in Paris by Robert Delpire, 1958.

I have been frequently accused of deliberately twisting subject matter to my point of view. Above all, I know that life for a photographer cannot be a matter of indifference. Opinion often consists of a kind of criticism. But criticism can come out of love. It is important to see what is invisible to others—perhaps the look of hope or the look of sadness. Also, it is always the instantaneous reaction to oneself that produces a photograph.

My photographs are not planned or composed in advance and I do not anticipate that the on-looker will share my viewpoint. However, I feel that if my photograph leaves an image on his mind—something has been accomplished.

It is a different state of affairs for me to be working on assignment for a magazine. It suggests to me the feeling of a hack writer or a commercial illustrator. Since I sense that my ideas, my mind and my eye are not creating the picture but that the editors' minds and eyes will finally determine which of my pictures will be reproduced to suit the magazines' purposes.

I have a genuine distrust and "mefiance" toward all group activities. Mass production of uninspired photojournalism and photography without thought becomes anonymous merchandise. The air becomes infected with the "smell" of photography. If the photographer wants to be an artist, his thoughts cannot be developed overnight at the corner drugstore.

I am not a pessimist, but looking at a contemporary picture magazine makes it difficult for me to speak about the advancement of photography, since photography today is accepted without question, and is also presumed to be understood by all—even children. I feel that only the integrity of the individual photographer can raise its level.

The work of two contemporary photographers, Bill Brandt of England and the American, Walker Evans, have influenced me. When I first looked at Walker Evans' photographs, I thought of something Malraux wrote: "To transform destiny into awareness." One is embarrassed to want so much for oneself. But, how else are you going to justify your failure and your effort?

DOROTHEA LANGE (1895-1965) *On my darkroom door for many years I had posted the words of Francis Bacon: "The contemplation of things as they are, without substitution or imposture, without error or confusion, is in itself a nobler thing than a whole harvest of invention." (From a Memo to Nancy Newhall, April 13, 1958.)*

DOCUMENTARY PHOTOGRAPHY   1940
A Pageant of Photography, San Francisco, p. 28.

Documentary photography records the social scene of our time. It mirrors the present and documents for the future. Its focus is man in his relation to mankind. It records his customs at work, at war, at play, or his round of activities through twenty-four hours of the day, the cycle of the seasons, or the span of a life. It portrays his institutions—family, church, government, political organizations, social clubs, labor unions. It shows not merely their facades, but seeks to reveal the manner in which they function, absorb the life, hold the loyalty, and influence the behavior of human beings. It is concerned with methods of work and the dependence of workmen on each other and on their employers. It is pre-eminently suited to build a record of change. Advancing technology raises standards of living, creates unemployment, changes the face of cities and of the agricultural landscape. The evidence of these trends—the simultaneous existence of past, present, and portent of the future—is conspicuous in old and new forms, old and new customs, on every hand. Documentary photography stands on its own merits and has validity by itself. A single photographic print may be "news," a "portrait," "art," or "documentary"—any of these, all of them, or none. Among the tools of social science—graphs, statistics, maps, and text—documentation by photograph now is assuming place. Documentary photography invites and needs participation by amateurs as well as by professionals. Only through the interested work of amateurs who choose themes and follow them can documentation by the camera of our age and our complex society be intimate, pervasive, and adequate.

PHOTOGRAPHING THE FAMILIAR   1952
(with Daniel Dixon) *Aperture*, Vol. 1, No. 2, pp. 4-15.

Photography today appears to be in a state of flight.

This is clearly a harsh judgment. Some will feel it to be a false judgment; others will think it clumsy or ill-considered. But still others may feel it to have merit. They, perhaps less devoutly enlisted in this or that photographic cause, may find in their uncertainties a reason to believe the judgment sound. Themselves in disorder, they may sense some design of a larger disorder. It is in an effort to explain that design—and in the conviction that there can be found for disorder a remedy—that we say what we do: that photography appears to be in a state of flight.

But why flight? What in flight from? If in flight, what can be done?

To begin with, photography is still a very young technique—one that has found power and expression in the mastery of its own mechanics. This is not only true of photography. It applies equally to all young techniques—to the steam engine and the camera alike. During the early years, all photographers were in a sense inventors, and photography as a field is still infant enough to have undeveloped in it some of the features of invention. Color, for instance, is beginning now to assert itself as a photographic value; there is excited talk of a new dimension in the motion picture; in an age perhaps more than any other dedicated to techniques, science presents to the photographic technician a challenge more important than any he has had to face before.

But, on the whole, the day is gone when the photographer could find in exploration of his equipment the expression he sought. Settled to a different pace, technical advance has permitted the photographer to catch up. The ranges of technique have been largely conquered; and that exploration ended, the photographer must seek another.

Now it is no accident that the photographer becomes a photographer any more than the lion tamer becomes a lion tamer. Just as there is a necessary element of hazard in one, in the other is a necessary element of the mechanical. For better or for worse, the destiny of the photographer is bound up with the destinies of a machine. In this alliance is presented a very special problem. Ours is a time of the machine, and ours is a need to know that the machine can be put to creative human effort. If it is not, the machine can destroy us. It is within the power of the photographer to help prohibit this destruction, and help make the machine an agent more of good than of evil. Though not a poet, nor a painter, nor a composer, he is yet an artist, and as an artist undertakes not only risks but responsibility. And it is with responsibility that both the photographer and his machine are brought to their ultimate tests. His machine must prove that it can be endowed with the passion and the humanity of the photographer; the photographer must prove that he has the passion and the humanity with which to endow the machine.

This certainly is one of the great questions of our time. Upon such an endowment of the mechanical device may depend not only the state of the present but the prospects of the future. The photographer is privileged that it is a question which in his work he can help to answer.

But does he?

Unfortunately, very often not. For in his natural zeal to master his craft, he has too long relied upon the technical to engage his energies. Now the technical has relaxed its challenge, he is often left with the feeling that there is nowhere to go. He is lost; he is confused; he is bewildered. Accustomed to discovery, now suddenly he is obliged to interpret.

But, his history being that of the inventor, he is often unprepared to interpret. So he plunges off in search of new discoveries. Hoping to preserve his tradition of invention, this time he gropes, not for the new chemical or lens, but for what he calls the "new angle." He searches among the complexities of approach for an experience kindred to that he had known in technical experiment. The harshest demand of his own art—the demand that he serve it as an artist— he seeks to escape along the frontiers of shock. Thus the spectacular is cherished above the meaningful, the frenzied above the quiet, the unique above the potent. The familiar is made strange, the unfamiliar grotesque. The amateur forces his Sundays into a series of unnatural poses; the world is forced by the professional into unnatural shapes. Landscape, season, occasion—these are compelled to a twisted service in which they need not be interpreted but, like a process, invented.

In this unwillingness to accept a familiar world photography puts invention to a destructive work. That the familiar world is often unsatisfactory cannot be denied, but it is not, for all that, one we need abandon. Awkward though it may be, ours is a world that still confers upon the artist an energy and sometimes even a comfort. We need not refuse to recognize that world any more than we need blow it up. We need not be seduced into evasion of it any more than we need be appalled by it into silence. We need not, for fear of the world's image, either hide in or ruin technique. We need take neither the view of angel nor devil. We can, instead, take the view of man. We can concern ourselves with presence rather than with phantom, image rather than with conjure. Bad as it is, the world is potentially full of good photographs. But to be good, photographs have to be full of the world.

So it can be seen how, in its distrust of the familiar, photography appears to be in flight—in flight as much from itself as from anything else. The question remains: what can be done about it?

As we have suggested, many photographers may find an answer to this question in a refreshed relationship with the world—or worlds—they know best. This for some would mean loneliness and privacy, their most familiar territories seldom entered by any but themselves. These, though, are few, for the camera does not easily capture the image of a secret, though when it does we are, as always, warmed with the honor of being told. Most of us, however, live in worlds at least cousin to each other, worlds that visit and entertain, quarrel and gossip, worlds that cannot keep a secret and wouldn't if they could.

So what is familiar to one of us may very likely be familiar to another. Sweat in the eyes, sun on the back, cold in the heart—these things we all know. More important, we all know something of what they mean. Hard work, warm weather, pain, we all have enough in common to make most of our many worlds companion to each other. We eating, we sleeping, we mourning and rejoicing, we hating, we loving—it is the same with these. These we know; so knowing, these we see; and it is in these that a great photograph speaks, not of eating and sleeping, but of ourselves. Whether of a board fence, an eggshell, a mountain peak or a broken sharecropper, the great photograph first asks, then answers, two questions. "Is that my world? What, if not, has that world to do with mine?"

Yet even though we live in worlds familiar to each other, there is in the photography of how they are familiar a very special difficulty.

If not by nature, then at least by tradition the artist is individual. His art, he insists, finds its expression in individuality. His gift is not that which brings together but which sets apart. But in working with a world of the familiar this is not so much so. Then the photographer must himself become a familiarity. He cannot enter the household as a man from Mars. He must, instead, become a member of the family. In order to see the familiar, he must act and feel the familiar. His impulse can be a movement of the common; his instinct can be a gesture of the ordinary; his vision can be a focus of the usual. Through his lens must be transmitted not only detail but volume; in his print must appear not only the specific but the general.

This does not mean that the photographer need make a sacrifice of his right to express himself. On the contrary, he expresses himself— perhaps more fully—in a different way. Among the familiar, his behavior is that of the intimate rather than of the stranger. Rather than acknowledge, he embraces; rather than perform, he responds. Moving in a world so much composed of himself, he cannot help but express himself. Every image he sees, every photograph he takes, becomes in a sense a self-portrait. The portrait is made more meaningful by intimacy—an intimacy shared not only by the photographer with his subject but by the *audience*.

For these same reasons, the photographer need not suspect the familiar for fear of the domestic. The two are not the same. Nobody likes to look at dull photographs; boredom, in the end, is as outlandish as outrage; and certainly the tedious is as easily registered as the outrageous. While there is perhaps a province in which the photograph can tell us nothing more than what we see with our own eyes, there is another in which it proves to us how little our own eyes often permit us to see. And here again it is the photographer's sense of the familiar that provides the proof. For in that intimacy, even with the commonplace, will be discovered passages and openings denied to the outsider. The intimate will be admitted to subtleties and complexities shut to the stranger. He will find the simple to be complicated, the miniature to be enormous, the insignificant decisive. Through familiarity the photographer will find not only the familiar but the strange, not only the ordinary but the rare; not only the mutual but, the singular. In a search for these there is, in photography or in anything else, no loss of self, no surrender to the domestic. There are instead those qualities—challenge, purpose, and promise— which more than any others nourish the personality, and without which even the most unique expression would soon become humdrum.

These, then, are the issues: whether we, as photographers, can make of our machine an instrument of human creation, whether we, as artists, can make of our world a place for creation. Too, these are issues we have sometimes failed to meet. For whatever reasons of fear, worship, convenience or custom, photography seems often more concerned with illusion than reality. It does not reflect but contrives. It lives in a world of its own. Living in a world of its own, it is not, either as art or science, successful.

We believe that photography must reconsider its function. It is the nature of the camera to deal with what *is*—we urge those who use the camera to retire from what *might be*. We suggest that, as photographers, we turn our attention to the familiarities of which we are a part. So turning, we in our work can speak more than of our subjects —we can speak with them; we can more than speak about our subjects —we can speak for them. They, given tongue, will be able to speak with and for us. And in this language will be proposed to the lens that with which, in the end, photography must be concerned—time, and place, and the works of man.

LÁSZLÓ MOHOLY-NAGY (1895-1946) *Photography has not yet achieved anything like its full stature, has not articulated its own intrinsic structure. Yet this lack of "results" does not contradict the almost unbelievable impact which photographic vision has had upon our culture.* VISION IN MOTION, *Chicago, Paul Theobald,* 1947, p. 178.

LIGHT—A MEDIUM OF PLASTIC EXPRESSION 1923
Broom, Vol. 4, pp. 283-84.

Since the discovery of photography virtually nothing new has been found as far as the principles and technique of the process are concerned. All innovations are based on the aesthetic representative conceptions existing in Daguerre's time (about 1830), although these conceptions, i.e., the copying of nature by means of the photographic camera and the mechanical reproduction of perspective, have been rendered obsolete by the work of modern artists.

Despite the obvious fact that the *sensitivity to light* of a chemically prepared surface (of glass, metal, paper, etc.) was the most important element in the photographic process, i.e., containing its own laws, the sensitized surface was always subjected to the demands of a *camera obscura* adjusted to the traditional laws of perspective while the full possibilities of this combination were never sufficiently tested.

The proper utilization of the plate itself would have brought to light phenomena imperceptible to the human eye and made visible only by means of the photographic apparatus, thus perfecting the eye by means of photography. True, this principle has already been applied in certain scientific experiments, as in the study of motion (walking, leaping, galloping) and zoological and mineral forms, but these have always been isolated efforts whose results could not be compared or related.

It must be noted here that our intellectual experience complements spatially and formally the optical phenomena perceived by the eye and renders them into a comprehensible whole, whereas the photographic apparatus reproduces the purely optical picture (distortion, bad drawing, foreshortening).

One way of exploring this field is to investigate and apply various chemical mixtures which produce light effects imperceptible to the eye (such as electro-magnetic rays, x-rays).

Another way is by the construction of new apparatus, first by the use of the *camera obscura;* second by the elimination of perspective. In the first case using apparatus with lenses and mirror-arrangements which can cover their environment from all sides; in the second case, using an apparatus which is based on new optical laws. This last leads to the possibility of "light-composition," whereby light would be controlled as a new plastic medium, just as color in painting and tone in music.

This signifies a perfectly new medium of expression whose novelty offers an undreamed of scope. The possibilities of this medium of composition become greater as we proceed from static representation to the motion pictures of the cinematograph.

I have made a few primitive attempts in this direction, whose initial results, however, point to the most positive discoveries (and as soon as these attempts can be tested experimentally in a laboratory especially devised for the purpose, the results are certain to be far more impressive).

Instead of having a plate which is sensitive to light react mechanically to its environment through the reflection or absorption of light, I have attempted to *control* its action by means of lenses and mirrors, by light passed through fluids like water, oil, acids, crystal, metal, glass, tissue, etc. This means that the filtered, reflected or refracted light is directed upon a screen and then photographed. Or again, the light-effect can be thrown directly on the sensitive plate itself, instead of upon a screen. (Photography without apparatus.) Since these light effects almost always show themselves in motion, it is clear that the process reaches its highest development in the film.

FROM PIGMENT TO LIGHT   1936
Telehor, Vol. 1, No. 2, pp. 32-36.

The terminology of art "isms" is truly bewildering. Without being exactly certain what the words imply, people talk of impressionism, neo-impressionism, pointillism, expressionism, futurism, cubism, suprematism, neoplasticism, purism, constructivism, dadaism, superrealism—and in addition there are photography, the film, and light displays. Even specialists can no longer keep abreast of this apocalyptic confusion.

It is our task to find the common denominator in all this confusion. Such a common denominator exists. It is only necessary to study the lessons of the work of the last hundred years in order to realize that the consistent development of modern painting has striking analogies in all other spheres of artistic creation.

THE COMMON DENOMINATOR

The invention of photography destroyed the canons of representational, imitative art. Ever since the decline of naturalistic painting, conceived as "color morphosis," unconsciously or consciously sought to discover the laws and elementary qualities of color. The more this problem emerged as the central issue, the less importance was attached to representation. *The creator of optical images learned to work with elementary, purely optical means.*

Approached from this point of view all the manifold "isms" are merely the more or less individual methods of work of one or more artists, who in each case commenced with the destruction of the old representational image in order to achieve new experiences, a new *wealth of optical expression.*

SIGNS OF THE NEW OPTICS

The elements of the new imagery existed in embryo in this very act of destruction. Photography with its almost dematerialized light, and especially the use of direct light rays in camera-less photography and in the motion picture, made clarification an urgent necessity.

Investigations, experiments, theories of color and light, abstract displays of light-images—as yet far too fragmentary and isolated—point towards the future, though they cannot as yet provide a precise picture of anything like the future's scope.

But one result has already emerged from these efforts: the clear recognition that apart from all individual emotion, apart from the purely subjective attitude of the spectator, objective factors determine the effectiveness of an optical work of art: factors conditioned by the material qualities of the optical medium of expression.

MINIMUM DEMANDS

Our knowledge concerning light, brightness, darkness, color, color harmony—in other words our knowledge of the elementary foundations of optical expression is still very limited (in spite of the tireless work of the numerous artists). Existing theories of harmony are no more than the painters' dictionary. They were elaborated to meet the needs of traditional art. They do not touch our present aesthetic sensibilities, our present aims, much less the entire *field of optical expression.* Uncertainty reigns even with regard to the most elementary facts. Innumerable problems of basic importance still confront the painter with the need for careful experimental enquiry: What is the nature of light and shade? Of brightness—darkness? What are light values? What are time and proportion? New methods of registering the intensity of light? The notion of light? What are refractions of light? What is color (pigment)? What are the media infusing life with color? What is color intensity? The chemical nature of color and effective lights? Is form conditional on color?— On its position in space?—On the extent of its surface area? Biological functions? Physiological reactions? Statics and dynamics of composition? Spraying devices, photo and film cameras, screens? The technique of color application? The technique of projection? Specific problems of manual and machine work? etc., etc., etc. Research into the physiological and psychological properties of the media of artistic creation is still in its elementary stages, compared with physical research. Practical experience in the creative use of artificial color (light) as yet scarcely exists.

THE FEAR OF PETRIFICATION

Artists frequently hesitate to apply the results of their experiments to their practical work, for they share the universal fear that mechanization may lead to a petrification of art. They fear that the open revelation of elements of construction, or any artificial stimulation of the intellect or the introduction of mechanical contrivances may sterilize all creative efforts.

This fear is unfounded, since the conscious evocation of *all* the elements of creation must always remain an impossibility. However, many optical canons are elaborated in detail, all optical creation will retain the unconscious spontaneity of its experience as its basic element of value.

Despite all canons, all inflexible laws, all technical perfection, this inventive potency, this genetic tension which defies analysis, determines the character of every work of art. It is the outcome of intuitive knowledge both of the present and of the basic tendencies of the future.

ART AND TECHNIQUE

The attempt was made, at least partially, to restore the capacity for spontaneous color experience—which had been lost through the spread of the printed word and the recent predominance of literature—by intellectual means. This was only natural, for in the first phase of industrial advance the artist was overwhelmed by the intellectual achievements of the technician, whose achievements embodied the constructive side of creation.

Given a clear determination of function, the latter could without difficulty (at least in theory) produce objects of rational design. The same was assumed to be true in art, until it became apparent that an exaggerated emphasis on its determinable intellectual aspects merely served as a smoke-screen, once the elements of optical expression as such—quite apart from their "artistic" qualities—had been mastered. It was, of course, necessary first to develop a standard language of optical expression, before really gifted artists could attempt to raise the elements thus established to the level of "art." That was the basic aim of all recent artistic and pedagogic efforts in the optical sphere. If today the sub-compensated element of feeling revolts against this tendency, we can only wait until the pendulum will react in a less violent manner.

FROM PAINTING TO THE DISPLAY OF LIGHT

All technical achievements in the sphere of optics must be utilized for the development of this standard language. Among them the *mechanical and technical* requisites of art are of primary importance.

Until recently they were condemned on the grounds that manual skill, the "personal touch," should be regarded as the essential thing in art. Today they already hold their own in the conflict of opinions; tomorrow they will triumph; the day after tomorrow they will yield results accepted without question. Brushwork, the subjective manipulation of a tool is lost, but the clarity of formal relationships is increased to an extent almost transcending the limitations of matter; an extent in which the objective context becomes transparently clear. Maximum precision, the law of the norm, replaces the misinterpreted significance of manual skill.

It is difficult today to predict the formal achievements of the future. For the formal crystallization of a work of art is conditioned not merely by the incalculable factor of talent, but also by the intensity of the struggle for the mastery of its medium (tools, today machines). But it is safe to predict even today that the optical creation of the future will not be a mere translation of our present forms of optical expression, for the new implements and the hitherto neglected medium of light must necessarily yield results in conformity with their own inherent properties.

PURPOSIVE PROGRESS OF THOUGHT, CIRCULAR ADVANCE OF TECHNIQUE

During the intermediary stages, however, we must not overlook a well-known factor retarding the advance of art: individual pioneers invent new instruments, new methods of work, revolutionizing the traditional forms of production. But usually a long time must elapse before the new can be generally applied. The old hampers its advance. The creative potentialities of the new may be clearly felt, but for a certain time it will appear clothed in traditional forms that are rendered obsolete by its emergence.

Thus in the sphere of music we must for the present content ourselves with the noisy triumphs of the mechanical piano and of the cinema organ, instead of hearing the new electro-mechanical music that is entirely independent of all previously existing instruments. In the sphere of painting the same revolutionary significance already applies to the use of spraying devices, of powerful enamel reflectors and of such reliable synthetic materials as galalith, trolit, bakelite, zellon, or aluminum. The situation is similar in the realm of the cinema, where a method of production is regarded as "revolutionary," whose creative achievements are scarcely greater than those that might be obtained could classical paintings be set in motion.

This situation is unsatisfactory and superannuated when judged in terms of a future in which light displays of any desired quality and magnitude will suddenly blaze up, and multicolored floodlights with transparent sheaths of fire will project a constant flow of immaterial, evanescent images into space by the simple manipulation of switches. And in the film of the future we shall have constant change in the speed and intensity of light; space in motion constantly varied through the medium of light refracted from efflorescent reflectors; flashes of light and black-outs; chiaroscuro, distance and proximity of light; ultra-violet rays, infra-red penetration of darkness rendered visible—a wealth of undreamt-of optical experiences that will be profoundly stirring to our emotions.

A NEW INSTRUMENT OF VISION

In photography we possess an extraordinary instrument for reproduction. But photography is much more than that. Today it is in a fair way to bringing (optically) something entirely new into the world. The specific elements of photography can be isolated from their attendant complications, not only theoretically, but tangibly, and in their manifest reality.

THE UNIQUE QUALITY OF PHOTOGRAPHY

The photogram, or camera-less record of forms produced by light, which embodies the unique nature of the photographic process, is the real key to photography. It allows us to capture the patterned interplay of light on a sheet of sensitized paper without recourse to any apparatus. The photogram opens up perspectives of a hitherto wholly unknown morphosis governed by optical laws peculiar to itself. It is the most completely dematerialized medium which the new vision commands.

WHAT IS OPTICAL QUALITY?

Through the development of black-and-white photography, light and shadow were for the first time fully revealed; and thanks to it, too, they first began to be employed with something more than a purely theoretical knowledge. (Impressionism in painting may be regarded as a parallel achievement). Through the development of reliable artificial illumination (more particularly electricity), and the power of regulating it, an increasing adoption of flowing light and richly gradated shadows ensued; and through these, again a greater animation of surfaces, and a more delicate optical intensification. This manifolding of gradations is one of the fundamental "materials" of optical formalism: a fact which holds equally well if we pass beyond the immediate sphere of black-white-grey values and learn to think and work in terms of colored ones.

When pure color is placed against pure color, tone against tone, a hard, poster-like decorative effect generally results. On the other hand the same colors used in conjunction with their intermediate tones will dispel this poster-like effect, and create a more delicate and melting impression. Through its black-white-grey reproductions of all colored appearances photography has enabled us to recognize the most subtle differentiations of values in both the grey and chromatic scales: differentiations that represent a new and (judged by previous standards) hitherto unattainable quality in optical expression. This is, of course, only one point among many. But it is the

point where we have to begin to master photography's inward properties, and that at which we have to deal more with the artistic function
of expression than with the reproductive function of portrayal.

SUBLIMATED TECHNIQUE

In reproduction—considered as the objective fixation of the semblance of an object—we find just as radical advances and transmogri-
fications, compared with prevailing optical representation, as in direct
records of forms produced by light (photograms). These particular
developments are well known: bird's-eye views, simultaneous inter-
ceptions, reflections, elliptical penetrations, etc. Their systematic
co-ordination opens up a new field of visual presentation in which
still further progress becomes possible. It is, for instance, an immense extension of the optical possibilities of reproduction that we
are able to register precise fixations of objects, even in the most difficult circumstances, in a hundredth or thousandth of a second. Indeed,
this advance in technique almost amounts to a psychological transformation of our eyesight*, since the sharpness of the lens and the
unerring accuracy of its delineation have now trained our powers
of observation up to a standard of visual perception which embraces
ultra-rapid snapshots and the millionfold magnification of dimensions employed in microscopic photography.

IMPROVED PERFORMANCE

Photography, then, imparts a heightened, or (in so far as our eyes
are concerned) increased, power of sight in terms of time and space.
A plain, matter-of-fact enumeration of the specific photographic
elements—purely technical, not artistic, elements—will be enough to
enable us to divine the power latent in them, and prognosticate to
what they lead.

THE EIGHT VARIETIES OF PHOTOGRAPHIC VISION

1. Abstract seeing by means of direct records of forms produced by
light: the photogram which captures the most delicate gradations of
light values, both chiaroscuro and colored.

2. Exact seeing by means of the normal fixation of the appearance
of things: reportage.

3. Rapid seeing by means of the fixation of movements in the short-
est possible time: snapshots.

4. Slow seeing by means of the fixation of movements spread over a
period of time: e.g., the luminous tracks made by the headlights of
motor cars passing along a road at night: prolonged time exposures.

5. Intensified seeing by means of:

a) micro-photography;

b) filter-photography, which, by variation of the chemical composition of the sensitized surface, permits photographic potentialities

*Helmholtz used to tell his pupils that if an optician were to succeed in making a
human eye, and brought it to him for his approval, he would be bound to say:
"this is a clumsy job of work."

to be augmented in various ways—ranging from the revelation of far-distant landscapes veiled in haze or fog to exposures in complete darkness: infra-red photography.

6. Penetrative seeing by means of X-rays: radiography.

7. Simultaneous seeing by means of transparent superimposition: the future process of automatic photomontage.

8. Distorted seeing: optical jokes that can be automatically produced by:

   a) exposure through a lens fitted with prisms, and the device of reflecting mirrors; or

   b) mechanical and chemical manipulation of the negative after exposure.

WHAT IS THE PURPOSE OF THE ENUMERATION?

What is to be gleaned from this list? That the most astonishing possibilities remain to be discovered in the raw material of photography, since a detailed analysis of each of these aspects furnishes us with a number of valuable indications in regard to their application, adjustment, etc. Our investigations will lead us in another direction, however. We want to discover what is the essence and significance of photography.

THE NEW VISION

All interpretations of photography have hitherto been influenced by the aesthetic-philosophic concepts that circumscribed painting. These were for long held to be equally applicable to photographic practice. Up to now, photography has remained in rather rigid dependence on the traditional forms of painting; and like painting it has passed through the successive stages of all the various art "isms"; though in no sense to its advantage. Fundamentally new discoveries cannot for long be confined to the mentality and practice of bygone periods with impunity. When that happens all productive activity is arrested. This was plainly evinced in photography, which has yielded no results of any value except in those fields where, as in scientific work, it has been employed without artistic ambitions. Here alone did it prove the pioneer of an original development, or of one peculiar to itself.

In this connection it cannot be too plainly stated that it is quite unimportant whether photography produces "art" or not. Its own basic laws, not the opinions of art critics, will provide the only valid measure of its future worth. It is sufficiently unprecedented that such a "mechanical" thing as photography, and one regarded so contemptuously in an artistic and creative sense, should have acquired the power it has, and become one of the primary objective visual forms, in barely a century of evolution. Formerly the painter impressed his own perspective outlook on his age. We have only to recall the manner in which we used to look at landscapes, and compare it with the way we perceive them now! Think, too, of the incisive sharpness of those camera portraits of our contemporaries, pitted with pores and furrowed by lines. Or an air-view of a ship at sea moving through waves that seem frozen in light. Or the enlargement of a woven tissue, or the chiselled delicacy of an ordinary sawn block of wood. Or, in fact, any of the whole gamut of splendid details of structure, texture and "factor" of whatever objects we care to choose.

THE NEW EXPERIENCE OF SPACE

Through photography, too, we can participate in new experiences of space, and in even greater measure through the film. With their help, and that of the new school of architects, we have attained an enlargement and sublimation of our appreciation of space, the comprehension of a new spatial culture. Thanks to the photographer, humanity has acquired the power of perceiving its surroundings, and its very existence, with new eyes.

THE HEIGHT OF ATTAINMENT

But all these are isolated characteristics, separate achievements, not altogether dissimilar to those of painting. In photography we must learn to seek, not the "picture," not the aesthetic of tradition, but the ideal instrument of expression, the self-sufficient vehicle for education.

SERIES (PHOTOGRAPHIC IMAGE SEQUENCES OF THE SAME OBJECT)

There is no more surprising, yet, in its naturalness and organic sequence, simpler form than the photographic series. This is the logical culmination of photography. The series is no longer a "picture," and none of the canons of pictorial aesthetics can be applied to it. Here the separate picture loses its identity as such and becomes a detail of assembly, an essential structural element of the whole which is the thing itself. In this concatenation of its separate but inseparable parts a photographic series inspired by a definite purpose can become at once the most potent weapon and the tenderest lyric. The true significance of the film will only appear in a much later, less confused and groping age than ours. The prerequisite for this revelation is, of course, the realization that a knowledge of photography is just as important as that of the alphabet. The illiterate of the future will be ignorant of the use of camera and pen alike.

MAN RAY (1890-) *Of course, there will always be those who look only at technique, who ask "how," while others of a more curious nature will ask "why." Personally, I have always preferred inspiration to information.* MAN RAY, *Modern Photography,* November 1957, p. 85.

THE AGE OF LIGHT   1934
Preface to *Man Ray Photographs 1920-1934, Paris,*
Hartford, James T. Soby.

In this age, like all ages, when the problem of the perpetuation of a race or class and the destruction of its enemies, is the all-absorbing motive of civilized society, it seems irrelevant and wasteful still to create works whose only inspirations are individual human emotion and desire. The attitude seems to be that one may be permitted a return to the idyllic occupations only after meriting this return by solving the more vital problems of existence. Still, we know that the incapacity of race or class to improve itself is as great as its incapacity to learn from previous errors in history. All progress results from an intense individual desire to improve the immediate present, from an all-conscious sense of material insufficiency. In this exalted state, material action imposes itself and takes the form of revolution in one form or another. Race and class, like styles, then become irrelevant, while the emotion of the human individual becomes universal. For what can be more binding amongst beings than the discovery of a common desire? And what can be more inspiring to action than the confidence aroused by a lyric expression of this desire? From the first gesture of a child pointing to an object and simply naming it, but with a world of intended meaning, to the developed mind that creates an image whose strangeness and reality stirs our subconscious to its inmost depths, the awakening of desire is the first step to participation and experience.

It is in the spirit of an experience and not of experiment that the following autobiographical images are presented. Seized in moments of visual detachment during periods of emotional contact, these images are oxidized residues, fixed by light and chemical elements, of living organisms. No plastic expression can ever be more than a residue of an experience. The recognition of an image that has tragically survived an experience, recalling the event more or less clearly, like the undisturbed ashes of an object consumed by flames, the recogntion of this object so little representative and so fragile, and its simple identification on the part of the spectator with a similar personal experience, precludes all psychoanalytical classification or assimilation into an arbitrary decorative system. Questions of merit and of execution can always be taken care of by those who hold themselves aloof from even the frontiers of such experiences. For, whether a painter, emphasizing the importance of the idea he wishes to convey introduces bits of ready-made chromos alongside his handiwork, or whether another, working directly with light and chemistry, so deforms the subject as almost to hide the identity of the original, and creates a new form, the ensuing violation of the medium employed is the most perfect assurance of the author's convictions. A certain amount of contempt for the material employed to express an idea is indispensable to the purest realization of this idea.

Each one of us, in his timidity, has a limit beyond which he is outraged. It is inevitable that he who by concentrated application has extended this limit for himself, should arouse the resentment of those who have accepted conventions which, since accepted by all, require no initiative of application. And this resentment generally takes the form of meaningless laughter or of criticism, if not of persecution. But this apparent violation is preferable to the monstrous habits condoned by etiquette and aestheticism.

An effort impelled by desire must also have an automatic or subconscious energy to aid its realization. The reserves of this energy within us are limitless if we will draw on them without a sense of shame or of propriety. Like the scientist who is merely a prestidigitator manipulating the abundant phenomena of nature and profiting by every so called hazard or law, the creator dealing in human values allows the subconscious forces to filter through him, colored by his own selectivity, which is universal human desire, and exposes to the light, motives and instincts long repressed, which should form the basis of a confident fraternity. The intensity of this message can be disturbing only in proportion to the freedom that has been given to automatism or the subconscious self. The removal of inculcated modes of presentation, resulting in apparent artificiality or strangeness, is a confirmation of the free functioning of this automatism and is to be welcomed.

Open confidences are being made every day, and it remains for the eye to train itself to see them without prejudice or restraint.

HENRY P. ROBINSON (1830-1901) *Photography would be better if its elements were not so easily comprehended as to make it almost a frivolous pursuit, and to cause it to be included with amusements and recreations.* THE ELEMENTS OF A PICTORIAL PHOTOGRAPH, *London, Percy Lund & Co.*, 1896, p. 163.

PARADOXES OF ART, SCIENCE, AND PHOTOGRAPHY   1892
Wilson's Photographic Magazine, Vol. 29, pp. 242-45.

"Stick to nature, my boy!" is an admonition often heard among artists, yet it is most true that, beyond a certain point, the closer the imitation is to nature the further it is from art.

Art is not so much a matter of fact as of impression; even realists admit this. Their objections to what is called impressionism is that the impressionists seldom say anything worth saying, and sometimes nothing at all, leaving a shrewd suspicion that they have nothing to say, and glory in having no mission except to upset the experience and practice of centuries.

No possible amount of scientific truth will in itself make a picture. Something more is required. The truth that is wanted is artistic truth —quite a different thing. Artistic truth is a conventional representation that looks like truth when we have been educated up to accepting it as a substitute for truth. The North American Indian did not understand a portrait less than life size or a profile with one eye only; he was not educated up to the conventional.

Of late years there has been a great demand for truth in art, whatever that dark saying may mean. We have been impressed by literalists to be faithful to nature. To quote Mr. Oscar Wilde, "They call upon

Shakespeare—they always do—and quote that hackneyed passage about Art holding the mirror up to Nature, forgetting that this unfortunate aphorism is deliberately said by Hamlet in order to convince the bystanders of his absolute insanity on all art matters . . .", reducing genius to the position of a looking-glass. On the other hand, it is sometimes said, perhaps jokingly—for we should not take Mr. Brett or Mr. Pennell too seriously—that photography cannot be art because it has no capacity for lying. Although the saying is wrong as regards our art, this is putting the semblance of a great truth in a coarse way. In other and more polite words, no method can be adequate means to an artistic end that will not adapt itself to the will of the artist. The reason is this, if it can be reduced to reason: admit that all art must be based on nature; but nature is not art, and art, not being nature, cannot fail to be more or less conventional. This is one of those delightful contradictions that make the study of art an intellectual occupation. Men naturally turn to nature. We have evidence of this from prehistoric times. The ornament of all time, of all nations, with scarcely an exception, has been based on nature—the Greeks and Moors are the important exceptions—yet the ornament that approached nearest to exact imitation of nature has always been the most debased and worst. It is the lowest intellects that take the most delight in deceptive imitation. Mr. Lewis F. Day puts this very admirably in one of his recent publications: "Those who profess to follow Nature," he says, "seem sometimes to be rather dragging her in the dust. There is a wider view of nature, which includes human nature, and that selective and idealizing instinct which is natural to man. It is a long way from being yet proved that the naturalistic designer is more 'true to nature' than another. It is one thing to study nature, and another to pretend that studies are works of art. In no branch of design has it ever been held by the masters that nature was enough. It is only the very callow student who opens his mouth to swallow all nature, whole; the older bird knows better."

It is clear, then, that a method that will not admit of the modifications of the artist cannot be an art, and therefore is photography in a perilous state if we cannot prove that it is endowed with possibilities of untruth. But they who, looking perhaps only at their own limited experiments, say photography cannot lie, take a very narrow view and greatly underrate the capabilities of the art. All arts have their limits, and I admit that the limits of photography are rather narrow, but in good hands it can be made to lie like a Trojan. However much truth may be desirable in the abstract, to the artist there is no merit in a process that cannot be made to say the thing that is not.

Here I am bound to admit a considerable weakness in my argument. We are told by a writer in a popular new magazine, edited by a member of our Club, that it is "always the best policy to tell the truth—unless, of course, you are an exceptionally good liar!" This is, indeed, a misfortune, for there is not, I am ashamed to say, very great scope for sparkling unveracity in our art. That is to say, we cannot produce brilliant falsifications such as the painter may indulge in. One man may steal a horse, while another may not look over a hedge. A painter may unblushingly present us with an angel with wings that won't work, while a photographer is laughed at, very properly, if he gives us anything nearer an angelic form than that of a spook raised by a medium.

It must be confessed that it takes considerable skill to produce the best kind of lies. It is in the hands of first-class photographers only—and perhaps the indifferent ones—that photography can lie. With the first, possibly, graciously; with the latter, brutally. The photographers of only average attainments, and such as we should get turned out in quantities by an art-less Institute, seldom get beyond the plain, naked, uninteresting truth. Yet I think that many will agree with me that the very good and the very bad are much more interesting than the mediocre. That the best are interesting is clear; that the worst are often the cause of a good laugh is the experience of all; it is only the middling good that induce indifference.

There can be little doubt that, in this respect, and looking at it from this point of view, painting is a much greater art than photography; but what I am concerned to prove is that, although photography is only a humble liar, yet it is not the guileless innocent that some people suppose, and has a capacity for lying sufficient to enable it to worthily enroll its name among the noble arts. Nay, is it not the greater for its humility? Photography gives us the means of a nearer imitation of nature than any other art, yet has sufficient elasticity to show the directing mind, and therefore is the most perfect art of all. If we must have paradoxes, let us carry them to the bitter end.

"Let us have truth," says the conscientious writer who knows not what truth is. What should we get in art if we could capture it? We should have a representation of nature as we see it in a mirror, colors and all, and should tire of it as soon as the novelty wore off. The worst thing that could happen to photography as an art would be the discovery of a process giving the colors of nature—the one impossible thing in nature, I hope and believe. Its one great deviation from faultless virtue is, as I have endeavored to show, that it is more truthful than painting.

A writer, innocent of the resources of the art, and wishing to depreciate it, makes a point of the photographer having no control over the action of the developer so as to produce the variation from nature he desires. I can only reply that among my own pictures there is scarcely one that does not owe a good deal of any merit it may have to control of the developer. The possibilities of control were greater, perhaps, in the collodion process than the gelatine, but we are speaking of the capabilities of photography, not of any particular process.

The scientist may prove, beyond any possibility of doubt, that the relative values cannot be altered in development, but the photographer knows that variation in development varies the appearance of his results, and that should be quite enough for him. It is so difficult, and yet so tempting, to "find out what cannot be done, and then to go and do it!"

I feel serious promptings here to have a fling at science that will surely bring down the wrath of our President on my unfortunate head. I will try to ameliorate him by saying that science demands our greatest respect. No one can have more reverence for science than I have myself—when it keeps its place. But we are suffering from science, and fancy is dying out of the land. It is doing serious harm to photography as a picture-producing art. When a student ought to be studying the construction of a picture, and developing in his soul the art of lying, he is led away by the flickering *ignis fatuus* of science, and goes mad over developers. "Another new developer" has more effect on the tender feelings of the brethren of the camera than would the advent of a poet-photographer. This suggests a variation on Rejlander's *Two Ways of Life*. One youth travels along the pleasant and virtuous walks of art, not listening to the Sirens of Fact; but dozens of others are decoyed to the worser way, and are soon lost in the seductive vanities and subtleties of science. They last long enough, perhaps, to modify a developer—with which science, however, tells them they can do little or nothing—and are heard of no more, except in the multitudinous platitudes used in the endless discussions of abstractions in society papers; and the scientific dream of the future is an Institute of Photography from which art is to be excluded. Art will be very glad to part company.

Let us be generous and admit that science has its good points, but it is doing a good deal of harm in the world. It is robbing us of our illusions. The science of history has defrauded Richard III of his hump, made Henry VIII a moral character, and gone audaciously nigh to proving that Jack the Giant Killer never existed. We are bored by the tedious papers of those who "have not the wit to exaggerate nor the genius to romance," and a synonym for dullness is a lecture at the Royal Society. But scientists are not without their hilarious moments. In our own art I cannot help thinking that scientists are trifling with a serious subject when they tell us that we cannot do as we like with our developers or when they bring logarithms to bear on picture-making. But the humor is not all on one side, and we not unfrequently enjoy a smile at the prodigious engines they sometimes use to crack our poor little nuts.

What has science to do with art, except to provide materials for its use? It is only of late that art has, on the one hand, been made to depend on absolute scientific truth; and, on the other, by the same writers, been proved, in the case of photography, not to be an art because it cannot deviate from truth. It is merely an incident, an accident, a detail—call it what you will—that science, sometimes of the highest and most distracting kind, is connected with picture-making photography. The science that deals with the nature of the image or the calculation of the curve of a lens is a very distant cousin, indeed, to picture-making by the use of photographic materials. The use of materials invented by others for a definite purpose can scarcely be called science. No scientific theory should be allowed to have weight with an artist who has practised his art successfully for years and knows what he wants and how to get it. If, for instance, I was told that it was proved by science that the negative would not yield all the tones of nature, I should reply that many years' practice had convinced me of that well-known fact, but the mere fact of it being proved scientifically did not alter the facts or further limit the tones. When it was proved scientifically to Diogenes that he could not walk round his tub, that humorous philosopher settled the matter by walking round that desirable residence. I am afraid I have used this illustration somewhere before, but let it pass. In art the artist sees his results, and it is for him to judge, from his knowledge of art and nature, *not science*, whether his results are true, or, at any rate, if they lie properly and are what he wants. The artist has to do with appearances, the scientist with facts. It is not enough to say, This is not true. The question is, Is it true enough for artistic purposes?

I have alluded to development once or twice. Two very clever scientists, whom I much respect, Dr. Hurter and Mr. Driffeld, have proved to everybody's unsatisfaction that photographers have no control over the gradations; but this does not alter the fact that— to put the simplest case—he knows when a negative is over- or under-exposed or developed too dense or too thin to properly represent his idea of nature as far as in him lies and his art will allow. Then there has been another great attempt made to show that the perspective of photography is not scientifically true. If the attempt was successful, which is very doubtful, *who cares?* It has been true enough not to be found out for fifty years, and that is good enough for photography. Can it have been the want of truth that has unconsciously com-pelled artists since the beginning to admire the truth of photographic perspective and rely on its veracity? Here is another paradoxical nut to crack.

But my business is not to make a feature of the truth of any part of photography. On the contrary, I want to clear its character of the un-artistic virtue of being nothing but a truthful, inevitable, stupid purveyor of prosaic fact.

Painters sometimes trust to us for truth; the law courts are becom-ing more wary, and appreciate our deviations. I was once found fault with by an artist for "altering" a photograph, on the plea that it would mislead a painter if he wanted to copy it. I found he *had* copied it before he saw the scene, and when he afterward compared his picture with it, he found a clump of trees that should have appeared on the left transferred to the right. I had made the alteration by double printing, and improved the composition. *I did not* want a mere local view. I don't know that there is anything more exasperating than for a painter to take it for granted that it is a photographer's business to play jackal to his lion, and hunt up food for him; but it is a blessed truth that we can deceive him if we like. Painters ought to be more grateful to us than they are. Besides providing some of them with subjects, we have taught them what to avoid—educated them on the Spartan and Helot principle—and art has vastly improved during the half-century of our existence. We have made the column and curtain background absurd. When our art was born painters thought nothing of violating perspective by placing the horizon as low as the feet of their portraits, and made no difficulties about hanging heavy curtains from the sky, and we are still fulfilling our useful mission of showing artists the ridiculous things they ought not to do, but it is asking too much to provide subjects for them—idea, composition, and detail. A painter should never use photography until he is capable of getting on without it, and then he should make his own photographs. To copy another man's work is not honest, and is a lazy and mischievous method of attempting to make a living.

I am afraid I have filled my space without giving as many specimens as I could wish of the possible delinquencies and untruthfulnesses that art requires and photography can accomplish, but I hope I have shown that if it cannot lie like paint, it has the merit of approaching it in mendacity.

I will conclude with another illustration of the capabilities of our art for useful falsification. I once knew a photographer (it sounds better to put it that way) who was employed, for the purposes of a parliamentary committee, to make a series of photographs showing that one place was much more picturesque than another. Some ugly gas-works were to be erected, and it was desirable to place them on the least beautiful of two spots. It may be also mentioned that it was likewise necessary that they should be placed on the site that best suited the promoters. Both places were very picturesque, but in the photographs it was easy to see the one site was a little rustic paradise (with suitable figures and fine skies) and the other a dreary desert, all foreground of the plainest! Yet both were true to fact, and they had the intended effect.

In conclusion, let me express the pleasure I feel in being afforded the fascinating opportunity of saying a few humble words in praise of lying in a room which has been saturated with truth and fact for more than a hundred years—ever since, indeed, Barry "restored the antique spirit in art" by painting his anachronisms on the walls, and from which building emanates the prospectus of the Chicago Exhibition, which honors our art with the crowning paradox of classing photography with Instruments of Precision.

ARTHUR SIEGEL (1913-) *Painting and photography have both been affected by the same events and they have interacted on each other, but for nearly a hundred years "creative" photographers confused ends with means.* PHOTOGRAPHY IS, *Aperture, Vol. 9, No. 2, 1961, p. 48.*

FIFTY YEARS OF DOCUMENTARY 1951
American Photography, Vol. 45, No. 1, pp. 21-26.

In photography, documentary is the term used to describe a specific attitude which sees, in the creative production and use of photographs, a language for giving a fuller understanding of man as a social animal.

By examining closely, by isolating and relating his subjects, the documentary photographer penetrates the surface appearances and reveals the world about us. The documentary editor, either by working directly with the photographer or by assembling previously unrelated pictures, combines the photographic image with text to create meaning in some area of the social scene. In either case, the endeavor to influence human behavior by giving a deeper understanding of the social process is the same.

As we look through the major documentary works of the past 50 years, we find that each one, in order to fulfill this aim, has approached the problem through the analysis of a specific time period, a specific place or a specific aspect of human life. We find works which have concentrated on a period in time: a day, a year, a decade. Other works have concerned themselves mainly with the place: a dwelling, a street, a state, a nation.

The final and largest group, which places the emphasis on a particular segment of the social process, ranges from a study done in terms of one man's daily routine to the complex picture of a nation gripped by economic depression. This group includes intense studies on wars and racial conflicts, on problems of agriculture and industry, on transportation and communication. It also includes the more subtle works dealing with the symbols of past and present cultures and with the spiritual relationships existing between men. The creators of these visions understood the fact that human society is a constantly changing process and not a static thing. To produce understanding of society through photographs it was necessary to relate the pictures in a meaningful way.

In general, the history of photography, from its invention to the present, seems to be divided into three major periods. From 1839 to about 1885, the photographer tried to record the face of the world in an objective way. He roamed far and wide to capture the images of foreign people and places never before seen by his excited audience. But whether he traveled in exotic lands or remained at home, the photographer was satisfied with his records of surface appearances and felt no need to search beneath that surface with his camera.

From 1885 to about 1918, the great photographic movements, particularly the Photo-Secession, concerned themselves with the superimposition of the photographer's personality over the subject matter in terms of stylistic mannerisms. The personality of the "photographic artist" manifested itself by destroying the machine-made image by controlled handwork and the misguided copying of certain Victorian painters' vision. This ultimately led to the stereotyped seeing of the present-day pictorialists, whose work is usually devoid of any personal meaning.

From 1918 to the present, the flowering of mass production raised tremendous problems of distribution and the ownership of goods. Such new methods of communication and transportation as the radio and the airplane compressed the world and made neighbors of those who had never before heard of each other. New dynamic psychologies, such as Freud's studies, gave man the ability to explore more deeply than ever before his inner needs, wishes and fears. Science even gave man the power to destroy himself completely: the atom and hydrogen bombs. During that time the sincere photographers became increasingly aware of deeper implications. They consciously explored beneath the surface chaos of man's world to discover the relationships and significance of outer appearances.

The conscious documentary attitude toward photography developed in this last period and it is not surprising that, as a result of the complications of life in the 20th century, photography evolved a discipline that is directly concerned with these problems and attempts to suggest possible solutions. Who were the men who first adopted this attitude and what were the problems that challenged them?

As this century began, America's rapidly expanding machine economy with its promise of economic freedom set up a powerful attraction to the oppressed of Europe. They poured into New York City and other ports in an overwhelming flood. In the ten years between 1903 and 1913, ten million immigrants arrived in the land of plenty with high hopes. Ill equipped by language and training to cope with the new culture, they were forced to begin on the lowest rungs of the cultural ladder. Working in sweat shops and at backbreaking manual labor, exploited by landlord and employer, they created terrific problems of education, housing, health and integration into the new society.

Lewis Hine, trained as a sociologist, began photographing these people and their problems in 1903. His pictures made vivid the exploitation of children and adults alike. Penetrating into the miserable living and working conditions of slum tenements and the sweatshops, he exposed these sores to the conscience of the public. The resulting indignation helped, to some extent, to destroy these evils. After World War I, he documented the Red Cross relief activities in middle European countries and his pictures revealed the vast human suffering caused by the war and the great need for relief. In the later years of his life, Hine was concerned with the affirmation of the dignity of labor. His work portraits clearly showed the resourceful skill and the pride in a job well done.

Lewis Hine was the classic documentary photographer. His work at the beginning of the century provided a pattern to follow and develop. Working in a limited social area at a given time in history, photographic analysis provided a rich basis for understanding of and action upon many social problems. When he stated, "I wanted to show the things that had to be corrected. I wanted to show the things that had to be appreciated," he defined very simply the documentary attitude.

Across the continent in San Francisco in a tight ghetto, was an older immigrant, the Chinese. Imported in the early days of the gold rush and the building of the railroads, he was not allowed to assimilate into the general community. He functioned as servant, cook, fish-cutter, laundryman and small farmer. Gradually, he was built up to be menace to American labor, and Congress finally passed the Exclusion Law preventing him from becoming an American citizen.

Arnold Genthe photographed San Francisco's Chinatown for about ten years until it was destroyed in the earthquake of 1906. He used a small hand camera which allowed him to photograph his subjects unaware. He tried to show the Chinese as human beings, who traded, gambled, loved and hated in the manner of other people. His pictures of Chinatown are on the picturesque side, obviously influenced by the prevailing "artistic" photography, but they are a noble and early use of the candid camera. Genthe's photographs of the San Francisco earthquake must also be mentioned. They provided an insight into the effects of a great natural catastrophe. The disruption of normal community life was clearly shown and helped to bring aid to the stricken city.

Meanwhile, in Paris, working in obscurity from 1898 to 1927 was Eugène Atget. His influence on his photographic contemporaries was nil, and not until his rescue from oblivion by Berenice Abbott in the early 30's was his power felt. Essentially a romantic, he photographed Paris with the single-mindedness of a man in love. Working with a large camera on a tripod, he warmly examined its people, shops, buildings, interiors and exteriors, palace and pauper's place, street signs, vehicles and vegetation. Here are lyrical images, peaceful pictures. A man examining with tenderness and understanding the symbols of a fast vanishing 19th century. In the 30's, the widespread publication of Atget's pictures affected many photographers. His directness of vision, his richly organized tones and textures were adopted by many photographers for their own purposes.

From the end of the first world war until the 30's, America produced undreamed of physical bounty. Everyone worked, the stock market values steadily increased, women were emancipated from many previous moral, economic and political shackles, prohibition produced a disrespect for the law and everyone enjoyed more physical comforts. But there were a few questioning souls who wondered about the loss of spiritual values. Among these was Alfred Stieglitz.

From the early days of the 90's Stieglitz had used his camera as a tool for exploring men and their spiritual relationships. In the 20's, a series of one-man shows demolished the old concepts of portraiture. Previously, the photographer had made portraits in the imitation of the painter and tried to synthesize into one image all the qualities of the individual. Stieglitz demonstrated a new kind of portrait based on the camera's ability to analyze and to isolate small areas. Some of his portraits had as many as 45 images in a group. He showed that a portrait could be something more than a head and that a group of images consisting of parts of the body could together produce a new kind of portrait.

Photographic portraiture has never been the same since these exhibits. Aside from the portraits of people, he made portraits of the city. The city had become an overpowering group of monuments that were engulfing men. The human values were being devoured by the machine age. Apart from his photographic work, Stieglitz stood as a spiritual oasis in a materialistic desert. Writers, painters and photographers who were wondering and questioning gathered around him for stimulation and strength. Among these was Paul Strand, who in 1916 had already made huge candid closeups of the hurt and dwarfed city people.

In 1920, Strand continued his exploration of the city and made a poetic documentary motion picture of New York with Charles Sheeler. They looked down from the towers of Manhattan to the little ants below. New angles were exploited to jolt the observer into awareness. In 1929, Strand expanded his vision with a series made in the Gaspé. The formal and precise ordering of land, people, boats, houses, sky proclaimed that a new level of visual organization for the documentary photographer had been achieved.

In Mexico at this time was Edward Weston. Participating in the Mexican renaissance, he was developing an intensive portraiture and a feeling for landscape and its forms that greatly enriched the documentary tradition of the 30's. He also had discovered the powerful meaning of signs and the relation of buildings to people. All of these elements fused in his later work in *California and the West* to produce a new kind of lyrical documentary image.

At the same time Steichen was discovering and exploiting the rich potential of controlled artificial light sources. In a series of sculptural portraits and vivid advertisements, he added a new rich vocabulary of light use to the language of the photographs. With the invention and common use of flashbulbs in the 30's, this vocabulary was put to immediate use.

In 1925, the Leica began to come into common use. Here was a new tool that could be used almost as a direct extension of the eye. It was light in weight, precise in use and enabled the photographer to invade new domains previously denied to him because of his cumbersome camera or fearful flash powder. Pioneers like Dr. Erich Salomon and Paul Wolff used the little instrument to explore quick expressions and psychological situations that were the grandfathers of the later intensive and strange images of Cartier-Bresson and Helen Levitt. In 1927, Moholy-Nagy's book *Light: Photography: Film,* made conscious the power of photomontage and the new vision of the scientific image.

On Black Friday of October 1929, the bubble of easy living exploded, blowing America into a period of self-analysis and a search for a new set of values. Photographers like Berenice Abbott and Walker Evans returned to the United States from Europe and focused their eyes on their native land. Abbott documented a changing New York City, and Evans surveyed the East and South with the critical eye of a cultural anthropologist. Although he worked with a large camera, Evans produced a series of brilliant psychological portraits and his photographs of buildings had the flavor of the people living in them whether they were actually present or not. He produced a powerful series of cultural fragments and symbols that did for the social scene what Stieglitz had done for portraits in the 20's.

As the economic crisis deepened, it called forth reactions in terms of a new kind of large scale social planning. To explain these problems and the attempts at solutions it was necessary to inaugurate a new kind of collaborative interpretation of the American scene. Roy Stryker, as head of the Farm Security Administration's Historical Branch, was the brilliant midwife of this new conscious form of visual communication. Aware of the impact of photographs and words from his experimentation in teaching economics at Columbia University, Stryker conceived a vast portrait of America. He assembled a sensitive group of photographers, each of whom used his own photographic technique from Walker Evans' 8 x 10 to Arthur Rothstein's and Ben Shahn's Leica.

Stryker encouraged their social growth by providing facts in the form of maps, pamphlets and books. But most important, his own person was a constant challenge to the photographers to understand the hidden social process behind the obvious picture. Not the America of the unique, odd or unusual happening, but the America of how to mine a piece of coal, grow a wheat field or make an apple pie. The America of "what does it mean," not the America of "amuse me."

Out of this project came significant works like Walker Evans' *American Photographs*, Sherwood Anderson's *Hometown*, Richard Wright's and Ed Rosskam's *12,000,000 Black Voices*, Archibald Macleish's *Land of the Free* and Dorothea Lange and Paul S. Taylor's terrific study of the displaced tenant farmer, *An American Exodus*.

Other photographers were affected by the F.S.A. project. The Photo League in New York under the sensitive direction of Aaron Siskind produced some memorable group documentations such as the famous *Harlem Document*. Margaret Bourke-White with Erskine Caldwell examined the South in *You Have Seen Their Faces*. In England, Bill Brandt was looking into the structure of family life and the contrasts of social classes. Many of his pictures, taken with the Leica, are among the great, sensitive pictures of the time. In France, Brassaï was exploring the underworld and half-world of Paris. His pictures were penetrating analyses of the night creatures in a great metropolis. They were early forerunners of Weegee's raw and almost brutal *Naked City*, his study of New York's night life. In Germany Lerski made close-ups with an 11 x 14 camera and many sources of light to reveal the structure and surface of the human head in an almost terrifying way.

The new problems produced by the world wide depression profoundly influenced the moviemakers. England's brilliant John Grierson, trained as a sociologist, organized film groups for the Empire Marketing Board and the Post Office. Employing the creative editing principles developed by the Russians in the 20's, these films made the phrase "documentary film" a common term. In Holland, Joris Ivens was exploring the social impact of land changes caused by damming the Zyder Zee. America, too, was producing a new kind of film; Pare Lorentz produced the *Plow that Broke the Plains,* a searching study of the causes of the Dust Bowl, beautifully photographed by Paul Strand and Leo Hurwitz. Lorentz also produced that classic study of soil erosion, *The River*. Even Hollywood came through with the memorable *Grapes of Wrath*. However, it is only recently that the full impact of the documentary approach has dawned on the "Motion Pictures are Your Best Entertainment" producers.

In this period the creative editing of still pictures for social understanding came to its first flowering. At the bottom of the depression in 1932 appeared Charles Gross' little known, but still jolting, montages of pictures, charts, clippings *(A Picture of America)* which shocked the observer into economic awareness. In 1933 Roger and Allen showed in their *American Procession* the folkways of America from the Civil War to the World War. In the following year they dissected New York from a sociological point of view in the book, *Metropolis*.

That same year, Pare Lorentz presented *The Roosevelt Year,* an interpretive record of the first days of the New Deal. This book has become a landmark for those who are interested in the visualization of social history. In 1935, M. Lincoln Schuster edited *Eyes on the World*. Its prophetic implications of future war and analysis of the forces that were leading up to the catastrophe deserve special mention. Later Anita Brenner and George R. Leighton collaborated on *The Wind That Swept Mexico*, a profound and moving fusion of news, pictures and text.

By 1936, the editing method in books had been firmly established and the time was ripe for its use in a weekly periodical. *Life* magazine burst on the scene. From its lead story by Margaret Bourke-White on a Montana mining town through the recent wonderful issue devoted to education, *Life* has used and helped develop the documentary approach. Arthur Rothstein and John Vachon of F.S.A. fame have enriched the pages of *Look* with their pictures made in this spirit. *The Ladies Home Journal* picture editor, John Morris, has produced the notable series, "How America Lives."

As the depression disappeared under the impact of social planning and the new rearmament program, the world saw in Spain a preliminary to the main bout. In 1938, Robert Capa presented his haunting *Death in the Making*, pictures created by a man who was not only brave, but also sensitive to what was happening beneath the surface events. In Finland, Carl Mydans was probing the war and sharpening his eye for his brilliant later observations of the Pacific fighting. M. Therese Bonney's heart-wrenching pictures of *Europe's Children* appeared.

But these examples were lost on the armed forces in World War II. Photography was considered news-oriented record-making that could be taught in three months and was beneath the dignity of an officer's activity. Where previously trained documentary photographers were in the services, they were generally misused. With the sole exceptions of Steichen's wonderful documentary unit in the Navy (producing among many other projects, the long to be remembered *Fighting Lady*) and Pare Lorentz' unit in the Air Transport Command, the best pictures of the war were usually produced by photographers outside of the services like W. Eugene Smith who documented the Pacific soldier. Some signs of this news-oriented misconception are beginning to appear again in the present State Department's rapidly expanding Voice of America picture operation.

In 1939, Julian Bryan recorded the disintegration of Warsaw under the impact of the Nazi air force. His *Siege* brought home to the American observer the devastation of modern war. In 1941, Bourke-White recorded the war's impact on Moscow. Forcing us to consider what we were fighting for, this period brought out documentary collections of belief and affirmation like Alexander Aland's study of the fabric of different nationality groups that make the cloth of America. Ansel Adams' portraits of Japanese-Americans in *Born Free and*

Equal were a protest against the concentration camps on the West Coast.

With the end of the war new searchings began. Wayne Miller of Steichen's Navy unit produced an exciting, but as yet unpublished series on the Negro in the North. Wright Morris, on a Guggenheim grant, critically examined in sensitive words and pictures the effects of people on the structures they live in *(The Inhabitants)* and later made a nostalgic re-examination of the disappearing rural scene *(The Home Place)*. Todd Webb explored New York and found new facets of buildings and people. Paul Strand and Nancy Newhall have dug deep into the New England tradition in their just published *Time in New England.* In this series Strand attains new heights of observation and interpretation. John Collier's fruitful collaboration with an anthropologist resulted in *The Awakening Valley,* a fascinating study of an Indian culture in Ecuador. Published by the University of Chicago Press, it opened a new era of scholarly communication. Steinbeck and Capa presented the life of a common citizen in their *A Russian Journal.*

Using photographers such as Ester Bubley, John Vachon, Ed Rosskam, Harold Corsini, Arnold Eagle, John Collier, Charles Rotkin, Russell Lee, Gordon Parks and Todd Webb, Roy Stryker documented the social ramifications of the oil industry for Standard Oil of New Jersey in a manner never before attempted by industry. Out of this project came one of the most exciting documentary books ever made. Edwin and Louise Rosskam's *Towboat River,* a study of the Mississippi, is a new classic in the use of word and picture to capture the unique flavor of people at work and the environment that produces this work.

To sum up documentary photography of the last 50 years, the following trends are evident: 1. From physical appearance to spiritual relationships. 2. From accidental to formal visual organization. 3. From single techniques to multiple techniques. 4. From single pictures to creative editing. 5. From individual worker to group collaboration.

What of the future? As man lives he creates social problems. A fast expanding scientific technology, the clash of political and economic theories, Africa and Asia being brought from feudalism into the 20th century, all combine to produce tremendous problems of action and understanding. That the documentary attitude will expand its techniques and understandings is a foregone conclusion. The documentary photographer of the future bears a tremendous responsibility; let us hope he is adequate to his task.

AARON SISKIND (1903-) ... *as the language or vocabulary of photography has been extended, the emphasis of meaning has shifted—shifted from what the world looks like to what we feel about the world and what we want the world to mean.* PHOTOGRAPHY AS AN ART FORM. (*From an unpublished lecture delivered at The Art Institute of Chicago, November 7, 1958.*)

THE DRAMA OF OBJECTS   1945
Minicam Photography, Vol. 8, No. 9, pp. 20-23, 93-94.

Last year I spent the summer at the famous New England fishing village of Gloucester, and made a series of photographic still-lifes of rotting strands of rope, a discarded glove, two fishheads, and other commonplace objects which I found kicking around on the wharves and beaches. For the first time in my life, subject matter, as such, had ceased to be of primary importance. Instead, I found myself involved in the relationships of these objects, so much so that these pictures turned out to be deeply moving and personal experiences.

This work was a new departure for me. I used one camera and one lens throughout (familiar enough to be an extension of my hand and eye), a limited number of types of film, no filters. The daily working time (2½ hours) was as regular as the weather permitted (it did), and I left the studio each day with six pictures to be taken and film enough to give each picture three exposures. The purpose of this procedure was to clear my way for complete absorption in the problem—and this is about the heart of what I want to say.

Curiously enough, these still-lifes were an outgrowth of my documentary practice. Producing a photographic document involves preparation in excess. There is first the examination of the idea of the project. Then the visits to the scene, the casual conversations, and more formal interviews—talking, and listening, and looking, looking. You read what's been written, and dig out facts and figures for your own writing. Follows the discussions to arrive at a point of view and its crystallization into a statement of aim. And finally, the pictures themselves, each one planned, talked, taken, and examined in terms of the whole.

I worked pretty much this way in making "Harlem Document." However, I cautioned my co-workers on this job to become as passive as possible when they faced the subject, to de-energize for the moment their knowledge of the ideas about the subject, to let the facts fall away and at that crucial moment to permit the subject to speak for itself and in its own way.

For some reason or other there was in me the desire to see the world clean and fresh and alive, as primitive things are clean and fresh and alive. The so-called documentary picture left me wanting something.

It is a pretty uncomfortable feeling for a documentary photographer to find himself working without a plan. But the initial drive coupled with simple, precise work habits carried me along for a while. Then certain ideas began to emerge from the work, a predilection for certain kinds of objects, and for certain kinds of relationships. That carried me along further. And they shall continue to carry me along until these ideas begin to become fixed, resulting in clichés. When that happens, I shall have to chuck them and start out freshly again.

As the saying goes, we see in terms of our education. We look at the world and see what we have learned to believe is there. We have been conditioned to expect. And indeed it is socially useful that we agree on the function of objects.

But, as photographers, we must learn to relax our beliefs. Move on objects with your eye straight on, to the left, around on the right. Watch them grow large as you approach, group and regroup themselves as you shift your position. Relationships gradually emerge, and sometimes assert themselves with finality. And that's your picture.

What I have just described is an emotional experience. It is utterly personal: no one else can ever see quite what you have seen, and the picture that emerges is unique, never before made and never to be repeated. The picture—and this is fundamental—has the unity of an organism. Its elements were not put together, with whatever skill or taste or ingenuity. It came into being as an instant act of sight.

Pressed for the meaning of these pictures, I should answer, obliquely, that they are informed with animism—not so much that these inanimate objects resemble the creatures of the animal world (as indeed they often do), but rather that they suggest the energy we usually associate with them. Aesthetically, they pretend to the resolution of these sometimes fierce, sometimes gentle, but always conflicting forces.

Photographically speaking, there is no compromise with reality. The objects are rendered sharp, fully textured, and undistorted (my documentary training!). But the potent fact is not any particular object; but rather that the meaning of these objects exists only in their relationship with other objects, or in their isolation (which comes to the same thing, for what we feel most about an isolated object is that it has been deprived of relationship).

These photographs appear to be a representation of a deep need for order. Time and again "live" forms play their little part against a backdrop of strict rectangular space—a flat, unyielding space. They cannot escape back into the depth of perspective. The four edges of the rectangle are absolute bounds. There is only the drama of the objects, and you, watching.

Essentially, then, these photographs are psychological in character. They may or may not be a good thing. But it does seem to me that this kind of picture satisfies a need. I may be wrong, but the essentially illustrative nature of most documentary photography, and the worship of the object *per se* in our best nature photography is not enough to satisfy the man of today, compounded as he is of Christ, Freud, and Marx. The interior drama is the meaning of the exterior event. And each man is an essence and a symbol.

There are, I suppose, many ways of getting at reality. Our province is this small bit of space; and only by operating within that limited space—endlessly exploring the relationships within it—can we contribute our special meanings that come out of man's varied life. Otherwise, our photographs will be vague. They will lack impact, or they will deteriorate into just "genre" as so many documentary shots do.

CREDO   1956
Spectrum, Vol. 6, No. 2, pp. 27-28.

When I make a photograph I want it to be an altogether new object, complete and self-contained, whose basic condition is order—(unlike the world of events and actions whose permanent condition is change and disorder).

The business of making a photograph may be said in simple terms to consists of three elements: the objective world (whose permanent condition is change and disorder), the sheet of paper on which the picture will be realized, and the experience which brings them together. First, and emphatically, I accept the flat plane of the picture surface as the primary frame of reference of the picture. The experience itself may be described as one of total absorption in the object. But the object serves only a personal need and the requirements of the picture. Thus, rocks are sculptured forms; a section of common decorative iron-work, springing rhythmic shapes; fragments of paper sticking to a wall, a conversation piece. And these forms, totems, masks, figures, shapes, images must finally take their place in the tonal field of the picture and strictly conform to their space environment. The object has entered the picture, in a sense; it has been photographed directly. But it is often unrecognizable; for it has been removed from its usual context, dissassociated from its customary neighbors and forced into new relationships.

What is the subject matter of this apparently very personal world? It has been suggested that these shapes and images are underworld characters, the inhabitants of that vast common realm of memories that have gone down below the level of conscious control. It may be they are. The degree of emotional involvement and the amount of free association with the material being photographed would point in that direction. However, I must stress that my own interest is immediate and in the picture. What I am conscious of and what I feel is the picture I am making, the relation of that picture to others I have made and, more generally, its relation to others I have experienced.

HENRY HOLMES SMITH (1909-) *In the present state of things, each one must conserve the photography he understands, permitting, when his tolerance is sufficient the remainder of the art to be conserved and examined elsewhere. Ultimately each of us may find, to our surprise, that our intolerance often rests on ignorance and our misunderstandings, our accusations of obscurity, unintelligibility, or falseness spring from too narrow a view of a medium that offers an intensity of expression and a range of images much greater than is generally seen.* IMAGE, OBSCURITY & INTERPRETATION, *Aperture, Vol. 5, No. 4, 1957, p.* 141.

PHOTOGRAPHY IN OUR TIME: A NOTE ON SOME   1961
PROSPECTS FOR THE SEVENTH DECADE
Three Photographers, Kalamazoo Art Center,
Bulletin No. 2. (revised 1966)

Before I can make any estimate of photography's present state and future prospects, I need to know what a photograph should look like and I am not at all certain that I do. When I voiced this doubt to a distinguished American historian of photography several years ago, he declared, "Some of us think we do!" True. Yet by his rules we must exclude a good many photographs I find memorable, and work by several important living photographers, so I think my doubt is justified.

The historian, of course, had in mind the "classical" photograph when he spoke. But we cannot judge all photographs by that standard; the rules for the sonnet do not apply to all poems.

The classical photograph requires us to use a camera with a conventional lens with conventional corrections to render the subject's grays and blacks and light and shadow in conventional tonal passages of monochrome. The classical photograph invariably points to a more or less "untouched" object more or less clearly located in time and space. It depicts this object with a special, often "edgy" intensity and clarity. When done superbly, this kind of photograph follows the tradition brought to its highest development by Alfred Stieglitz. It has been refined in some ways by others, particularly Walker Evans, in brilliant work of twenty-five years ago. Photographs by Francis Bruguière, Harry Callahan and Frederick Sommer, on the other hand, depart from this tradition in quite different ways. The discussion that follows will touch on some reasons for whatever discontent is expressed with photography's traditional limitations and demonstrate that there is no need for them to hold us spellbound. I hope also to suggest some kinds of imagery that do not depend on this tradition and to indicate some of the themes which turn photographers toward new images.

To distinguish the non-traditional kinds of photographs by their imagery and style, we should also have some idea of the nature of photography, both as to its accepted major limitations and its unexplored potentialities, which photographers break out of the tradition to work with.

As for the limitations, the first two are imposed by photography's closeness to nature. First, in no other art does subject matter enter upon a picture plane, usually in miniature, and scurry about until the instant when the artist imposes his will and freezes it in place. The result is his image. Since his final goal is to produce an artifact, he is involved with the question of how much credit he can take for the imagery he uses. For more than a century this important problem belonged to camera and lens photography alone; now, with the advent of "action painting," some other artists share it. Second, the physico-chemical process, which records the image, is always under only partial control, just like natural growth and aging. This fact gives the act of making a photograph some of the dignity and importance of a natural process. It is no more practical to try to reverse this process (to put the picture back on the object) than to pack a plant back into its seed. I imagine some of the excessively sober-sided posturing about photography (the "untouched" or "undirected" subject) stems from a half-understood awareness of this characteristic.

Another limitation arises from the way in which photography satisfies "the most problematic dogma of aesthetic theory," as Panofsky describes the notion that a "work of art is the direct and faithful representation of a natural object." (See "Codex Huygens and Leonardo Da Vinci's Art Theory." p. 90, footnote.) This dogma has become the unjustifiable basis for much worthless praise and superficial criticism of photography. Public and photographer alike know that pictures are derived directly from objects by the action of light. Consequently a majority of both groups have come to expect at least a slight family resemblance between the object and its picture. (This is the picture as "faithful witness"; how could anyone cherish or come to the defense of an unfaithful one?) A limitation this narrow and arbitrary would be only a minor annoyance if it did not support so perfectly a characteristic defect of our time: As Denis de Rougemont has pointed out (*Love in the Western World*, p. 53) "The superstition of our time expresses itself in a mania for equating the sublime with the trivial . . ." and to take whatever is lower to be more real.

Resemblance (the ability to mimic the appearance of objects) is the lowest common denominator of the classical photograph. It should occasion no great surprise, then, if a large portion of our present-day audience should regard resemblance as the most "real" characteristic of photography. To single out the obvious and most easily identified function of the image as more "real" than some others is sufficient folly; to regard this same function as the entire task of the image is inexcusably simple-minded. Both attitudes make it impossible to examine photography as it is being used in other important ways today.

Further, photography combines a natural process with several compelling conventions derived from the science, technology, and art of the past five centuries. It is, for example, an explicit answer of the sciences of physics and chemistry to one aspect of the Renaissance artist's view of nature. "Distortions," and "aberrations" of simple lenses must be corrected according to certain conventional rules before they are useful in photography. What aesthetic dominated the thinking of these lens designers, or those geniuses of the 19th Century who preceded them and established once and for all the visual standards we now cling to? What ideal draftsman had they in mind? What paintings were on their walls?

A fifth limitation is related to photography's exceptional candor, for nearly a hundred years looked upon as unpleasant and indecent, and today only partly tolerated. The 19th Century, far more than we, preferred euphemism to fact and blinked at many of the embarrassments of the human predicament. This attitude governed photography pretty completely until the 1930's. As I see it, not until the decision permitting the legal publication of James Joyce's *Ulysses,* in the United States did the English-speaking public begin to qualify as an audience for photography. This was 1933.

Photography is the most rigorously logical of man's methods of making images, although its structure is less complex than, say, music or poetry and it is far more rigid than painting. Nonetheless, in its newer forms, it is not quite as simple as some people make it out to be. Traditional photography is in some ways analogous to formal verse, rhymed and in regular meter. The newer form, freed from many of the old conventions, obeys rules more like those of free verse or the sprung rhythms of Hopkins. It depends heavily on structures we now recognize in nature as symbols of power we respect: the action of water, wind, temperature, of growth and destruction and chance (the random scattering of leaves on grass, boulders tumbled in a river bed). The new work is quite close both to nature and to man's nature as we now think of it.

As to certain potentialities unexplored or only partly explored: the first is to face squarely the embarrassments of the human predicament. No other medium is so open in its candor, so able to emphasize the peculiarly relevant detail, underline an essential vulgarity, make us aware of some shocking crudity. This thematic material, in the tradition of Bosch and the Brueghels, is eternally true. It may become the 20th Century's counterpart of the homely subject matter of earlier times. (Possibly we are now ready for more surgical detail from the everyday world.) The term "scrupulous meanness," which James Joyce applied to the style of *Dubliners,* may best describe the approach outlined here. ("Meanness," in the sense of smallness of spirit, inferior, shabby, contemptible, stingy, malicious.) For such themes more is to be learned from Evans than from Stieglitz. Second, the view of the natural world which takes into account much more than traditional optimism allows for. The themes of Melville and Ryder point toward nature's implacability, impersonality, and indifference to the fate of man. If we agree with T. S. Eliot that beneath both beauty and ugliness we may see "the boredom, the horror, and the glory," of human experience, we may recognize that conventional perspective can render accurately the boredom, but it is inadequate for the horror and the glory. Hints as to the quality of this imagery abound in the arts of prehistoric times, primitive peoples, and in fetishes from many places.

Thematically, the world of dreams and metamorphosis also occupies the photographer's imagination today. Lewis Carroll and other 19th Century writers drew freely on this material. (The "Nighttown" section of *Ulysses,* by Joyce, is a 20th Century landfall in this same region.) The claims of Laughlin and Telberg have been staked hereabouts in our time, but much uncharted territory remains. These subjects call for a less definite sense of scene or place than we are accustomed to in photography. Some of Siskind's photographs with the blank white or deep black grounds achieve this sense of enlarged, indefinite or ambiguous setting. Multiple exposure can be used also to this same end; combining conventional camera and lens images in this way, however, involves such a neat balance between the rational and the irrational that it has baffled most photographers who try it.

Photographers today are also interested in maintaining a special equilibrium between the world of ordinary objects in familiar time and space and the intensely-felt subjective image, which is always the reason for making a first-rate picture. ("Image" refers here to "the reproduction in memory or imagination of experience of the senses." If one does not restrict the photographer to the reproduction of sight experience alone, his imagery gains an enormous new range of meaning.)

The equilibrium referred to above is maintained between two poles. At one end, the commonplace aspect of the subject matter dominates the picture, a public image results and the intensity of the experience of the artist is obscured or diminished. At the opposite extreme, the photographer's private or personal imagery completely obscures the original subject matter; most viewers then lose faith in their ability to deal with the picture and abandon it before they have a chance to see it. For better than forty-five years some photographers have been involved with this problem; on the one hand seeking to exploit the witness-like power of the medium and, on the other, to take advantage of a potential for images that are derived from, but lean only slightly on, the object pictured. (Strand's "White Fence, 1916" is one of the early examples with which I am familiar.)

I have tried to distinguish, in some ways, the photograph as *fact* (the image as witness) from the photograph as *artifact* (the image as image). Yet both fact and artifact are present in every photograph, and it is only the emphasis—now more of one, now more of the other —that makes any distinction possible. They are seldom in equal balance; probably such exact equilibrium is undesirable.

Contrary to widespread belief, the unfamiliar or difficult image may actually be a complete and important human utterance. Frederick Sommer has noted that "Photographs of penetrating perception do not easily lend themselves to misuse. . . ." For this, and similar reasons, the unabridged photographic statement is rarely printed and receives limited circulation. Consequently, we may see too few of them to learn the difference between the difficult and the garbled. Sommer puts it well when he says, "The possibilities of interesting people through photography in the life about them has . . . hardly been realized. . . . Fact is only fact when we have taken its spiritual measure." In our difficult and complicated world, we should be wary of the easy message; the plain one will be hard enough to believe. In my view what Stieglitz left us to *use* was neither his style nor his imagery, although they are both inspiring. Rather it was a tradition of faith in our own vision, whatever it may be, and a desire to use it with a passion for truth as strong as we possess.

If we do keep faith with our vision, we will be equally able to protect old photographic traditions against senseless onslaughts and see to it that new imagery and styles of younger artists are not recklessly destroyed. Opposition in such circumstances will take the form of public cat and dog fights, with differences plainly seen, battle lines drawn and ideas knee-deep in the streets.

W. EUGENE SMITH (1918-) *Somehow, somewhere there must be a continuing base from which, with practical idealism, real study can be applied— through which, growth with the clear view and the steady purpose can be nurtured by those willing to dedicate their lives to bringing into fact the best potentials of photographic journalism.* ONE WHOM I ADMIRE, DOROTHEA LANGE 1895-1965, *Popular Photography, Vol.* 58, *No.* 2, 1966, *p.* 88.

PHOTOGRAPHIC JOURNALISM   1948
Photo Notes, (June) pp. 4-5.

Photography is a potent medium of expression. Properly used it is a great power for betterment and understanding; misused, it can kindle many troublesome fires. Photographic journalism, because of the tremendous audience reached by publications using it, has more influence on public thinking and opinion than any other branch of photography. For these reasons, it is important that the photographer-journalist have (beside the essential mastery of his tools) a strong sense of integrity and the intelligence to understand and present his subject matter accordingly.

Those who believe that photographic reportage is "selective and objective, but cannot interpret the photographed subject matter," show a complete lack of understanding of the problems and the proper workings of this profession. The journalistic photographer can have no other than a personal approach; and it is impossible for him to be completely objective. Honest—yes. Objective—no.

Working with different techniques, all of which are common to others in the field, photographers Lisette Model, Cartier-Bresson, Gjon Mili, rise far above mere technical proficiency. Yet each of the three, were they to handle the same subject matter, would be capable of giving the world fine and individual interpretations. Cartier-Bresson and Leonard McCombe are two photographers who work almost exclusively with 35mm cameras and natural light. Here again, it could almost be guaranteed that their interpretations of the same subject would be quite different. Which is the objective truth? Perhaps all of these photographers are telling the truth—truth being "many things to many people."

Up to and including the instant of exposure, the photographer is working in an undeniably subjective way. By his choice of technical approach (which is a tool of emotional control), by his selection of the subject matter to be held within the confines of his negative area, and by his decision as to the exact, climactic instant of exposure, he is blending the variables of interpretation into an emotional whole which will be a basis for the formation of opinions by the viewing public.

It is the responsibility of the photographer-journalist to take his assignment and examine it—to search with intelligence for the frequently intangible truth; and then very carefully (and sometimes very rapidly) work to bring his insight, as well as the physical characteristics of the subject, to his finished pictures.

It is important that the inspiration for the interpretation should come from a study of the people or places to be photographed. The mind should remain as open and free from prejudice as possible, and the photographer should never try to force the subject matter into his or the editor's preconceived idea. Too often, an assignment is given, the photographer reads the instructions and the suggestions, and then follows them without much more thought—except to photograph as closely as possible to what he believes are the desires of the editors. All too frequently, due to faulty research, to inadequate knowledge or to the preconceived notions just mentioned, the directional theme of the assignment is a misconception of the living actuality. But because he does not wish to offend the editors who pay him his bread money, the photographer frequently tries to make his story conform to someone else's shortsighted or warped judgment.

The photographer must bear the responsibility for his work and its effect. By so much as his work is a distortion (this is sometimes intangible, at other times shockingly obvious), in such proportion is it a crime against humanity. Even on rather "unimportant" stories, this attitude must be taken—for photographs (and the little words underneath) are molders of opinion. A little misinformation plus a little more misinformation is the kindling from which destructive misunderstandings flare.

The majority of photographic stories require a certain amount of setting up, rearranging and stage direction, to bring pictorial and editorial coherency to the pictures. Here, the photo-journalist can be his most completely creative self. Whenever this is done for the purpose of a better translation of the spirit of the actuality, then it is completely ethical. If the changes become a perversion of the actuality for the sole purpose of making a "more dramatic" or "saleable" picture, the photographer has indulged in "artistic license" that should not be. This is a very common type of distortion. If the photographer has distorted for some unethical reasons, it obviously becomes a matter of the utmost gravity.

A personal belief of mine is that all the events in the world which cause great emotional upheavals, such as wars, riots, mine disasters, fires, the death of leaders (such as the reaction to the death of Ghandi)—these and similar happenings which tend to release human emotions from control should be photographed in a completely interpretational manner. *Under no circumstances should an attempt be made to recreate the moods and happenings of these moments.*

I prefer this unposed interpretive approach in the doing of all stories—that is, wherever possible. Regardless of the "how" of interpretations, the journalistic field must find men of integrity, openminded and sincere in purpose, with the intelligence and insight to penetrate to the vital core of human relationships—and with the very rare ability to give the full measure of their unbiased findings to the world. Few men are so completely equipped, but the standards of journalism should be measured high. And the individual striving for this perfection should not compromise. He must not knuckle down to those publications which would have it otherwise. He should be held accountable for any prolonged misuse of his work, and cannot seek refuge in the whine that he is just a working man doing his assigned job.

To have his photographs live on in history, past their important but short lifespan in a publication, is the final desire of nearly every photographer-artist who works in journalism. He can reach this plane only by combining a profound penetration into the character of the subject with a perfection of composition and technique—a consolidation necessary for any photographic masterpiece.

EUGENE SMITH PHOTOGRAPHY   1954
Exhibition Catalogue, University of Minnesota.

I would dream of being an artist in an ivory tower. Yet it is imperative that I speak to people, so I must desert that ivory tower. To do this I am a journalist—a photographic journalist. In result, I am constantly torn between the attitude of the conscientious journalist who is a recorder of, an interpreter of facts, and of the creative artist who often is necessarily at poetic odds with the literal facts.

My principal concern is for an honesty of interpretation to be arrived at by careful study and through the utmost possible sensitivity of understanding. I would further, if the strength of talent be within me, have my accomplished image transcend literal truth by intensifying its truthful accuracy, indicating even of the spirit and symbolizing more. And my only editor would be my conscience and my conscience would be of my responsibilities—in constant disciplined rejudgment of my failures and of my fulfillments.

THE WORLD'S 10 GREATEST PHOTOGRAPHERS   1958
Popular Photography, Vol. 42, No. 5, p. 84.

I doubt the existence of any perfection, although I am for trying the rise to this the impossible and would take measure from such failure rather than from the convenience of a safe but mundane success. (I do not deplore success.) I would experience ever deeper, and endeavor to give out from this experience. My photographs at best hold only a small strength, but through them I would suggest and criticize and illuminate and try to give compassionate understanding. And through the passion given into my photographs (no matter how quiet) I would call out for a spiritualization that would create strength and healing and purpose, as teacher and surgeon and entertainer, and would give comment upon man's place and preservation within this new age—a terrible and exciting age. And with passion. Passion, yes, as passion is in all great searches and is necessary to all creative endeavors—whether of statesman, or scientist, or artist, or freedom, or devil—and Don Juan may have been without passion, for sex and sentiment and violence can very much be without passion. Question this? Take note of the values around you, everywhere thrust upon you—and wade awhile, with this question in thought, through publications and publications from cover to cover.

EDWARD STEICHEN (1879-) *The use of the term art medium is, to say the least, misleading, for it is the artist that creates a work of art not the medium. It is the artist in photography that gives form to content by a distillation of ideas, thought, experience, insight and understanding.* MY LIFE IN PHOTOGRAPHY, *Saturday Review, Vol. 42, 1959, p. 18.*

ON PHOTOGRAPHY   1960
Daedalus, Vol. 42, pp. 136-37.

Mankind is faced with a staggering abundance of words and images adding up to a complexity of political, scientific, economic, social, and cultural problems which no single human being can possibly assimilate. From birth to death we all function on the basis of our individual and unique genetic make-up. The future artist, as an infant, comes without an IBM card that lists and qualifies his aptitudes or indicates how the enormous influences of environment will shape his native equipment. It is only in the retrospective consideration of the artist's life work that the germ of the ultimate masterwork becomes evident even in his earliest work.

In a somewhat similar manner each period in the arts is the result of its inheritance of a past subjected to the conditioning pressures of the present, and it is only in the distant future that we shall be able to measure and evaluate the importance of what the art of our recent decades has contributed or added to the history of the arts and the culture of our period. The works of individual artists in any period or in relationship to works of other periods are only momentarily avant-garde devices. These soon become academic routine, and are often used to saddle the next generation. The fundamental relationship of great art in all periods has more basic similarities than differences. The images created in the caves of Lascaux and Altamira have a deep kinship with those coming from the studio of Picasso, and if we can skip conditioning and prejudices, what looks like radical differences between Li Lung Mien and Mark Tobey can also be translated into kinships.

Today it would seem that the painting and sculpture of our time has achieved an almost complete break from the long accepted traditions of literal representation, and has assumed an individual and personal freedom that discards all past disciplines.

Long before the birth of a word language the caveman communicated by visual images. The invention of photography gave visual communication its most simple, direct, universal language. We are only beginning to recognize generally and accept the potentialities of photography as an art medium, but as a visual means of mass communication it has become a force, and stands without a peer.

The importance of the art of photography as mass communication has been amply demonstrated by the exhibition produced by the Museum of Modern Art under the title, "The Family of Man." This exhibition, in nine editions, has already been seen by some seven million people in twenty-eight countries—and it is still circulating. The audiences not only understand this visual presentation, they also participate in it, and identify themselves with the images, as if in corroboration of the words of a Japanese poet, "When you look into a mirror, you do not see your reflection, your reflection sees you."

Almost from the beginning, photographers have experimented with the production of images that imitated, or were inspired by, the prevalent concepts of other art media. Today a sizable percentage of the more talented younger photographers are probing and experimenting in new areas, creating images carrying connotations and meanings beyond, and often only indirectly related to, the objects represented. The photographers working in motion pictures with animated images in the realm of abstraction and surrealism, and with the added advantages of sound, are making a signal contribution to the modern use of photography as an art medium. As photography I would include color images directly projected on a screen by colored beams of light, even when made without the intervention of the camera.

It is quite possible that some richly imaginative and energetic young abstract painter may be even now experimenting with the highly developed photographically animated cartoon techniques coupled with related sound to open new horizons and areas in the domain of aesthetic imagery. In recording this as a possibility, I must give emphasis to the fact that a few photographers who have been exposed to the same heritage as the painters, as well as to the present-day impingements of science and of aesthetics in the arts, are now taking advantage also of the available technical advances to carry them toward these beckoning new image horizons.

ALFRED STIEGLITZ (1864-1946) *I detest tradition for tradition's sake; the half-alive; that which is not real. I feel no hatred of individuals, but of customs, traditions; superstitions that go against life, against truth, against the reality of experience, against the spontaneous living out of the sense of wonder—of fresh experience, freshly seen and communicated.* ALFRED STIEG-LITZ, *quoted by Dorothy Norman, Aperture, Vol. 8, No. 1, 1960, p. 25.*

THE HAND CAMERA—ITS PRESENT IMPORTANCE 1897
The American Annual of Photography, pp. 18-27.

Photography as a fad is well-nigh on its last legs, thanks principally to the bicycle craze. Those seriously interested in its advancement do not look upon this state of affairs as a misfortune, but as a disguised blessing, inasmuch as photography had been classed as a sport by nearly all of those who deserted its ranks and fled to the present idol, the bicycle. The only persons who seem to look upon this turn of affairs as entirely unwelcome are those engaged in manufacturing and selling photographic goods. It was, undoubtedly, due to the hand camera that photography became so generally popular a few years ago. Every Tom, Dick and Harry could, without trouble, learn how to get something or other on a sensitive plate, and this is what the public wanted—no work and lots of fun. Thanks to the efforts of these persons hand camera and bad work became synonymous. The climax was reached when an enterprising firm flooded the market with a very ingenious hand camera and the announcement, "You press the button, and we do the rest." This was the beginning of the "photographing-by-the-yard" era, and the ranks of enthusiastic Button Pressers were enlarged to enormous dimensions. The hand camera ruled supreme.

Originally known under the odious name of "Detective," necessarily insinuating the owner to be somewhat of a sneak, the hand camera was in very bad repute with all the champions of the tripod. They looked upon the small instrument, innocent enough in itself, but terrible in the hands of the unknowing, as a mere toy, good for the purposes of the globe-trotter, who wished to jot down photographic notes as he passed along his journey, but in no way adapted to the wants of him whose aim it is to do serious work.

But in the past year or two all this has been changed. There are many who claim that for just the most serious work the hand camera is not only excellently adapted, but that without it the pictorial photographer is sadly handicapped.

The writer is amongst the advocates who cannot too strongly recommend the trial of the hand camera for this class of photography. He frankly confesses that for many years he belonged to that class which opposed its use for picture making. This was due to a prejudice which found its cause in the fact that the impression had been given him that for hand camera exposures strong sunlight was *sine qua non*. The manufacturer is chiefly to be blamed for this false impression, as it was he who put up the uniform rule that the camera should be held in such a position that the sunlight comes from over one of the shoulders, in order to insure such lighting as to fully expose the plate. In short, the manufacturer himself did not realize the possibilities of his own ware and invention.

In preparing for hand camera work, the choice of the instrument is of vital importance. Upon this subject that able artist, J. Craig Annan, of Glasgow, who does much of his work with the hand camera, says: "Having secured a light-tight camera and suitable lens, there is no more important quality than ease in mechanical working. The adjustments ought to be so simple that the operator may be able to bring it from his satchel and get it in order for making an exposure without a conscious thought. Each worker will have his own idea as to which style of camera comes nearest to perfection in this respect, and having made his choice he should study to become so intimate with it that it will become a second nature with his hands to prepare the camera while his mind and eyes are fully occupied with the subject before him."

To this let me add, that whatever camera may be chosen let it be waterproof, so as to permit photographing in rain or shine without damage to the box. The writer does not approve of complicated mechanisms, as they are sure to get out of order at important moments, thus causing considerable unnecessary swearing, and often the loss of a precious opportunity. My own camera is of the simplest pattern and has never left me in the lurch, although it has had some very tough handling in wind and storm. The reliability of the shutter is of greater importance than its speed. As racehorse scenes, express trains, etc., are rarely wanted in pictures, a shutter working at a speed of one-fourth to one-twenty-fifth of a second will answer all purposes. Microscopic sharpness is of no pictorial value. A little blur in a moving subject will often aid in giving the impression of action and motion.

As for plates, use the fastest you can get. They cannot be too fast. Do not stop down your lens except at the seashore, and set your shutter at as slow speed as the subject will permit. This will ensure a fully exposed plate. Under exposures are best relegated to the ash-barrel, as they are useless for pictorial work.

The one quality absolutely necessary for success in hand camera work is *Patience*.

This is really the keynote to the whole matter. It is amusing to watch the majority of hand camera workers shooting off a ton of plates helter-skelter, taking their chances as to the ultimate result. Once in a while these people make a hit, and it is due to this cause that many pictures produced by means of the hand camera have been considered flukes. At the same time it is interesting to note with what regularity certain men seem to be the favorites of chance— so that it would lead us to conclude that, perhaps, chance is not everything, after all.

In order to obtain pictures by means of the hand camera it is well to choose your subject, regardless of figures, and carefully study the lines and lighting. After having determined upon these watch the passing figures and await the moment in which everything is in balance; that is, satisfies your eye. This often means hours of patient waiting. My picture, "Fifth Avenue, Winter," is the result of a three hours' stand during a fierce snow-storm on February 22nd, 1893, awaiting the proper moment. My patience was duly rewarded. Of course, the result contained an element of chance, as I might have stood there for hours without succeeding in getting the desired picture. I remember how upon having developed the negative of the picture I showed it to some of my colleagues. They smiled and advised me to throw away such rot. "Why, it isn't even sharp, and he wants to use it for an enlargement!" Such were the remarks made about what I knew was a piece of work quite out of the ordinary, in that it was the first attempt at picture making with the hand camera in such adverse and trying circumstances from a photographic point of view. Some time later the laugh was on the other side, for when the finished picture was shown to these same gentlemen it proved to them conclusively that there was other photographic work open to them during the "bad season" than that so fully set forth in the photographic journals under the heading, "Work for the Winter Months." This incident also goes to prove that the making of the negative alone is not the making of the picture. My hand camera negatives are all made with the express purpose of enlargement, and it is but rarely that I use more than part of the original shot.

Most of my successful work of late has been produced by this method. My experience has taught me that the prints from the direct negatives have but little value as such.

The hand camera has come to stay—its importance is acknowledged.

A word to the wise is sufficient.

HOW I CAME TO PHOTOGRAPH CLOUDS

1923
The Amateur Photographer & Photography,
Vol. 56, No. 1819, p. 255.

As for the cloud series perhaps it will interest you how that came about.

Last summer when manuscripts were sent in by the various contributors for the issue of the publication, "M.S.S." devoted to photography, and its aesthetic significance, Waldo Frank—one of America's young literary lights, author of *Our America,* etc.—wrote that he believed the secret power in my photography was due to the power of hypnotism I had over my sitters, etc.

I was amazed when I read the statement. I wondered what he had to say about the street scenes—the trees, interiors—and other subjects, the photographs of which he had admired so much: or whether he felt they too were due to my powers of hypnotism. Certainly a lax statement coming from one professing himself profound and fair thinking, and interested in enlightening.

It happened that the same morning in which I read this contribution my brother-in-law (lawyer and musician) out of the clear sky announced to me that he couldn't understand how one as supposedly musical as I could have entirely given up playing the piano. I looked at him and smiled—and I thought: even he does not seem to understand. He plays the violin. The violin takes up no space: the piano does. The piano needs looking after by a professional, etc. I simply couldn't afford a piano, even when I was supposedly rich. It was not merely a question of money.

Thirty-five or more years ago I spent a few days in Murren (Switzerland), and I was experimenting with ortho plates. Clouds and their relationship to the rest of the world, and clouds for themselves, interested me, and clouds which were difficult to photograph—nearly impossible. Ever since then clouds have been in my mind, most powerfully at times, and I always knew I'd follow up the experiment made over 35 years ago. I always watched clouds. Studied them. Had unusual opportunities up here on this hillside. What Frank had said annoyed me: what my brother-in-law said also annoyed me. I was in the midst of my summer's photographing, trying to add to my knowledge, to the work I had done. Always evolving—always going more and more deeply into life—into photography.

My mother was dying. Our estate was going to pieces. The old horse of 37 was being kept alive by the 70-year-old coachman. I, full of the feeling of today: all about me disintegration—slow but sure: dying chestnut trees—all the chestnuts in this country have been dying for years: the pines doomed too—diseased: I, poor, but at work: the world in a great mess: the human being a queer animal—not as dignified as our giant chestnut tree on the hill.

So I made up my mind I'd answer Mr. Frank and my brother-in-law. I'd finally do something I had in mind for years. I'd make a series of cloud pictures. I told Miss O'Keeffe of my ideas. I wanted to photograph clouds to find out what I had learned in 40 years about

photography. Through clouds to put down my philosophy of life—
to show that my photographs were not due to subject matter—not to
special trees, or faces, or interiors, to special privileges—clouds were
there for everyone—no tax as yet on them—free.

So I began to work with the clouds—and it was great excitement—
daily for weeks. Every time I developed I was so wrought up, always
believing I had nearly gotten what I was after—but had failed. A
most tantalizing sequence of days and weeks. I knew exactly what I
was after. I had told Miss O'Keeffe I wanted a series of photographs
which when seen by Ernest Bloch (the great composer) he would
exclaim: Music! Music! Man, why that is music! How did you ever
do that? And he would point to violins, and flutes, and oboes, and
brass, full of enthusiasm, and would say he'd have to write a symphony called "Clouds." Not like Debussy's but *much, much more.*

And when finally I had my series of ten photographs printed, and
Bloch saw them—what I said I wanted to happen happened *verbatim.*

Straight photographs, all gaslight paper, except one palladiotype.
All in the power of every photographer of all time, and I satisfied
I had learnt something during the 40 years. It's 40 years this year
that I began in Berlin with Vogel.

Now if the cloud series are due to my powers of hypnotism I plead
"Guilty." Only some "Pictorial photographers" when they came to
the exhibition seemed totally blind to the cloud pictures. My photographs look like photographs—and in their eyes they therefore can't
be art. As if they had the slightest idea of art or photography—
or any idea of life. My aim is increasingly to make my photographs
look as much like photographs that unless one has *eyes* and *sees,* they
won't be seen—and still everyone will never forget them having once
looked at them. I wonder if that is clear.

ALFRED STIEGLITZ: FOUR HAPPENINGS   1942
Twice-A-Year, edited by Dorothy Norman, No. 8/9, pp. 105-36.

I. WHY I GOT OUT OF BUSINESS

In September, 1890, I returned from nine years' stay in Europe.
My eldest sister had died in childbirth in Los Angeles and my parents
felt it was time for me to come home.

I had hoped to remain in Europe. The life there was congenial.
My father had assured me a small annual income and I felt I could
live on that with comfort.

My demands were modest—traveling third class on slow trains,
eating in inexpensive restaurants, standing at the Royal Opera House
downstairs for thirty-seven and a half cents—as a student, getting
rebates on books, on Roman baths—a rebate even on tickets to the
race track, and a rebate on tickets for the best theatres and music,
in addition to having all the advantages of the University and the
Polytechnic, havens of perfect freedom—having no social aspirations,

being passionately devoted to photography and crazy about billiards, as well as about race horses—what more could life offer anywhere?

Intuitively I felt that it would be very different in my own country, even though I had always loved it as an idea. "The Boys of Seventy-Six" had been my bible as I was growing up, with Nathanael Greene as my hero; I, feeling that wonderful as George Washington was, Greene satisfied something in my nature that Washington didn't. Greene seemed always to be beaten in the battles with the English, but to me it was ever a victory and not a defeat, for in his battles it was so and so many hundred Englishmen killed, so and so many prisoners taken, while Greene retreated with but a handful of Americans killed and but a handful of Americans falling into English hands. This is at least the way it seemed to me as I'd read the story of Greene over and over again. There seemed to be a sense of humor in Greene's strategy. And as far as Washington was concerned, I had always been told that he was the quintessence of perfection, never even having told a lie. This implied that everybody else did tell a lie at some time or other. This, to me, made Washington not quite human and I knew that if I had lived in the days of the American Revolution, I'd have preferred to fight under Greene than to fight under Washington. Of course later in life I realized that a fairytale had been passed on to me and I was gullible—or should I call it innocent enough—to take it literally. But Greene was a human being like myself. Washington was made to appear a God and I knew that I didn't belong amongst Gods. But at the same time I had believed in the fairytale of America.

In my various rooms in Berlin—rooms which I gave up during the summer months while I was foot-trotting Switzerland, the Tyrol, the Bavarian highlands, upper Italy—I always had a painting of my mother which a friend of mine, a German artist, who had lived with my family in New York for some years, had painted for me for my twenty-first birthday, hanging over an upright piano. I was never without a piano during those years.

On the open piano there always were scores of "Carmen," of Wagner, of Gluck—my favorites. And over my mother's picture there was draped an American flag twelve feet long.

This flag was made by a friend of mine, poor in money, very poor. He was the son of a Konigsberg professor. He was the youngest in the family—he had seven sisters.

He had a stipend of six hundred marks a year. He was as gifted as he was poor. He was brilliant. He played piano, he played violin and the flute, he was studying engineering, he was as homely as sin and in six weeks I had taught him sufficient English so that he could read Washington Irving's *Alhambra*.

He knew of my passion for my home country. Because of this he one day surprised me in bringing me the American flag I have mentioned. He had made it himself.

And now—in 1890—I was back in America. I was a forlorn soul, even though I lived with my parents. One day my father said, "Don't you think you ought to be earning your own living?"

I felt I should, but how? I seemed like a fish out of water. Yes, I had an international reputation as a photographer, but what of it? How could it be put to use, that is, turned into money? That didn't seem to interest me.

One day Mr. Foord, a friend of the family for years, asked to see me, invited me to lunch with him at the old Astor House. (It was opposite this place that two years later I photographed "The Car Horses.")

Mr. Foord at twenty-six—he was a Scotchman by birth—had been editor of the *New York Times*. When we had lunch together at this time, he was editor of *Harper's Weekly*. Later on he became editor of *Asia*.

In some way or other, in 1889, he had been induced to become interested in establishing a company devoted to making three-color photographic reproductions. He had become interested in this even though he was still editor of *Harper's Weekly*.

A man named Gast, son of the founder of the old Gast Lithograph Company, had been working with the Colortype Company which was the first company in America to produce three-color printing. (I know this is sometimes disputed.)

Mr. Gast had been working with the Colortype Company when it was founded. He had somehow managed to come into contact with Mr. Foord and had told Mr. Foord that he had discovered a new process for printing color on the printing press, and that there were millions in it.

Mr. Foord listened, went to his friends, Nathan Straus, Isidore Straus and Oscar Straus, told them of the process and they had taken stock in the new company that was then formed. At the time they had built a Lakewood Hotel as a protest against some Jewish question which had arisen in the most fashionable of the Lakewood hotels. Lakewood at the time was a fashionable center. Posters for the hotel enterprise had subsequently been ordered from the Heliochrome Company, which was the name of the new company that was founded by Mr. Gast with the money that Foord had gotten the Strauses to put up.

When I met Mr. Foord at lunch that day he told me that my father had taken a thousand dollar interest in the new venture. He had done this because he felt that I might be tempted to become interested in such a company, as I was such a great photographer.

I told Mr. Foord that I knew nothing about business—I knew nothing about process work—as a matter of fact, photography as business didn't interest me—that I felt completely unfit for any such job.

He told me I was much too modest, that a gifted person like myself could quickly learn what was essential to develop such a company.

He frankly told me that the Heliochrome Company he had organized was about to go on the rocks—that the big posters that the company had made for the big Lakewood Hotel were finished and had been paid for, but that there was practically no money left in the bank, and there were no orders in sight.

Didn't I think that I could reorganize the company and make a good thing of it for all concerned, including myself?

When I came home I told my father what had happened and I told my ex-roommates of Berlin, both of whom had taken their degrees as doctors of philosophy. Both were chemists—both their fathers had died about a year or two before, and had left them independent young men.

Neither of them wished to work as chemists for a paltry hundred dollars a month—so when they had heard of the offer to me, my father said to us, "Why can't you three go into this company and do something with it?"

My friends had no business experience of any kind, but they felt that they'd like to do something and if I'd go in they'd go in with me.

I went to Mr. Foord and told him that we would take over the concern provided that we would take over none of the liabilities and that we would become sole owners of the new concern. I said that if I did reorganize it, I would drop the old name and call the new company the Photochrome Engraving Company.

After hemming and hawing he finally agreed. In reality there were no assets except a camera, a hand-proofing press and some chemicals.

There were six workmen to be taken care of if we wished to continue using them in the business.

Mr. Gast was the artist—that is, he was the man who seemed to know about the process. There was a salesman—an Irishman, Mr. Murphy, who was guaranteed forty dollars a week for soliciting orders on a commission basis. Mr. Gast received, if I remember correctly, seventy-five dollars a week—the others averaged something like thirty dollars each a week. The proofman was a Scotchman—an ardent Salvation Army man. The photographer of the half-tone plates was a German, who was full of brilliant theories and not very perfect as a photographer.

We started with a capital of ten thousand dollars. I called in the workmen and told them how things stood. First of all, that the three of us knew nothing whatsoever of business nor of the processes of the company—that none of us would draw a single cent of salary until we felt we had earned it. That we were pupils and that they, the workmen, were our teachers. That the books would ever be open to them and that I felt we were one family working together for a common good.

Nearly a year passed before a single order came in. We had started business at a frightful time, for business generally was at a low ebb. There was practically no business in nearly all fields. We had been making sample plates—heaven knows how many—both in black and white and in color. I was the one to make prices and estimates, and was technical head. I was learning. I had a gift for figures.

Our concern quickly got the reputation of doing some of the best work in the city. Also that our quotations, or estimates, were high. For what we were ready to give they were really low. I rarely added anything to the actual cost. All I wanted was to cover the expense of rent, which was relatively nominal, and the cost of the working men. That was relatively high, for we did not deduct for holidays, nor for illness, nor did we put anybody on part time. Other firms did. Times, we were told, were hard. They certainly were hard for us.

At the end of the year practically all the capital was gone. I had learned enough and I wanted to get out, but my partners induced me to continue. There seemed to be a "beginning."

My father was willing that I should go on. A few men were added to our list of working people.

When I was persuaded to go on we moved from the ramshackle building we had been in on Fulton Street—a fire trap—an old five-story brownstone house—to Leonard Street, a new loft building between Baxter and Center streets. So we were around the corner from the Tombs and within a stone's throw of the Baxter Street Jewish clothing peddlers—in a pretty rough neighborhood—not far from the notorious Five Points.

We had as our first real customer the *Cassier Magazine* which was primarily devoted to mechanical engineering. We also had as customer the *Police Gazette*—Mr. Carey, the manager of the *Police Gazette,* being friendly towards Mr. Murphy. This solicitor also brought in an order one day for fifty thousand small color portraits. Cards about 2½ by 3½ inches. These little cards were colored pictures of actors and actresses of the Murphy Comedy Company, a traveling theatrical company. Our agent told us this order ought to run into hundreds of thousands of cards being needed in time; that we were to send a thousand cards to each of the places at which the Murphy Comedy Company was to give performances. We were to be paid every month for cards sent. I did not like the idea of our company taking the whole risk and there not even being any collateral whatsoever. So I was opposed to accepting this order. But my friends voted me down, saying that we'd never get under way if we didn't take risks. So we began filling the order and sent out thousands of cards to various parts of the country. Our letters asking for some payment remained unanswered, but still more and more orders came in. I finally balked and said I refused to go on, that I felt we were being swindled. There was quite a heated argument between myself and my partners. I finally decided to go to see Mr. Carey of the *Police Gazette* as I knew he could give me some advice, he being accustomed to dealing with theatrical people. I had never met Mr. Carey, but I had great faith in the integrity of sporting people. So I saw Mr. Carey and told him the story of the order from the Murphy Comedy Company. He listened attentively, and when I was through he said, "Your concern has been the laughing stock of the printers and engravers of the city. You mustn't trust theatrical people. You'll never see a cent of this money owed to you." I was rather horror-stricken at his generalization about theatrical people and I naïvely said, "You don't mean to say, Mr. Carey, that Augustin Daly isn't good for whatever he contracts for?" Augustin Daly was in the hey-day of the Daly Theater and this theater was at the top of all the theaters in New York. Mr. Carey smiled and said, "Even Mr. Daly must pay cash. His credit is very limited." As a matter of fact he advised that we keep away from all theatrical people. We were too naïve. I said to Mr. Carey, "But you are identified with the theatrical business on a large scale. How do you manage?" He said, "Well, we know how to take care of ourselves. You don't." He added, "Your feeling not to trust the Murphy Comedy Company was right. And your feeling that you could trust practically all sporting people is also right."

When I reported this to my partners they were not convinced that I was right in questioning the Murphy Comedy Company order. I felt there and then that I should withdraw from the business, but I was persuaded to continue in it, much against my better wisdom.

Then one day an order came in from the Wagner Palace Car Company for colored advertisements—small cards. I don't remember how many, but I believe the order was five thousand dollars—this figure may not be accurate but it was for us a huge amount—truly a beginning.

I informed the workmen of what had happened. I had hardly returned to the office when one of the engravers named Klomberg, a well set-up six footer knocked at the door and came in and said, "Mr. Stieglitz, I represent the men. Having heard of the wind-fall for the company they ask for a ten per-cent increase in wages."

"Klomberg," I said, "aren't you fellows going to give us a chance to get on our feet?"

He shrugged his shoulders and he said, "I'm simply representing the men."

I told him to come back in fifteen minutes. My partners asked me what I was going to do. I told them to wait and see.

In fifteen minutes Mr. Klomberg returned and I informed him that wages would be raised ten per-cent but with the understanding that the men would have to be put on the same basis as men in other engraving plants—that is, that holidays were not to be paid for, nor days of sickness—that only the time spent in the shop at work would count, and the only difference between our shop and the others would be that we would have no time-clock. Every man was to be on his honor.

When he left, I said to him, "Tell the men and report to me if they are satisfied with the conditions."

In a few minutes he had returned and informed us that everything was satisfactory.

At the time we also were working on a job for the publishing house of Putnam. It amounted to about a thousand dollars. We were making, I don't remember how many, half-tone plates and line cuts. I had made the estimate on an absolute cost basis.

When the work was brought in I found that there were twelve more originals than we had estimated on and I called the solicitor's attention to it. He laughed and said, "Well, just average these things, that will be all right."

When the job was done and the cuts and proofs were sent to Putnam, word came back that we had done a grand job. About four weeks later a cheque came for our bill with the amount for the twelve extra things deducted.

I told the solicitor what had happened and told him we'd have to be paid for our work.

He smiled and said, "Of course they'll pay for the work. Some smart aleck has done this."

To make a long story short, we were not to be paid. I insisted on pay. Putnam's paid, and I received a letter telling me that we would get no more orders from them as we seemed to be so illiberal and did not understand our business.

This had hardly happened when I felt I'd call in Mr. Klomberg to find out whether the new regime was working to the satisfaction of the men. He came in and I asked him, "Are the men satisfied with the new regime? Are the wives, sweethearts, aunts, sisters, grandmothers satisfied?"

He laughed and he said, "Yes, they're all satisfied."

And in reply I said, "So are we."

When he had left the office my partners asked me, "What's the meaning of all this theatre?"

I said, "Between the people who give us work like Putnam's and the workmen, I don't see where I come in. I'd better get out. I just don't belong. To do business in this country it seems necessary to have a policeman on one side and a lawyer on the other and even though I respect each I prefer other company. Do you realize that the workmen will have received about six per-cent less in pay on the new basis than they would have received on the old? No, I can't remain with such people."

Even my partners seemed surprised, and were not aware of these facts. In due season I quit "business." I had learned my lesson. I had had five or six years of business experience, the only business experience I have ever had in my life. During that time I had received no salary and no interest or dividends on the capital invested by my father for me, but I had come into contact with New York. I had begun photographing it during this period, as early as 1892, when I photographed the steaming "Car Horses" at the Terminal—Astor House, and "Winter, Fifth Avenue"—the lumbering stagecoach with its horses and driver moving northward through a blizzard on Fifth Avenue. These pictures formed a landmark, not only in my own life, but in photographic history as well.

My share of the business eventually was turned over to the workmen; my one partner retired not long after I did, the other continued the photogravure branch under a new name, until he finally also got out. So eventually the workmen became the sole owners of the business.

II. THE ORIGIN OF THE PHOTO-SECESSION AND HOW IT BECAME "291"

1

The *Camera Club of New York* was in its hey-day.

I had taken the dying *Society of Amateur Photographers* and the all but dead *N. Y. Camera Club* and called forth a live body. An amalgamation of the dying and the dead. The members of both bodies believed that photography as a passion had come to an end for all time. This was in the 1890's.

I gave the *Camera Club* all my time and thought. I had founded *Camera Notes* as a quarterly organ of the *Camera Club*. It was the making of the *Camera Club*.

As always, without a break, from 1883 in Berlin on, I was fighting for photography. *Camera Notes* was a battlefield as well as a bugle call. Members of the club received *Camera Notes* free of charge and many sold the four numbers of a year for twenty to thirty dollars, so covering their membership dues to the *Camera Club,* which were twenty dollars a year. The edition was limited to a thousand.

The battle of photography was raging in this country as well as in Europe. Art institutions had become involved. I had very definite ideas, without any formula. From the very beginning I felt convinced that photography could be a new, additional medium of expression, possibly a creative one.

Gertrude Käsebier, Holland Day, Clarence H. White, Frank Eugene, Joseph T. Keiley, Steichen, Coburn, all unknown at the time, were gradually discovered by me and became an integral part of my fight for photography, as I understood photography. They were all Americans.

There was warfare finally in the club itself. The bulk of the members did not see why I shouldn't consider the *Camera Club* primarily as a social institution before considering photography itself.

It so happened that I had helped draw up the constitution of the club. Its first article read—"The Camera Club is founded to further the art and science of photography." I was guided by that.

Everywhere in the world where photography played any role I was looked upon as the leading spirit in American photography, and as such I was called upon to send collections of American photographs to this and that international exhibition.

Such collections were never sent unless the conditions that I laid down were accepted without reservation. Only in this way, I felt, would the Art Institutions (for it was these that I was dealing with) respect the spirit of my endeavor. I was ever really fighting for a new spirit in life that went much deeper than just a fight for photography. Steichen's work, and that of Clarence White, Keiley and Käsebier was so "new" as photography, that their work was looked upon in the conservative ranks that were in control in the world, as preposterous, as so much insolence—a challenge to the decencies of photography and good taste. It was the old story of a new vision supplanting the dead, or supplanting the lack of all vision.

I did not know that in time I would be broadening the fight, a fight that involved painters, sculptors, literary people, musicians, and all that is genuine in every sphere of life.

A club had been formed called the *National Arts Club*—Charles de Kay, the art editor and associate editor of the *New York Times,* brother-in-law of Richard Watson Gilder, the poet, and editor of the *Century Magazine* when the *Century Magazine* was a real force, was its founder and its director. As the latter he received a munificent salary.

One day he appeared at the *Camera Club* and said, "Stieglitz, why don't you show these American photographs in New York—the photographs that you send abroad to art institutions and that are creating such a stir there?"

I told him that there was no place in New York fit to hold such a show, and there wasn't. At the time the American prints I had sent to the opening of the New Glasgow Art Galleries at the request of J. Craig Annan, a great photographer himself, were on their way back to this country.

De Kay said, "Why can't we have those prints that were shown in Glasgow?"

"Well, de Kay," I said, "if your club will give me a room, in your gallery, to show such prints as I see fit, and let me hang them in my own way, not a soul coming into the room before I open the doors, it's a go."

"But how about our art committee?"

"I do not recognize committees. Either you want to show or you don't. Your committee will probably say, 'Let that crazy man go ahead.' "

The next day he came and he said, "I was told, 'Let that crazy man go ahead.' "

So the exhibition found its way to the walls there. I made Steichen the concert master of the orchestra. Steichen himself was in Paris—when I say Steichen, I mean his prints.

As soon as de Kay had given me permission to go ahead he said, "Now we've got to have some publicity. What will we call this?"

I said, "Anything you like—preferably *An Exhibition of American Photographs.*"

"That will attract no attention," he said. "Why not *Exhibition of American Photographs arranged by the Camera Club of New York?*"

"Why, the members of the *Camera Club,* the big majority, hate the kind of work I'm fighting for."

"Well, why not *Exhibition of American Photographs arranged by Alfred Stieglitz?*" he said.

"No, no, they'd hang me on the first lamp post.—That I wouldn't mind, but I don't want my name exploited. De Kay," I said, "I've got it—it's a good one—call it *An Exhibition of American Photography arranged by the Photo-Secession.*"

"What's that?" he asked. "Who is it?"

"Yours truly, for the present, and there'll be others when the show opens. The idea of Secession is hateful to the American—they'll be thinking of the Civil War. I'm not. *Photo-Secession* actually means a seceding from the accepted idea of what constitutes a photograph; besides which, in Europe, in Germany and in Austria, there've been splits in the art circles and the moderns call themselves Secessionists, so *Photo-Secession* really hitches up with the art world. There is a sense of humor in the word Photo-Secession."

He raced away and the next morning there was a long editorial in the *New York Times* about the coming exhibition of American photographs arranged by the *Photo-Secession* and to be held at the *National Arts Club.*

At the opening, when Käsebier appeared—it was a blizzard night—she said to me, "What's this Photo-Secession? Am I a photo-secessionist?"

My answer was, "Do you feel you are?"

"I do."

"Well, that's all there is to it," I said.

Then a man who was secretary of the *Architectural League* and a member of the *Camera Club,* a future president of the *Camera Club,* and who was on several committees in the *National Arts Club* and occasionally made a photograph of a nude which was half-way acceptable—one of them hanging on the walls of this exhibition—came to me and said, "Stieglitz, am I a secessionist?"

I said, "No."

It didn't take long before the *Photo-Secession* was known all over the world. It was a force for light.

2

In 1904, though a very sick man, I went with my wife, my six-year old daughter, and her nurse to Europe. I had been on the firing-line for fourteen years in New York, fighting the fight of photography. The fight I am still fighting.

This fight includes everything in life as far as I am concerned. A fight for my own life as well as a fight for the lives of all true workers, whether American or any other—with perhaps an emphasis on Americans because I believe they have needed it most, since the true worker in America has seemed to become rarer and rarer in the sense in which I use the term "true worker." In other countries—Europe, or China or Japan—at the time, there was an understanding of the true worker which did not exist in America. By that I mean the "quality worker," not in a theoretical but in a living sense.

American photography had been placed on the map. Steichen, Käsebier, White, Coburn, Eugene and others had been given to the world. Their work had made the rounds of art museums in Europe. The exhibitions of the group under my direction—the Photo-Secession—had aroused great interest, relatively as much interest as later on was aroused by so-called "modern art."

Eventually there were factions in the making. Photography was being made safe for Democracy as early as 1902. I was considered a tyrant, un-American and heaven knows what not. While I was in Europe, Mr. Curtis Bell, who was a photographer, and steward of the *Lotus Club,* became imbued with the idea that it was time to save photography from Stieglitz and what Stieglitz represented. As I had said, it was time for him to milk the cow and castrate the bull.

Mr. Curtis Bell was going to go into the business of photography, and as an introduction he created an organization with the purpose of holding a photographic exhibition as a challenge to all I had stood for and worked for in my country. He gathered about him "all of America," including the Morgans, the Goulds, the Havemeyers—people of that class. They were the patrons. They were to give the money and prestige. He gathered about him as jury the great artists, I do not know how many of them. They included La Farge and John Alexander and, I believe, Kenyon Cox. It was to be a great international affair.

Announcements were sent all over the world. While I was in Europe, prominent and revolutionary photographers who had been in touch with my work for years, and who were following my lead in the battle for photography, wrote to me and asked whether the invitation they had received had any connection with me. My reply was a simple one. I wrote a letter to the *London Times* and to some London photographic weeklies. I let it be known that neither I nor any of the Photo-Secession could in any way be identified with this noisy project for popularizing the "art" side of photography, under the auspices of the so-called professional art patrons and the professional artists. Finally, when I returned to America, I, imagining that the exhibition would be held in some very large place, was informed that it was to take place on the top floor of a small brownstone building owned by Clausen, the art dealer, the same Clausen who some years later was forced to go out of business because he had been found selling fictitious Innesses and Wyants and Blakelocks to members of the *Lotus Club* and other art clubs. Clausen may have been innocent but he had to go out of business nevertheless.

In the meantime there was quite some excitement among the shining lights about me. The names of Morgan and Gould and Vanderbilt seemed to symbolize much money. Of the men about me, many were poor. And if I, holding aloof should be making a mistake, it would be fatal possibly to their future. So one night at the corner of 31st Street and 5th Avenue (the *Camera Club* was in 31st Street and Steichen was living at 291 Fifth Avenue), Steichen said to me, "Look here, Stieglitz, don't you think you are making a terrible mistake in standing up against the *Lotus Club* with the Morgans, the Goulds, the Vanderbilts and Astors backing this enterprise of Curtis Bell's?" And I said, "If you feel that way, you still have a chance to join with that crowd and show your work, but personally I feel that these people have no more to do with that exhibition than I have. They lend their names in courtesy to Mr. Bell. The American likes to be courteous, especially when it costs him nothing. It is part of his education."

Whether Steichen would decide to show or not, I didn't know. He was his own master. After a moment or so, he suddenly asked, "Stieglitz, haven't you any ideas? We ought to have an exhibition in New York, but where is the place for it? You always insist that it is impossible to show photographs as they really should be shown—I mean, shows like you arranged in all those European cities, and even for some American cities—like the *Chicago Art Institute's,* the *Pennsylvania Academy's* in Philadelphia, and the *Carnegie's* in Pittsburgh. Something must be done to give New York at least a chance to see what we have been doing all these years."

And as we stood there he suddenly said, "There is a room in my house, a couple of rooms, where two women artists are living. The whole building seems to be filled with the odor of their cooking. I think that they have a monthly lease and could be persuaded to vacate and I have a feeling that these two rooms plus a front room could be had for not a very large amount of money—for about six hundred dollars a year—and the rooms could be turned into galleries and a series of photographic exhibitions could take place there covering a year, and in that way New York would at least have a chance to understand what we have been talking about, as well as what we have already done." So I said to Steichen, "We'll look into the matter and when I see you tomorrow give me a definite idea of what you feel can be done."

The next day Steichen was filled with enthusiasm. He told me that he had seen the agent of the landlord (at the time Marshall Field). The rent would be $600 a year—$50 a month. Steichen himself would decorate the rooms and get them into shape for exhibitions. The cost of installing the electric fixtures and the necessary carpentry would not be more than three hundred dollars. Mrs. Steichen lived across the hall. She would have the key and could take care of the visitors who wanted to see the galleries.

As I was eager to have New York see the photographs made in all countries and see them in the proper way and in the proper surroundings, and relying on Steichen's enthusiasm, and, above all, on his ability, I then and there told him we would go ahead. I signed a lease.

In due time—actually in 1905—what were then called the *Photo-Secession Galleries* were opened and these galleries were a revelation to all of New York. Columns were devoted in the editorial pages of the daily press to this new spirit. In the course of a year the masterpieces of photography of the world, from the earliest days to the most recent, were shown in these small and beautiful rooms.

The rooms were also started with the idea that there might be things shown there other than photography so that photography could be measured in juxtaposition to other media of expression. These exhibitions were the beginning of what gradually evolved into what was later known as "291." I might add that the great enterprise of Curtis Bell that Steichen seemed so afraid of, turned out to be a flat failure from every point of view.

Curtis Bell's venture—to make photography safe for Democracy—was really the beginning of the popularization of photography of a very low standard. Popularization inevitably means low standards. Mr. Bell opened his professional gallery with his American Salon exhibition and Mrs. Clarence Mackey as his chief patroness. He became a flourishing photographer on Fifth Avenue. The great combination of Morgan, Vanderbilt, Astor, Mackey, Clausen *et al* had in no way interfered with the development of that work which was my life. Nor with Steichen's, nor White's, nor any of the other Secessionists.

That is the story of the beginning of "291."

3

The *Photo-Secession* became the leading factor in the international pictorial photographic world. Its "founding" had led to the opening of its own gallery at 291 Fifth Avenue.

At the end of the series of exhibitions held there—at the end of the first year—Steichen, who had had a one-man show in our *Photo-*

Secession galleries and a one-man painting show in the "high class" galleries of Eugene Glaenzer not a block away on Fifth Avenue, decided that America was no place for him. He would go to Paris with his wife and his child.

When I came home and told my wife that Steichen was going, she said, "Thank God, he's going. Now we two can travel and you can give up all that nonsense, for without Steichen you can't go ahead."

The very next morning I told Steichen of what had happened.

So I called up the real estate agent and asked him whether he could renew the lease for two years at the same rate we had been paying, which was six hundred dollars a year. My proposition was accepted.

When I came home and told my wife what I had done she burst out crying.

"You can thank yourself," I said. "I had no idea of doing this until you spoke as you did."

Steichen moved to Europe and I continued with the *Photo-Secession Gallery.*

Jealousies had been developing over the years amongst the Secessionists. I was getting sick and tired of the arrogance of the photographers who had banded about me. They had come to believe that my life was to be dedicated solely to them and did not realize that my battle was for an idea bigger than any individual. Although the battle of photography had been established from my point of view, it had not yet been clearly won. Then one day a strange woman appeared, Pamela Coleman Smith. She had several portfolios of drawings. She imagined that the *Photo-Secession Gallery* might be interested in her work. There was a drawing in washes, an illustration called "Death in the House." The moment I saw this picture I decided to show her work. "Death in the House" really illustrated my feeling at the time.

Steichen, whom I kept in close touch with what I had been doing, one day wrote to me from Paris: "You seem to have opened the doors of the *Photo-Secession* to things not photography. Do you want an exhibition of selected Rodin drawings?" I cabled back: "Yes." Then Steichen arrived shortly afterwards with a wonderful lot of selected Rodin drawings—Steichen being very close to Rodin, a sort of foster son. He had photographed Rodin innumerable times and had photographed his sculpture. When Steichen arrived he had brought with him a collection of the evolution of a painter I had never heard of: Matisse. The evolution in the form of drawings, watercolors, and an oil contributed by George F. Of, the painter. This was the real introduction of modern art to America.

It was in those *Photo-Secession* rooms that the ice was broken for modern art in America, and that the series of demonstrations of photography as I understood photography were continued. And I came more and more in touch with people, with the world—I, with nothing but the thought of liberating the people from superstition, from labels, from bias and the idea that money could buy everything.

And then, when finally, after three years, the rent was to be doubled, and a lease of three years had to be taken, it was then that I called quits, even though a young girl named Agnes Ernst working for the *Sun,* appeared on the scene, and hearing what was about to happen volunteered to get ten thousand dollars for us. She knew where she could get it. This girl became Mrs. Eugene Meyer, Jr., within a few years. Of course I couldn't possibly entertain her proposition that she get money to support my ideas.

In reality I told her that if she respected what I was doing she would make no attempt to get any money.

It was at the Rodin show that she had first appeared—when she had been commissioned to interview me for the *New York Sun.* I had denied her the interview, but she had insisted.

"It's my first order, my first chance. I'm heart and soul with you. Do give me a chance."

So the interview took place.

During the Rodin show two tall handsome young men with unusually fine faces had appeared on the scene and both had acquired Rodin drawings, waxing enthusiastic—Paul Haviland and his brother, Frank Haviland (later known as Frank Burty).

When finally in 1908 the *Photo-Secession* had to be given up because of the raise of the rent, Paul Haviland came to me and said, "I've taken a lease for three years on a room opposite the ones you have had." (The tailor who'd been in the one that Haviland had taken had moved into the ones I had had—a fashionable ladies' tailor. It happened that before the tailor occupied those quarters they were the home of Steichen and his wife and his newborn child.)

Where we had been was 291 Fifth Avenue. Across the hallway was 293 Fifth Avenue.

I told Haviland I could not accept the lease he had taken. It was five hundred dollars a year. I told him I was too tired to go on and I was.

He said, "You don't have to do anything. I'll have the place cleaned and painted" (it needed both badly), "and I'll put in a small table with a couple of chairs and benches and thus fellows like myself and others will have an opportunity to talk with you."

I couldn't believe my ears.

Haviland's father was American. His mother was French, the daughter of Burty, the art critic, who fought for Meryon, the great etcher. Haviland was a graduate of Harvard.

I told him I was going to Lake George and I'd see what I would do.

At Lake George I had a very hard summer. My child was ill and there was general family excitement, but somehow or other the lake, the row-boat and I were great friends. Everything became clear to me.

Why not continue the "work" in one room? Why not turn that room virtually into a facsimile of the main older room, so that when people came, who'd been accustomed to come, they would feel at home? Why not focus even more intensely on quality?

And so, when I came to New York, the room that Haviland had taken was turned into a "gallery"—the exact duplication of the old main room, and it was in this gallery that eventually Maurer and Marin, Cézanne, Picasso, Lautrec, Sharaku, the first exhibited work of untaught children from two to ten, who had never been to school, Negro art, Matisse sculpture, Weber, Hartley, Dove, Marius de Zayas, Walkowitz, Strand photographs, de Meyer photographs, S. MacDonald Wright, Katharine Rhoades, Marion Beckett and finally Georgia O'Keeffe were introduced, etc., etc.

Before opening the gallery I called in my friend, J. B. Kerfoot, a literary critic of *Life*, when the original *Life* was still in its hey-day.

I told him about Haviland and said, "I cannot let him carry the whole load. It makes me feel uncomfortable."

I hadn't a cent of my own. My little capital I had blown in on the *Photo-Secession* and *Camera Work* and the like. I told Kerfoot I'd like to have a fund of twelve hundred dollars, five hundred to pay the rent, seven hundred dollars for light and printing and other overhead.

So he invited George D. Pratt of the Standard Oil, who was interested in photography, and Herbert G. French, treasurer of Proctor and Gamble, who was a member of the *Photo-Secession* and photographed, his brother-in-law, Hunter, a collector of rare Japanese prints and early American glass, a wealthy man, married but without children, and, naturally, Haviland and one or two other people. It was all very impromptu and unofficial.

At tea at the Holland House, Pratt guaranteed a hundred dollars a year, Herbert G. French, fifty. Hunter subscribed fifty, Kerfoot also subscribed fifty, and finally, in time, Agnes Meyer, when marrying Eugene Meyer, Jr., chipped in five hundred a year.

My father had died and left me ten thousand dollars. I had sworn to myself that if ever I got any money again I'd not touch the capital and yet as twelve hundred dollars a year were not guaranteed for three years I decided to go into my new capital and make up the difference. I could not let the idea of money get in the way of doing work properly.

Of course there was always *Camera Work* which I carried alone, but that's another story.

The new gallery created even more of a sensation than had the old one. I did not like the idea of having it known as the *Photo-Secession* for it was no longer merely that.

My photographic friends could not make out what I was doing. They charged me with having lost interest in photography.

Steichen who was back in Paris seemed to understand. He was big enough. He worked, produced, co-operated spontaneously and didn't carp when he didn't understand. He absolutely trusted me. We were working together even though over three thousand physical miles apart.

Haviland and Marius de Zayas, who had come into my life, were the two great co-workers with me at the time, from the time the new gallery opened until Haviland had to leave for France in 1915 because of the war, and de Zayas in the autumn of 1916 opened his *Modern Gallery* as an art dealer. As a matter of fact, I was so disgusted with the turn affairs had taken at "291," principally because of the war, that I had announced at this time that I was going to quit. And I would have quit in 1916 if de Zayas, in opening the *Modern Gallery* with the help of Picabia and Agnes Meyer, had not given me to understand that the *Modern Gallery* was to be dedicated exclusively to abstract art—which meant that only the abstract paintings of Marin would be acceptable. All of the other Marins would have to find a place elsewhere. Walkowitz, Hartley and Dove were not to be acceptable either. Certain of my photographs would be acceptable. Realizing the situation I was not going to desert Marin and Walkowitz and Dove and Hartley. So I had no choice but to continue "291" at 291 Fifth Avenue.

When we had first opened the new gallery, I had said to Haviland one day, *"Photo-Secession* won't do any more. Let's speak of the gallery as '291'."

Haviland had looked at me and seemed to understand.

What was "291"? Where did it come from?

The original *Photo-Secession Gallery* was in 291 Fifth Avenue—the new gallery was in 293. The wall between 291 and 293 had been taken out so that one elevator could feed both houses and a tiny elevator it was, so "291" should really have been 293, but somehow "291" sounded more euphonious to me than 293, so "291" it had come to be.

I spoke of it as "291" perfectly naturally. So did Haviland and within a week—this is no exaggeration—"291" was commonplace amongst the frequenters of the place and "291" still lives—for, in spite of the interim between the place "291" and the *Intimate Gallery* and *An American Place,* it is the spirit of "291" that is alive and functioning. That is the spirit that manifests itself at *An American Place* still. Whoever was of the spirit of "291" at any time is still functioning in *An American Place*—whether he is aware of it or not.

That is my way of seeing. And in my way of seeing lies my way of action. Underlying all is a natural law and on this natural law rests the hope of mankind.

III. HOW *THE STEERAGE* HAPPENED

Early in June, 1907, my small family and I sailed for Europe. My wife insisted upon going on the *Kaiser Wilhelm II*—the fashionable ship of the North German Lloyd at the time. Our first destination was Paris. How I hated the atmosphere of the first class on that ship. One couldn't escape the *nouveaux riches*.

I sat much in my steamer chair the first days out—sat with closed eyes. In this way I avoided seeing faces that would give me the cold shivers, yet those voices and that English—ye gods!

On the third day out I finally couldn't stand it any longer. I had to get away from that company. I went as far forward on deck as I could. The sea wasn't particularly rough. The sky was clear. The ship was driving into the wind—a rather brisk wind.

As I came to the end of the deck I stood alone, looking down. There were men and women and children on the lower deck of the steerage. There was a narrow stairway leading up to the upper deck of the steerage, a small deck right at the bow of the steamer.

To the left was an inclining funnel and from the upper steerage deck there was fastened a gangway bridge which was glistening in its freshly painted state. It was rather long, white, and during the trip remained untouched by anyone.

On the upper deck, looking over the railing, there was a young man with a straw hat. The shape of the hat was round. He was watching the men and women and children on the lower steerage deck. Only men were on the upper deck. The whole scene fascinated me. I longed to escape from my surroundings and join these people.

A round straw hat, the funnel leaning left, the stairway leaning right, the white draw-bridge with its railings made of circular chains —white suspenders crossing on the back of a man in the steerage below, round shapes of iron machinery, a mast cutting into the sky, making a triangular shape. I stood spellbound for a while, looking and looking. Could I photograph what I felt, looking and looking and still looking? I saw shapes related to each other. I saw a picture of shapes and underlying that the feeling I had about life. And as I was deciding, should I try to put down this seemingly new vision that held me—people, the common people, the feeling of ship and ocean and sky and the feeling of release that I was away from the mob called the rich—Rembrandt came into my mind and I wondered would he have felt as I was feeling.

Spontaneously I raced to the main stairway of the steamer, chased down to my cabin, got my Graflex, raced back again all out of breath, wondering whether the man with the straw hat had moved or not. If he had, the picture I had seen would no longer be. The relation-ship of shapes as I wanted them would have been disturbed and the picture lost.

But there was the man with the straw hat. He hadn't moved. The man with the crossed white suspenders showing his back, he too, talking to a man, hadn't moved, and the woman with the child on her lap, sitting on the floor, hadn't moved. Seemingly no one had changed position.

I had but one plate holder with one unexposed plate. Would I get what I saw, what I felt? Finally I released the shutter. My heart thumping. I had never heard my heart thump before. Had I gotten my picture? I knew if I had, another milestone in photography would have been reached, related to the milestone of my "Car Horses" made in 1892, and my "Hand of Man" made in 1902, which had opened up a new era of photography, of seeing. In a sense it would go beyond them, for here would be a picture based on related shapes and on the deepest human feeling, a step in my own evolution, a spontaneous discovery.

I took my camera to my stateroom and as I returned to my steamer chair my wife said, "I had sent a steward to look for you. I wondered where you were. I was nervous when he came back and said he couldn't find you." I told her where I had been.

She said, "You speak as if you were far away in a distant world," and I said I was.

"How you seem to hate these people in the first class." No, I didn't hate them, but I merely felt completely out of place.

As soon as we were installed in Paris I went to the Eastman Kodak Company to find out whether they had a dark room in which I could develop my plate. They had none. They gave me an address of a photographer. I went there. The photographer led me to a huge dark room, many feet long and many feet wide, perfectly appointed.

He said, "Make yourself at home. Have you developer? Here's a fixing bath—it's fresh."

I had brought a bottle of my own developer. I started developing. What tense minutes! Had I succeeded, had I failed? That is, was the exposure correct? Had I moved while exposing? If the negative turned out to be anything but perfect, my picture would be a failure.

Finally I had developed and washed and rinsed the plate. In looking at it, holding it up to the red light it seemed all right, and yet I wouldn't know until the plate had been completely fixed.

The minutes seemed like hours. Finally the fixing was completed. I could turn on the white light. The negative was perfect in every particular. Would anything happen to it before I got to New York?

I washed it. No negative could ever receive more care, and when the washing was finished, I dried the negative with the help of an electric fan. I waited until it was bone dry, and when it was completely dry I put the glass plate into the plate holder which originally held it. In that way I felt it was best protected. I would not remove it from that place till I had returned to New York. I had sufficient plate holders with me to permit myself that luxury—or, should I say, that insurance?

I wanted to pay the photographer for the use of his dark room, but he said, "I can't accept money from you. I know who you are. It's an honor for me to know you have used my dark room."

How he happened to know me I couldn't understand. Later on I discovered that my name was written on a package which I had left in his office while in the dark room.

And when I got to New York four months later I was too nervous to make a proof of the negative. In making the negative I had in mind enlarging it for *Camera Work,* also enlarging it to eleven by fourteen and making a photogravure of it.

Finally this happened. Two beautiful plates were made under my direction, under my supervision, and proofs were pulled on papers that I had selected. I was completely satisfied. Something I not often was, or am.

The first person to whom I showed "The Steerage" was my friend and co-worker Joseph T. Keiley. "But you have two pictures there, Stieglitz, an upper one and a lower one," he said.

I said nothing. I realized he didn't see the picture I had made. Thenceforth I hesitated to show the proofs to anyone, but finally in 1910 I showed them to Haviland and Max Weber and de Zayas and other artists of that type. They truly saw the picture, and when it appeared in *Camera Work* it created a stir wherever seen, and the eleven by fourteen gravure created still a greater stir.

I said one day, "If all my photographs were lost and I'd be represented by just one, *The Steerage,* I'd be satisfied."

I'm not so sure that I don't feel much the same way today.

IV. THE MAGAZINE *291* AND *THE STEERAGE*

1

In January, 1915, Paul Haviland and de Zayas came into "291" and said, "Stieglitz, we and Agnes Meyer feel that "291" is in a rut. The war has put a damper on everything. We must do something. We have the idea that "291" should publish a monthly magazine devoted to the most modern art and to satire, presented in a spirit related to some of the most modern publications in France."

I'd always been hoping that there would be a magazine in this country devoted to real satire. The American is afraid of satire. Afraid of true caricature. He enjoys cartoons. Those everlasting cartoons. Was there a place for true caricature in the United States?

Had not Marius de Zayas made some grand caricatures and were they not shown at "291"? They had met with little response.

So this proposition that "291" publish a sheet devoted to satire and caricature met with my fullest approval. Maybe such a publication might bring some new life into "291."

Haviland and de Zayas were ready to act at once. It was really their idea. They had in mind a monthly publication that would cost a hundred dollars a month. The numbers were to be sold at ten cents a piece, the subscription price to be a dollar a year.

Would I sanction the use of the name "291" as the name of the magazine and would I be one of the three guarantors assuming responsibility for the paying of bills—the two other guarantors to be Paul Haviland and Agnes Meyer?

I assented.

Of course I realized that by the end of the year each of us would probably have to foot a liability of at least fifty percent more than the original estimates.

My interest in the magazine was primarily based on the fact that I felt it would give de Zayas a free opportunity to use his genius as a caricaturist and satirist, and that it would give Agnes Meyer and Paul Haviland and Katharine N. Rhoades opportunities which I felt they should have.

Agnes Ernst Meyer's dream had been, before she was married and when she was working on the *Morning Sun* as a reporter, to write on art matters, to become an authority on the history of art and on the creative arts of the day. But having married a rich man and having become a mother, she was prevented from devoting much time to her original ambitious aspirations. Maybe a "291" magazine would give her a chance to do some Agnes Ernst work, for it was Agnes Ernst I originally was interested in.

Paul Haviland was in a position to afford the risk and would be heart and soul a real worker.

Katharine Rhoades wrote and painted. In her, too, I was deeply interested. Here was a possible outlet for her.

Then, also, there were Marin, Hartley, Walkowitz, Dove and many others I hoped might find an added outlet. In short, "291," the magazine, I saw as a real instrument of expression of the time.

One Sunday morning Agnes Meyer, living at the St. Regis Hotel, invited de Zayas, Haviland and myself to come to see her and talk over the magazine proposition.

Agnes Meyer asked how we were to determine what should be published in "291"—what was the policy to be—was the majority to rule? As we were four, I asked her what would happen in case of a tie.

I pointed out to her and the men that "291" was founded on a new idea, so why think of obsolete methods. I suggested that anything that might be thought worthy of publication by any one of the four of us should be sufficient reason to incorporate it in the new publication. If we didn't have that much faith in each other, why begin?

Meetings and minutes and endless discussions were really anti-"291." Agnes Meyer was elated with the idea, as were de Zayas and Haviland.

The difficult problem of majorities and discussions had been simply solved. Our meeting lasted less than ten minutes.

De Zayas and Haviland immediately set to work on the first issue. So did Agnes Meyer.

Soon thereafter I was told that Eugene Meyer, Jr., the husband of Agnes Meyer, thought that too much satire, too much truth telling about how the game of art and its business were played, should not appear in "291." Meyer thought it would be a very bad policy.

Of course, I disagreed for I felt that the youngsters—for as such I looked upon them—should have their way. In a sense I was more or less an onlooker, but fully aware. I was curious to see what the young ones would do if left to themselves, how they would represent the spirit of "291."

The magazine 291 quickly came into being. It created great excitement. It was truly an eye-opener, not only for the United States, but for Europe. Instead of its being the sheet originally contemplated, it became more or less a de luxe affair as Haviland, de Zayas, and myself had rather expensive tastes—that is, we wanted good paper, good ink, careful printing, careful mailing—that meant the cost would be greater than originally figured on. Regardless, we went ahead. The result was what counted with us.

291, the magazine, was launched. There were eight single issues and two double issues. These soon were to play a role in the development of happenings in France. This, because Picabia arrived from France in June, 1915, directly from the war. When he saw what we were doing at 291, in magazine form, he immediately became an active factor. Several of the issues became primarily Picabia issues. We sent innumerable copies to France. It was these copies that helped crystallize the original Dada Movement when Picabia returned to France some months later.

Haviland was called to France. De Zayas eventually went into the art business, so split from 291. Agnes Meyer had become a "Freerite" with passionate Chinese art aspirations. But before the final disintegration of the group, Haviland and de Zayas came to me one day and said, "Stieglitz, we feel that a double number of 291 should be devoted to photography, with 'The Steerage' as a basis." "The Steerage" was considered by many the most significant photograph I had ever made. It had even attracted the attention of Picasso in 1912. De Zayas had taken a print to Paris to show it to Picasso. Picasso was reported to have said, "This photographer is working in the same spirit as I am."

The print shown to Picasso was an eleven by fourteen photogravure proof of "The Steerage" made under my supervision.

A similar proof Dr. Jessen of the Berlin Museum had bought for his museum for a hundred dollars. There were nine other photogravures for which he also had paid a hundred dollars each. Several of the proofs were also bought by other collectors for a hundred dollars apiece. Whenever I have received money for any of my work I have turned it over to artists of one kind or another. I never have kept any of such money for myself.

Haviland and de Zayas claimed that for the sake of photography, for the sake of the idea we were all working for, it would be a great thing if I were to have five hundred proofs of the photogravure plate pulled on Imperial Japan paper for a small special "de luxe" edition on thin Japan tissue.

Haviland and de Zayas each wrote an essay on photography for this number taking "The Steerage" as a basis. I had the editions printed under my direction and paid for the cost. It was a special contribution of mine.

The double number containing the Imperial Japan proofs was sold to subscribers for twenty cents each. The thin Japan ones for a dollar each. Hundreds of people, rich and poor, had been clamoring for "Steerage" prints. The poor could not afford the hundred dollars and the rich could not afford the hundred dollars. I was in no position to give away the few proofs I had, before printing this edition for *291*.

I really printed the edition for *291* to see what would happen. The subscribers to *291*—there were about a hundred to the ordinary edition—duly received their copies. There were eight subscribers to the de luxe edition and they received their copies. These eight subscribers paid one dollar for their copies. The two editions called forth great admiration from all classes of people. No attempt was made to solicit subscribers or to sell the magazine. What interested me most was to see what the American people would do if left to themselves. That has been an underlying principle in everything I've touched for all these years.

When, in 1917, the place "291" had come to an end, and I had lost practically all of my friends—certainly those identified with the magazine *291*—I didn't know what to do with the upward of eight thousand copies of the magazine *291*. I called a rag picker. It was war time. The cost of paper was high. I had never done anything like this before. Maybe the gesture was a satirical one. The rag picker offered five dollars and eighty cents for the lot. This included the wonderful Imperial Japan "Steerage" prints.

I handed the five dollars and eighty cents to the girl who had been part-time secretary to me and said to her, "Here, Marie, this may buy you a pair of gloves, maybe two pairs."

I had no feeling whatsoever about this transaction—this act of mine. It was merely another lesson to me.

I kept most of the deluxe edition but even in time I destroyed most of that.

And now I asked myself why was a Dr. Jessen, director of the Berlin Museum, willing to pay a hundred dollars for a copy of "The Steerage," which my American friends did not seem to want even for one dollar, though for years they had been at me to give them a chance to acquire a print? Now that it was possible to get a print for a dollar they wondered why I didn't give them prints. As a matter of fact wasn't I "giving them away" at a dollar?

Outside of the hundred subscriptions to the regular edition of the magazine *291* and the eight subscriptions to the de luxe edition, how many single copies of either edition do you think were bought? Make your estimate as low as your imagination will permit—not a single one. This is America.

2

THE STEERAGE AT WEYHE'S

Mr. Weyhe, and Carl Zigrosser working with him, are two human beings. Somehow they had salvaged some copies of *Camera Work*. They also salvaged a few numbers of the heavy Japan "Steerage."

Not so many years later when I came into their shop on Lexington Avenue one day I saw my "Steerage" framed and hanging on the wall amongst etchings and lithographs—some very good etchings and lithographs.

"What's the price of 'The Steerage'?" I asked.

"Four dollars."

I was tempted to buy it. It looked so handsome, and how ridiculously low the price. I remembered that I was living on fifty cents a day for food and that four dollars meant eight days' food. Did I have a right to buy my own pictures under such conditions?

For at least three or four years this print hung on the walls of Weyhe's. I often frequented that shop as it seemed one of the few human places in New York.

One day while I was visiting the Weyhe shop, Zigrosser said, while talking about photography, "Stieglitz, a man the other day, a collector of Leonardo da Vincis, a man for whom Leonardo was the only thing in the world, saw 'The Steerage.' He asked what it was and where it came from. 'A photograph,' I told him. He looked at it again, asked the price—four dollars—and took it."

"Well," I thought, "it's in good company and maybe if Leonardo knew he wouldn't mind."

I was glad that I had not succumbed to the temptation and that I had had food for eight days—once in my life at least I had been wise. I had not succumbed to the temptation of buying a picture, even though the picture was my own.

PAUL STRAND (1890-) *It has always been my belief that the true artist, like the true scientist, is a researcher using materials and techniques to dig into the truth and meaning of the world in which he himself lives; and what he creates, or better perhaps, brings back, are the objective results of his explorations. The measure of his talent—of his genius, if you will—is the richness he finds in such a life's voyage of discovery and the effectiveness with which he is able to embody it through his chosen medium.* LETTER TO THE EDITOR, *Photographic Journal, Vol. 103, No. 7, 1963, p. 216.*

PHOTOGRAPHY   1917
Seven Arts, August, pp. 524-26.

    Photography, which is the first and only important contribution thus far, of science to the arts, finds its *raison d'être*, like all media, in a complete uniqueness of means. This is an absolute unqualified objectivity. Unlike the other arts which are really anti-photographic, this objectivity is of the very essence of photography, its contribution and at the same time its limitation. And just as the majority of workers in other media have completely misunderstood the inherent qualities of their respective means, so photographers, with the possible exception of two or three, have had no conception of the photographic means. The full potential power of every medium is dependent upon the purity of its use, and all attempts at mixture end in such dead things as the color-etching, the photographic painting and in photography, the gum-print, oil-print, etc., in which the introduction of hand work and manipulation is merely the expression of an impotent desire to paint. It is this very lack of understanding and respect for their material, on the part of photographers themselves which directly accounts for the consequent lack of respect on the part of the intelligent public and the notion that photography is but a poor excuse for an inability to do anything else.

    The photographer's problem therefore, is to see clearly the limitations and at the same time the potential qualities of his medium, for it is precisely here that honesty, no less than intensity of vision, is the prerequisite of a living expression. This means a real respect for the thing in front of him, expressed in terms of chiaroscuro (color and photography having nothing in common) through a range of almost infinite tonal values which lie beyond the skill of human hand. The fullest realization of this is accomplished without tricks of process or manipulation, through the use of straight photographic methods. It is in the organization of this objectivity that the photographer's point of view toward Life enters in, and where a formal conception born of the emotions, the intellect, or of both, is as inevitably necessary for him, before an exposure is made, as for the painter, before he puts brush to canvas. The objects may be organized to express the causes of which they are the effects, or they may be used as abstract forms, to create an emotion unrelated to the objectivity as such. This organization is evolved either by movement of the camera in relation to the objects themselves or through their actual arrangement, but here, as in everything, the expression is simply the measure of a vision, shallow or profound as the case may be. Photography is only a new road from a different direction but moving toward the common goal, which is Life.

    Notwithstanding the fact that the whole development of photography has been given to the world through *Camera Work* in a form uniquely beautiful as well as perfect in conception and presentation, there is no real consciousness, even among photographers, of what has actually happened: namely, that America has really been expressed in terms of America without the outside influence of Paris art-schools or their dilute offspring here. This development extends over the comparatively short period of sixty years, and there was no real movement until the years between 1895 and 1910, at which time an intense rebirth of enthusiasm and energy manifested itself all over the world. Moreover, this renaissance found its highest aesthetic achievement in America, where a small group of men and women worked with honest and sincere purpose, some instinctively and few consciously, but without any background of photographic or graphic formulae much less any cut and dried ideas of what is Art and what isn't; this innocence was their real strength. Everything they wanted to say had to be worked out by their own experiments: it was born of actual living. In the same way the creators of our skyscrapers had to face the similar circumstance of no precedent, and it was through that very necessity of evolving a new form, both in architecture and photography that the resulting expression was vitalized. Where in any medium has the tremendous energy and potential power of New York been more fully realized than in the purely direct photographs of Stieglitz? Where a more subtle feeling which is the reverse of all this, the quiet simplicity of life in the American small town, so sensitively suggested in the early work of Clarence White? Where in painting, more originality and penetration of vision than in the portraits of Steichen, Käsebier and Frank Eugene? Others, too, have given beauty to the world but these workers, together with the great Scotchman, David Octavius Hill, whose portraits made in 1840 have never been surpassed, are the important creators of a living photographic tradition. They will be the masters no less for Europe than for America because by an intense interest in the life of which they were really a part, they reached through a national, to a universal expression. In spite of indifference, contempt and the assurance of little or no remuneration they went on, as others will do, even though their work seems doomed to a temporary obscurity. The thing they do remains the same; it is a witness to the motive force that drives.

The existence of a medium, after all, is its absolute justification, if as so many seem to think, it needs one and all, comparison of potentialities is useless and irrelevant. Whether a water-color is inferior to an oil, or whether a drawing, an etching, or a photograph is not as important as either, is inconsequent. To have to despise something in order to respect something else is a thing of impotence. Let us rather accept joyously and with gratitude everything through which the spirit of man seeks to an ever fuller and more intense self-realization.

PHOTOGRAPHY AND THE NEW GOD

Broom, Vol. 3, No. 4, pp. 252-58.

Man having created the concept of God The Creator, found himself unsatisfied. For despite the proven pragmatic value of this image, through which the fine arts of music and literature, of architecture, painting, and sculpture, together with the less fine arts of murder, thievery and general human exploitation, had been carried to great heights, there was still something unfulfilled: the impulse of curiosity in man was still hungry.

In all ages therefore, we find the empirical thinker, the alchemist and astrologer, mathematician and philosophic experimenter, at work, frequently, as in the early Christian world, at considerable risk of his life, liberty and pursuit of happiness. Then, it was the artist alone who was able to indulge in the luxury of empirical thought under the camouflage of subject matter. In every other field of research, the scientific method was seen to be and no doubt was, inimical to all forms of Churchianity; the scientist was then, as his fellow-worker the artist is to-day, *persona non grata*.

But through the disintegration of the power of the Christian Church following the Reformation, scientific empirical thought found its opportunity of expression. Men's imaginations, weary of sectarian intrigue and of Holy Wars, kindled at the thought of the unknown in the form of unexplored trade routes and new sources of material wealth; and through them dreamed of a power over their fellows as potent as any which could be derived from a vested interest in God. With this change in the direction of thought, the scientist became indispensable, he began to function in society. For when it became apparent that craftsmanship as a means to trade growth was insufficient, that quantity and not quality of production was the essential problem in the acquisition of wealth, it was the scientist and his interpreter, the inventor who jumped into the breach.

Out of wood and metals he made hands that could do the work of a thousand men; he made backs that could carry the burden of a thousand beasts and chained the power which was in the earth and waters to make them work. Through him, men consummated a new creative act, a new Trinity: God the Machine, Materialistic Empiricism the Son, and Science the Holy Ghost.

And in the development and organization of this modern Church, the veritable artist, composer or poet, architect, painter or sculptor, has played no great part. His form of creativity based upon what Croce calls intuitive rather than intellectual knowledge, was clearly of no value in a fairly unscrupulous struggle for the possession of natural resources, for the exploitation of all materials, human and otherwise. As a consequence the artist has fallen considerably from his place of high seriousness as an integral and respected element in society, to that of a tolerated mountebank entertainer merely. With neither Popes, Princes nor any equivalent of the Rockefeller Foundation to support his experimental work, he is today in a position similar to that which the scientist occupied in the middle ages; that of heretic to existing values. That kind of life which has its being in the extension and projection of knowledge through the syntheses of intuitive spiritual activity, and its concomitant the *vita contemplativa,* is seen to be and no doubt is, a menace to a society built upon what has become the religious concept of possessiveness. It is natural therefore that the artist finds himself looked upon with a new sort of hostility which expresses itself, due possibly to the benign influence of civilization, in the form of indifference or contempt, and extends to him the privilege of starving to death. At the judgment seat of the new Trinity he has been found wanting as a waster and a non-producer.

With this increasing isolation of the seeker after intuitive knowledge, the scientist, working not so much in the field of philosophy as in those more "practical" expressions of conceptual knowledge, the natural sciences, has become more and more a part of this industrial society, nay, is largely responsible for it. Having created the new God, he has permitted himself to be used at every step and for every purpose by its interested devotees. Printing presses or poison gas, he has been equally blind or indifferent to the implications in the use or misuse of either, with the result that the social structure which he has so irresponsibly helped to rear, is today fast being destroyed by the perversion of the very knowledge contributed by him. Virtually yanked out of comparative obscurity by the forces of evolutionary circumstance, and considerably over-inflated by his Holy Ghostship, he has made possible the present critical condition of Western Civilization, faced as it is with the alternatives of being quickly ground to pieces under the heel of the new God or with the tremendous task of controlling the heel.

Signs of this imperative revaluation of the idea of the machine are beginning to manifest themselves. And significantly, one might almost say ironically enough, not among the least important is the emerging demonstration on the part of the artist of the immense possibilities in the creative control of one form of the machine, the camera. For he it is who, despite his social maladjustment, has taken to himself with love a dead thing unwittingly contributed by the scientist, and through its conscious use, is revealing a new and living act of vision.

In order to make this clear it is necessary to record briefly the development of the use of the camera by the seeker after intuitive knowledge. The first of these to become interested in the mechanism and materials of photography was David Octavius Hill, a painter, and member of the Royal Scottish Academy. Hill came upon photography about 1842 in the following way: he had received a commission to paint a large canvas on which were to appear the recognizable portraits of a hundred or more of the well-known people of the time. Faced with this difficult task and having heard of the then recently invented process of photography, he turned to it as a help to his painting. Three years of experimentation followed and it is interesting to learn that he became so fascinated by the new medium that he seriously neglected his painting. So much so in fact, that his wife and friends found it necessary to remind him that he was an "artist." They chided him about wasting his time and finally succeeded in giving him such a bad conscience that he never photographed again. Yet the results of Hill's experimenting have given us a series of amazing portraits which have not until recently been surpassed. They are built with the utmost simplicity upon large masses of light and dark, but unquestionably the element which makes these portraits live is the naïveté and freedom from all theory with which Hill approached his new medium. He was not concerned or hampered in his photographing by the academic standards of the time as he must have been in his painting, for as a painter he is of slight importance. Despite the primitive machine and materials with which he was compelled to work, the exposures of five to fifteen minutes in bright sunlight, this series of photographs has victoriously stood the test of comparison with nearly everything done in photography since 1845. They remain the most extraordinary assertion of the possibility of the utterly personal control of a machine, the camera.

A gap then of nearly forty years intervened during which these photographs made by Hill passed into obscurity and practically no similar experimentation was done. However, some time before their rediscovery photography had, about the year 1880, started upon a renascent and widespread development all over the world. With the invention of the dry plate, the improvements in lenses and printing papers, the process had been brought within the realm of greater certainty and ease of manipulation. And with this period begins that curious misconception of the inherent qualities of a new medium, on the part of almost everyone who has attempted to express himself through it. Without the slightest realization that in this machine, the camera, a new and unique instrument had been placed in their hands, photographers have in almost every instance, been trying to use it as a short cut to an accepted medium, painting. This misconception still persists today throughout Europe and to a large degree even here in America.

As a consequence the development of photography so beautifully and completely recorded in the numbers of *Camera Work*, is interesting not so much in the aesthetically expressive as in an historical sense. We find all through the work done in Germany, France and Italy, in England and much in America, the supreme altar of the new

God, a singular lack of perception and respect for the basic nature of the photographic machine. At every turn the attempt is made to turn the camera into a brush, to make a photograph look like a painting, an etching, a charcoal drawing or whatnot, like anything but a photograph; and always in imitation of the work of inferior painters. Moreover, with the production of this very considerable number of bastard photographs, interesting though they were temporarily, went an equally vast and foolish discussion as to whether photography was or was not an Art. Needless to say this discussion was usually as thoughtless and as uncritical of its terminology and of its standards as were the photographers of theirs. But partly through this evolution we are now fortunately becoming aware of the fact that nobody knows exactly what Art is; the word does not slip quite so glibly off the tongues of the serious-minded. And fortunately as well, a few photographers are demonstrating in their work that the camera is a machine and a very wonderful one. They are proving that in its pure and intelligent use it may become an instrument of a new kind of vision, of untouched possibilities, related to but not in any way encroaching upon painting or the other plastic arts. It has taken nearly eighty years for this clarification of the actual meaning of photography to reach from the remarkably true but instinctive approach of David Octavius Hill, to the conscious control embodied in the recent work of Alfred Stieglitz.

For it is in the later work of Stieglitz, an American in America, that we find a highly evolved crystallization of the photographic principle, the unqualified subjugation of a machine to the single purpose of expression. It is significant and interesting to note that this man is not a painter and has never felt any impulse to be one. From the very inception of his photographic work which covers a period of thirty-five years, he like Hill, was fascinated by the machine as a thing apart. In fact, Stieglitz knew nothing about painting until, as the guiding spirit in that little experimental laboratory known as "291," he gave Americans their first opportunity of seeing the development of modern painting together with that of photography. Yet with all this he has maintained in his own photographic work a unity of feeling uncontaminated by alien influences; in his own words, "no mechanicalization but always photography." In his later work, consisting almost exclusively of a series of portraits made during the past four years, the achievements possible to the camera pass out of the realm of theory and become objective realities in which certain affirmations emerge. For the first time we are given an opportunity of examining and of drawing some conclusions concerning the means of photographic expressiveness, an expressiveness the actual nature of which, together with that of other media, may be safely left to the aestheticians to fight about among themselves.

We find first of all in this man's work a space-filling and formal sense which, in many instances, achieves as pure a synthesis of objectivity as can be found in any medium. We perceive upon the loveliness of paper a registration in monochrome of tonal and tactile values far more subtle than any which the human hand can record. We discover as well, the actuality of a new sensitivity of line as finely expressive as any the human hand can draw. And we note that all these elements take form through the machine, the camera, without resort to the imbecilic use of soft focus or uncorrected lenses, or to processes in which manual manipulation may be introduced. Nay more, we see that the use of such lenses or processes weakens or destroys entirely the very elements which distinguish photography and may make it an expression. In the work of Stieglitz there is always a full acceptance of the thing in front of him, the objectivity which the photographer must control and can never evade.

But above all, we become aware in these photographs of his, of a new factor which the machine has added to plastic expression, the element of differentiated time. The camera can hold in a unique way, a moment. If the moment be a living one for the photographer, that is, if it be significantly related to other moments in his experience, and he knows how to put that relativity into form, he may do with a machine what the human brain and hand, through the act of memory cannot do. So perceived, the whole concept of a portrait takes on a new meaning, that of a record of innumerable elusive and constantly changing states of being, manifested physically. This is as true of all objects as of the human object. With the eye of the machine, Stieglitz has recorded just that, has shown that the portrait of an individual is really the sum of a hundred or more photographs. He has looked with three eyes and has been able to hold, by purely photographic means, space-filling, tonality and tactility, line and form, that moment when the forces at work in a human being become most intensely physical and objective. In thus revealing the spirit of the individual he has documented the world of that individual, which is today. In this sense portrait painting, already nearly a corpse, becomes an absurdity.

Now in all of this it should be well understood, that the machine is a passive and an innocent party. The control of its mechanism and materials, the fineness and sensitivity of its accomplishment are those of man. The new God shorn of its God-hood becomes an instrument of intuitive knowledge. Whether the results of its use will continue to live in the mind and spirit of the future, only time will tell. Whether or not these results come under the category of Art is irrelevant. The important fact to be noted is that today, painters, writers and musicians, even the scientists and sensitive people in every occupation, are reacting as profoundly before photographs, these untouched products of an intelligence and spirit channelling through a machine, as before any of the accepted forms of expression. So that when Croce in his

"Aesthetic" writes: "And if photography be not quite an Art, that is precisely because the element of nature in it remains more or less unconquered and ineradicable." When he asks: "Do we ever feel complete satisfaction before even the best of photographs? Would not an artist vary and touch up much or little, remove or add something to the best of photographs?" the conclusion and answer are obvious. Signor Croce is speaking of the shortcomings of *photographers* and not of photography. He has not seen, for the simple reason that it did not exist when he wrote his book, fully achieved photographic expression. In the meantime the twaddle about the limitations of photography has been answered by Stieglitz and a few others of us here in America, by work done. Granting the limitations which all media have in common, it is only when the limitations of *photographers* are under examination, that the discussion becomes realistic.

Thus the deeper significance of a machine, the camera, has emerged here in America, the supreme altar of the new God. If this be ironical it may also be meaningful. For despite our seeming wellbeing we are, perhaps more than any other people, being ground under the heel of the new God, destroyed by it. We are not, as Natalie Curtis recently pointed out in *The Freeman,* particularly sympathetic to the somewhat hysterical attitude of the Futurists toward the machine. We in America are not fighting, as it may be natural to do in Italy, away from the tentacles of a medieval tradition towards a neurasthenic embrace of the new God. We have it with us and upon us with a vengeance, and we will have to do something about it eventually. Not only the new God but the whole Trinity must be humanized lest it in turn dehumanize us. We are beginning perhaps to perceive that.

And so it is again the vision of the artist, of the intuitive seeker after knowledge, which, in this modern world, has seized upon the mechanism and materials of a machine, and is pointing the way. He it is who is again insisting, through the science of optics and the chemistry of light and metals and paper, upon the eternal value of the concept of craftsmanship, because that is the only way in which he can satisfy himself and because he knows that quality in work is prerequisite to quality in living. He has evolved through the conscious creative control of this particular phase of the machine a new method of perceiving the life of objectivity and of recording it. And he has done so in spite of the usual opposition and contempt with which the Accepted always greets the New, in spite of the actual deterioration of materials and in the face of a total absence of those monetary returns which work in other media occasionally brings.

In thus disinterestedly experimenting, the photographer has joined the ranks of all true seekers after knowledge, be it intuitive and aesthetic or conceptual and scientific. He has moreover, in establishing his own spiritual control over a machine, the camera, revealed the destructive and wholly fictitious wall of antagonism which these two groups have built up between themselves. Rejecting all Trinities and all Gods he puts to his fellow workers this question squarely: What is the relation between science and expression? Are they not both vital manifestations of energy, whose reciprocal hostility turns the one into the destructive tool of materialism, the other into anemic phantasy, whose coming together might integrate a new religious impulse? Must not these two forms of energy converge before a living future can be born of both?

THE ART MOTIVE IN PHOTOGRAPHY   1923
The British Journal of Photography, Vol. 70, pp. 612-15.

A discussion of all the ramifications of photographic methods in modern life would require more time and special knowledge than I have at my disposal. It would include all the diverse uses to which photography is being put in an essentially industrial and scientific civilization. Some of these applications of the machine, the camera, and the materials which go with it, are very wonderful. I need only mention as a few examples the X-ray, micro-photography, photography in astronomy as well as the various photo-mechanical processes which have so amazingly given the world access to pictorial communication in much the same revolutionary way that the invention of the printing press made extensive verbal communication possible and easy.

Of much less past importance than these in its relationship to life, because much less clearly understood, is that other phase of photography which I have particularly studied and worked with, and to which I will confine myself. I refer to the use of the photographic means as a medium of expression in the sense that paint, stone, words, and sound are used for such purpose. In short, as another set of materials which, in the hands of a few individuals and when under the control of the most intense inner necessity combined with knowledge, may become an organism with a life of its own, as a tree or a mountain has a life of its own. I say a few individuals because they, the true artists, are almost as rare a phenomenon among painters, sculptors, composers as among photographers.

Now the production of such living organisms in terms of any material is the result of the meeting of two things in the worker. It involves, first and foremost, a thorough respect and understanding for the particular materials with which he or she is impelled to work, and a degree of mastery over them, which is craftsmanship. And secondly, that indefinable something, the living element which fuses with craftsmanship, the element which relates the product to life and must therefore be the result of a profound feeling and experience of life. Craftsmanship is the fundamental basis which you can learn and develop provided you start with absolute respect for your materials, which, as students of photography, are a machine called camera and the chemistry of light and other agents upon metals. The living element, the plus, you can also develop if it is potentially there. It cannot be taught or given you. Its development is conditioned by your own feeling which must be a free way of living. By a free way of living I mean the difficult process of finding out what your own feeling about the world is, disentangling it from other people's feelings and ideas. In other words, this wanting to be what may truthfully be called an artist is the last thing in the world to worry about. You either are that thing or you are not.

Now the general notion of artist is quite a different matter. This notion uses the word to describe anyone who has a little talent and ability, particularly in the use of paint, and confuses this talent, the commonest thing in the world, with the exceedingly rare ability to use it creatively. Thus everybody who slings a little paint is an artist, and the word, like many other words which have been used uncritically, ceases to have any meaning as a symbol of communication.

However, when you look back over the development of photography, when you look at what is being done today still in the name of photography in *Photograms of the Year* in the year book of the pictorial photographers, it is apparent that this generally erroneous notion of artist has been and is the chief worry of photographers and their undoing. They, too, would like to be accepted in polite society as artists, as anyone who paints is accepted, and so they try to turn photography into something which it is not; they introduce a paint feeling. In fact, I know of very few photographers whose work is not evidence that at bottom they would prefer to paint if they knew how. Often, perhaps, they are not conscious of their subjugation to the idea of painting, of the absence of all respect and understanding of their own medium which this implies and which sterilizes their work. But, nevertheless, either in their point of view toward the things they photograph, or more often in the handling of certain unphotographic materials, they betray their indebtedness to painting, usually second-rate painting. For the pathetic part is that the idea which photographers have had of painting is just as uncritical and rudimentary as this popular notion of the artist. There is every evidence in their work that they have not followed the whole development of painting as they have not perceived the development of their own medium.

You need not take my word for this. The record is there. You can see for yourself the whole photographic past, its tradition, in that extraordinary publication, *Camera Work*. For photography has a tradition, although most of those who are photographing today seem to be unaware of the fact. That is at least one of the reasons why they are prey to the weaknesses and misconceptions of that tradition and are unable to clarify or to add one iota to its development. So if you want to photograph, and if you are not living on a desert island, look at this tradition critically, find out what photography has meant to other people, wherein their work succeeds or fails to satisfy, whether you think you could hang it on the same wall with a Dürer woodcut, a painting by Rubens or even Corot, without the photograph falling to pieces. For this is, after all, the test, not of Art, but of livingness.

In my own examination of the photographic tradition I have found out for myself, and I think it can be demonstrated, that there are very few photographs which will meet this test. And they will not because, although much of the work is the result of a sensitive feeling for life, it is based, nevertheless, on that fundamental misconception that the photographic means is a short cut to painting. But from the point of view of genuine and enthusiastic experimentation, however it may have been on the wrong track, this work will always have great historical importance, will be invaluable to the student. The gum prints of the Germans, Henneberg, Watzek, the Hofmeisters and Kühn, those of Steichen, will never happen again. Nobody will be willing to spend the time and energy or have the conviction necessary to the production of these things. And it is when one finds, as one does today, photographers all over the world, in England, Belgium, Germany, in this country, going right ahead as though nothing had ever happened, using this and other manipulative processes without one one-thousandth of the intensity or ability with which their predecessors worked, that such work ceases to have any meaning and becomes merely absurd.

Let us stop for a moment before discussing further the photographic past and present, to determine what the materials of photography really are; what, when they are not perverted, they can do. We have a camera, a machine which has been put into our hands by science. With its so-called dead eye, the representation of objects may be recorded upon a sensitive emulsion. From this negative a positive print can be made which without any extrinsic manual interference will register a scale of tonal values in black and white far beyond the power of the human hand or eye. It can also record the differentiation of the textures of objects as the human hand cannot. Moreover, a lens optically corrected can draw a line which, although different from the line drawn by hand, let us say the line of Ingres, for example, may nevertheless be equally subtle and compelling. These, the forms of objects, their relative colour values, textures, and line, are the instruments, strictly photographic, of your orchestra. These the photographer must learn to understand and control, harmonize. But the camera machine cannot evade the objects which are in front of it. No more can the photographer. He can choose these objects, arrange, and exclude, before exposure, but not afterwards. That is his problem, these the expressive instruments with which he can solve it. But when he does select the moment, the light, the objects, he must be true to them. If he includes in his space a strip of grass, it must be felt as the living differentiated thing it is, and so recorded. It must take its proper but no less important place as a shape and a texture, in relationship to the mountain, tree, or whatnot, which are included. You must use and control objectivity through photography because you cannot evade or gloss over by the use of unphotographic methods.

Photography so understood and conceived is just beginning to emerge, to be used consciously as a medium of expression. In those other phases of photographic method which I mentioned, that is, in scientific and other record making, there has been at least, perhaps of necessity, a modicum of that understanding and control of purely photographic qualities. That is why I said these other phases were nearer to a truth than all the so-called pictorialism, especially the unoriginal, unexperimental pictorialism which today fills salons and year-books. Compared with this so-called pictorial photography, which is nothing but an evasion of everything truly photographic, all done in the name of art and God knows what, a simple record in the *National Geographic Magazine,* a Druet reproduction of a painting or an aerial photographic record is an unmixed relief. They are honest, direct, and sometimes informed with beauty, however unintentional. I said a simple record. Well, they are not so simple to make, as most of the pictorial photographers would find out if they threw away their oil pigments and their soft-focus lenses, both of which cover a multitude of sins, much absence of knowledge, much sloppy workmanship. In reality they do not cover them for anyone who sees.

Gums, oils, soft-focus lenses, these are the worst enemies, not of photography, which can vindicate itself easily and naturally, but of photographers. The whole photographic past and present, with few exceptions, has been weakened and sterilized by the use of these things. Between the past and the present, however, remember that there is this distinction—that in the past these extrinsic methods were perhaps necessary as a part of photographic experimentation and clarification. But there is no such excuse for their continued use today. Men like Kühn and Steichen, who were masters of manipulation and diffusion, have themselves abandoned this interference because they found the result was a meaningless mixture, not painting, and certainly not photography. And yet photographers go right on today gumming and oiling and soft-focussing without a trace of that skill and conviction which these two men possessed, who have abandoned it. Of course, there is nothing immoral in it. And there is no reason why they should not amuse themselves. It merely has nothing to do with photography, nothing to do with painting, and is a product of a misconception of both. For this is what these processes and materials do—your oil and your gum introduce a paint feeling, a thing even more alien to photography than colour is in an etching, and Lord knows a coloured etching is enough of an abomination. By introducing pigment texture you kill the extraordinary differentiation of textures possible only to photography. And you destroy the subtlety of tonalities. With your soft-focus lens you destroy the solidity of your forms, likewise all differentiation of textures, and the line diffused is no longer a line, for a significant line, that is, one that really has a rhythmic emotional intensity does not vibrate laterally but back, in a third dimension. You see, it is not a question of pure or straight photography from a moral point of view. It is simply that the physical, demonstrable results from the use of unphotographic methods, do not satisfy, do not live, for the reasons I have mentioned. The formless halated quality of light which you get at such cost with a soft-focus lens will not satisfy. The simplification so easily achieved with it, and with these manipulative processes will not satisfy. It is all much too easy, as I know, because I have been through the mill myself. I have made gum prints, five printings, and I have Whistlered with a soft-focus lens. It is nothing to be ashamed of. I had to go through this experience for myself at a time when the true meaning of photography had not crystallized, was not so sharply defined as it is today, a crystallization, by the way, which is the result not of talk and theorizing, but of work actually done. Photography, its philosophy, so to speak, is just beginning to emerge through the work of one man, Alfred Stieglitz, of which I will speak later.

In short, photographers have destroyed by the use of these extrinsic methods and materials, the expressiveness of those instruments of form, texture and line possible and inherent in strictly photographic processes. And these instruments, although they are different in the source and manner of production, therefore different in the character of their expressiveness, from those of any other plastic method, are nevertheless related to the instrumentation of the veritable painter and etcher.

For if photographers had really looked at painting, that is, all painting, critically as a development, if they had not been content to stop with the superficial aspects of Whistler, Japanese prints, the inferior work of German and English landscape painters, Corot, etc., they might have discovered this—that the solidity of forms, the differentiation of textures, line, and colour are used as significant instruments in all the supreme achievements of painting. None of the painting just referred to comes in that category. Photographers, as I have said before, have been influenced by and have sought to imitate either consciously or not consciously the work of inferior painters. The work of Rubens, Michelangelo, El Greco, Cézanne, Renoir, Marin, Picasso, or Matisse cannot be so easily translated into photography, for the simple reason that they have used their medium so purely, have built so much on its inherent qualities that encroachment is well-nigh impossible. And it is being demonstrated today that a photograph likewise built upon the basic qualities of photography cannot be imitated or encroached upon in any way by painter or etcher. It is as much a thing with its own unalienable character, with its own special quality of expressiveness, as any fully realized product of other media.

The unintelligence of present-day photographers, that is of so-called pictorial photographers, lies in the fact that they have not discovered the basic qualities of their medium, either through the misconceptions of the past or through working. They do not see the thing which is happening, or which has happened, because they do not know their own tradition. This is proven by their continued puerile use of the unphotographic methods just dealt with, evidence that they are still dominated by a rudimentary, uncritical conception of painting, that they see in a half-baked, semi-photographic product, a short cut to what they conceive painting to be, and to the recognition of themselves as artists. But, above all, the lack of knowledge of their own tradition is proved by the fact that thousands of numbers of *Camera Work* lie idle today in storage vaults, in cellars, clutter up shelves. These marvellous books which have no counterpart or equal, which contain the only complete record of the development of photography and its relationship to other phases of life, to the publication of which Stieglitz devoted years of love and enthusiasm and hard work, photographers have left to rot on his hands, a constant weight upon him, physical and financial. That he has not destroyed every copy is a miracle. But he continues to preserve them as well as the collection of photographs representing this past development of photography, the only collection of its kind in existence, and most of which he purchased—all this he preserves perhaps, because he has faith in photography, in the work he has done, and in the young generations of students, who, he hopes, will seek them out and use them; that is, use all this past experiment, not to imitate, but as a means of clarifying their own work, of growing, as the painter who is also an artist can use his tradition. Photographers have no other access to their tradition, to the experimental work of the past. For whereas the painter may acquaint himself with the development and past achievements of his medium, such is not the case for the student-worker in photography. There is no place where you can see the work of Hill, White, Käsebier, Eugene, Stieglitz as well as the work of Europe, on permanent exhibition. Yet the photographers do not seem to be interested. They have done nothing to help preserve or use these things. This is in itself a criticism of their intensity, and it shows in the quality of their work. All the way through there is this absence of faith in the dignity and worth of their own medium however used or misused, and, at the same time, the absurd attempt to prove to the world that they, too, are artists. The two things do not jibe. So I say to you again, the record is there, accessible to anyone sufficiently interested. If when you have studied it, you still have to gum, oil, or soft-focus, that is all right, that is your experience to go through with. The human animal seems unable for some reason or other to learn much from either the blunders, or the wisdom of the past. Hence the war. But there are, nevertheless, laws to which he must ultimately conform or be destroyed. Photography, being one manifestation of life, is also subject to such laws. I mean by laws those forces which control the qualities of things, which make it impossible for an oak tree to bring forth chestnuts. Well, that is what photographers have been trying to make photography do—make chestnuts, and usually old chestnuts, grow on an oak tree. I won't say it can't be done, but it certainly has not been done. I don't care how you photograph—use the kitchen mop if you must, but if the product is not true to the laws of photography, that is, if it is not based on the inherent qualities I have mentioned, as it will not, you have produced something which is neither an acorn or a chestnut, something which is dead. Of course, it does not follow that if you do make what has been called a good straight photograph, you will thereby automatically create a living organism, but, at least, you will have done an honest piece of work, something which may give the pleasure of craftsmanship.

And if you can find out something about the laws of your own growth and vision as well as those of photography you may be able to relate the two, create an object which has a life of its own, which transcends craftsmanship. That is a long road, and because it must be your own road nobody can teach it to you or find it for you. There are no short cuts, no rules.

Perhaps you will say: But wait, how about design and composition, or, in painter's lingo, organization and significant form? My answer is that these are words which, when they become formulated, signify, as a rule, perfectly dead things. That is to say when a veritable creator comes along, he finds the only form in which he clothes his feelings and ideas. If he works in a graphic medium he must find a way to simplify the expression and eliminate everything that is irrelevant to it. Every part of his picture, whether a painting, etching, or a photograph, must be meaningful, related to every other part. This he does naturally and inevitably by utilizing the true qualities of his medium in its relation to his experience of life. Now when he has done this transcendent thing, after much hard work, experiment, and many failures, the critic and the professors, etc., appear on the scene, usually fifteen or twenty years after the man has died, and they deduce from his work rules of composition and design. Then the school grows and academic imitation, until finally another man comes along, and, also naturally and inevitably, breaks all the rules which the critics and the professors have neatly tied up with blue ribbons. And so it goes. In other words, composition, design, etc., cannot be fixed by rules, they are not in themselves a static prescription by which you can make a photograph or anything that has meaning. They signify

merely the way of synthesis and simplification which creative individuals have found for themselves. If you have something to say about
life, you must also find a way of saying it clearly. And if you achieve
that clarity of both perception and the ability to record it, you will
have created your own composition, your own kind of design, personal to you, related to other people's, yet your own. The point I
want to make is that there is no such thing as THE way; there is only
for each individual, his or her way, which in the last analysis, each
one must find for himself in photography and in living. As a matter
of fact, your photography is a record of your living, for anyone who
really sees. You may see and be affected by other people's ways, you
may even use them to find your own, but you will have eventually to
free yourself of them. That is what Nietsche meant when he said,
"I have just read Schopenhauer, now I have to get rid of him." He
knew how insidious other people's ways could be, particularly those
which have the forcefulness of profound experience, if you let them
get between you and your own vision. So I say to you that composition and design mean nothing unless they are the moulds you yourselves have made, into which to pour your own content, and unless
you can make the mould, which you cannot if you do not respect
your materials and have some mastery over them, you have no chance
to release that content. In other words, learn to photograph first,
learn your craft, and in the doing of that you will find a way, if you
have anything to say, of saying it. The old masters were craftsmen
first, some of them artists, afterwards. Now this analysis of photography and photographers is not a theory, but derived from my own
experience as a worker, and more than that even, is based on the
concrete achievements of D. O. Hill, who photographed in 1843, and
of Alfred Stieglitz, whose work today is the result of thirty-five years
of experimentation. The work of these two men: Hill, the one photographic primitive, Stieglitz, who has been the leader in the fight
to establish photography, not photographers, stands out sharply from
that of all other photographers. It embodies, in my opinion, the only
two fully realized truly photographic expressions, so far, and is a
critical comment upon the misconceptions of the intermediary past
and the sterility of the present. The work of both disclaims any
attempt to paint, either in feeling or in handling.

The psychology of Hill is interesting. He himself was a painter, a
member of the Royal Scotch Academy, and one of his commissions
was to paint a picture in which were to appear recognizable portraits
of some one hundred or more notable people of the time. He had
heard of the lately invented process of photography, and it occurred
to him that it might be of considerable assistance in the painting of
his picture. He began to experiment with a crude camera and lens,
with paper negatives, exposures in the sun five or six minutes, and
he became so fascinated by these things that he neglected his painting.

He worked for three years with photography and then finally, when his wife and friends got at him and told him he was an artist wasting his time, in other words, gave him a bad conscience, he gave it up and, as far as we know, never photographed again. In other words, when Hill photographed he was not thinking of painting. He was not trying to turn photography into paint or even to make it do an equivalent. Starting with the idea of using photography as a means, it so fascinated him that it soon became an end in itself. The results of his experimentation reveal, therefore, a certain directness, a quality of perception which, with Hill's extraordinary feeling for the people whom he photographed, has made his work stand unsurpassed until today. And this, mind you, despite the crudity of the materials with which he had to work, the long exposures, etc., and in spite of the fact that George Eastman was not there to tell Hill that all he (Hill) had to do was to press the button and he (Eastman) would do the rest. He was not trying to paint with photography. Moreover, it is interesting to note that his painting, in which he was constrained by the academic standards of the time, has passed into obscurity. His photography, in which he was really free, lives.

The work of Stieglitz, from the earliest examples done thirty-five years ago, to the amazing things he is doing today, exhibits to even a more marked degree this remarkable absence of all interference with the authentic qualities of photography. There is not the slightest trace of paint feeling or evidence of a desire to paint. Years ago, when he was a student in Germany painters who saw his photographs often said, "Of course, this is not Art, but we would like to paint the way you photograph." His reply was, "I don't know anything about Art, but for some reason or other I have never wanted to photograph the way you paint." There you have a complete statement of the difference between the attitude of Stieglitz towards photography, and practically every other photographer. And it is there in his work, from the earliest to the latest. From the beginning Stieglitz has accepted the camera machine, instinctively found in it something which was part of himself, and loved it. And that is prerequisite to any living photographic expression for anyone.

I do not want to discuss in detail this work of Stieglitz, as another exhibition of his most recent photographs opens April 1 at the Anderson Galleries. Go and see these things yourselves. If possible, look at the earlier photographs in *Camera Work,* so that you can follow the development of his knowledge and of his perceptions. Stieglitz has gone much further than Hill. His work is much wider in scope, more conscious, the result of many more years of intensive experiment. Every instrument, form, texture, line, and even print colour are brought into play, subjugated through the machine to the single purpose of expression. Notice how every object, every blade of grass, is felt and accounted for, the full acceptance and use of the thing in front of it. Note, too, that the size and shape of his mounts become part of the expression. He spends months sometimes just trying to mount a photograph, so sensitive is the presentation. Observe also how he has used solarization, really a defect, how he has used it as a virtue consciously, made the negative with that in mind. That is truly creative use of material, perfectly legitimate, perfectly photographic.

In other words, go and see what photography really is, what it can record in the hands of one who has worked with intense respect and intelligence, who has lived equally intensely, without theories. Stieglitz fought for years to give other people a chance to work and to develop, and he is still fighting. The photographers failed. They did not develop, did not grow. Stieglitz has done for photography what they have not been able to do. He has taken it out of the realm of misconception and a promise, and made it a fulfilment.

In his exhibition two years ago he set aside the question of whether photography is or is not art as of no importance to him, just as he did thirty-five years ago. Exactly, because nobody knows what art is, or God or all the other abstractions, particularly those who make claims to such knowledge. There are a few, however, who do know what photography is and what painting is. They know that there is as much painting which is bad photography as most photography is bad painting. In short, they have some idea whether a thing is genuine and alive or false and dead.

In closing, I will say this to you as students of photography. Don't think when I say students that I am trying to talk down. We are all students, including Stieglitz. Some a little longer at it than the others, a little more experienced. When you cease to be a student you might as well be dead as far as the significance of your work is concerned. So I am simply talking to you as one student to others, out of my own experience. And I say to you, before you give your time, and you will have to give much, to photography, find out in yourselves how much it means to you. If you really want to paint, then do not photograph except as you may want to amuse yourselves along with the rest of Mr. Eastman's customers. Photography is not a short cut to painting, being an artist, or anything else. On the other hand, if this camera machine with its materials fascinates you, compels your energy and respect, learn to photograph. Find out first what this machine and these materials can do without any interference except your own vision. Photograph a tree, a machine, a table, any old thing; do it over and over again under different conditions of light. See what your negative will record. Find out what your papers, chloride, bromide, palladium, the different grades of these, will register. What differences in colour you can get with different developers, and how these differences affect the expression of your prints. Experiment with mounts to see what shape and size do to your photograph. The field is limitless, inexhaustible, without once stepping outside the natural boundaries of the medium. In short, work, experiment and forget about art, pictorialism, and other unimportant more or less meaningless phrases. Look at *Camera Work*. Look at it critically, know at least what photographers have done. Look also just as critically at what is being done and what you are doing. Look at painting if you will, but the whole development; don't stop with Whistler and Japanese prints. Some have said that Stieglitz' portraits were so remarkable because he hypnotised people. Go and see what he has done with clouds; find out whether his hypnotic power extends to the elements.

Look at all these things. Get at their meaning to you; assimilate what you can, and get rid of the rest. Above all, look at the things around you, the immediate world around you. If you are alive, it will mean something to you, and if you care enough about photography, and if you know how to use it, you will want to photograph that meaning. If you let other people's vision get between the world and your own, you will achieve that extremely common and worthless thing, a pictorial photograph. But if you keep this vision clear you may make something which is at least a photograph, which has a life of its own, as a tree or a matchbox, if you see it, has a life of its own. An organism which refuses to let you think about art, pictorialism, or even photography, it simply is. For the achievement of this there are no short cuts, no formulae, no rules except those of your own living. There is necessary, however, the sharpest kind of self-criticism, courage, and hard work. But first learn to photograph. That alone I find for myself is a problem without end.

EDWARD WESTON (1886-1958) *The photographer's power lies in his ability to re-create his subject in terms of its basic reality, and present this re-creation in such a form that the spectator feels that he is seeing not just a symbol for the object, but the thing itself revealed for the first time. Guided by the photographer's selective understanding, the penetrating power of the camera-eye can be used to produce a heightened sense of reality—a kind of super realism that reveals the vital essences of things.* WHAT IS PHOTOGRAPHIC BEAUTY? *Camera Craft, Vol. 46, 1939, p. 254.*

PHOTOGRAPHY—NOT PICTORIAL   1930
Camera Craft, Vol. 37, No. 7, pp. 313-20.

"Art is an interpreter of the inexpressible, and therefore it seems a folly to try to convey its meaning afresh by means of words." This thought from Goethe is so true to me, that I hesitate before adding more words to the volumes both written and spoken by eager partisans—or politicians. I have always held that there is too much talk about art—not enough work. The worker will not have time to talk, to theorize—he will learn by doing.

But I have started with art as subject matter, though I have been asked to write my viewpoint on "Pictorial Photography." Are they, or can they be analagous? I would say, "Let the pedants decide that!" And yet—that word "Pictorial" irritates me: as I understand the making of pictures. Have we not had enough picture making—more or less refined "Calendar Art" by hundreds of thousands of painters and etchers? Photography following this line can only be a poor imitation of already bad art. Great painters—and I have had fortunate contacts with several of the greatest in this country, or in the world— are keenly interested in, and have deep respect for photography *when it is photography* both in technique and viewpoint, when it does something they cannot do; they only have contempt, and rightly so, when it is an imitation painting. And that is the trouble with most photography—just witness ninety per cent of the prints in innumerable salons—work done by those who if they had no camera would be third rate, or worse, painters. No photographer can equal emotionally nor aesthetically the work of a fine painter, *both having the same end in view*—that is, the painter's viewpoint. Nor can the painter begin to equal the photographer *in his particular field.*

The camera then, used as a means of expression, must have inherent qualities either different or greater than those of any other medium, otherwise, it has no value at all, except for commerce, science, or as a weekend hobby for weary businessmen—which would be fine if they did not expose their results to the public as art!

William Blake wrote: "Man is led to believe a lie, when he sees with, not through the eye." And the camera—the lens—can do that very thing—enable one to see through the eye, augmenting the eye, seeing more than the eye sees, exaggerating details, recording surfaces, textures that the human hand could not render with the most skill and labor. Indeed what painter would want to—his work would become niggling, petty, tight! But in a photograph this way of seeing is legitimate, logical.

So the camera for me is best in close up, taking advantage of this lens power: recording with its one searching eye the very quintessence of the thing itself rather than a mood of that thing—for instance, the object transformed for the moment by charming, unusual, even theatrical, but always transitory light effects. Instead, the physical quality of things can be rendered with utmost exactness: stone is hard, bark is rough, flesh is alive, or they can be made harder, rougher, or more alive if desired. In a word, let us have photographic beauty!

Is it art—can it be? Who knows or cares! It is a vital new way of seeing, it belongs to our day and age, its possibilities have only been touched upon. So why bother about art—a word so abused it is almost obsolete. But for the sake of discussion, the difference between good and bad art lies in the minds that created, rather than in skill of hands: a fine technician may be a very bad artist, but a fine artist usually makes himself a fine technician to better express his thought. And the camera not only sees differently with each worker using it, but sees differently than the eyes see: it must, with its single eye of varying focal lengths.

I cannot help feeling—and others have too—that certain great painters of the past actually had photographic eyes—born in this age they might well have used the camera. For instance, Velazquez. Diego Rivera wrote of him: "The talent of Velazquez manifesting itself in coincidence with the image of the physical world, his genius would have led him to select the technique most adequate for the purpose: that is to say, photography."

And there is Vincent Van Gogh who wrote "A feeling for things in themselves is much more important than a sense of the pictorial." Living today he might not use a camera, but he surely would be interested in some present day photographs.

Photography has or will eventually, negate much painting—for which the painter should be deeply grateful; relieving him, as it were from certain public demands: representation, objective seeing. Rivera, I overheard in a heated discussion one day at an exhibit of photographs in Mexico: "I would rather have one of these photographs than any realistic painting: such work makes realistic painting superfluous."

For those who have been interested enough to follow me so far I will explain my way of working. With over twenty years of experience, I never try to plan in advance. Though I may from experience know about what I can do with a certain subject, my own eyes are no more than scouts on a preliminary search, for the camera's eye may entirely change my original idea, even switch me to different subject matter. So I start out with my mind as free from an image as the silver film on which I am to record, and I hope as sensitive. Then indeed putting one's head under the focussing cloth is a thrill, just as exciting to me today as it was when I started as a boy. To pivot the camera slowly around watching the image change on the ground glass is a revelation, one becomes a discoverer, seeing a new world through the lens. And finally the complete idea is there, and completely revealed. *One must feel definitely, fully, before the exposure.* My finished print is there on the ground glass, with all its values, in exact proportions. The final result in my work is fixed forever with the shutter's release. Finishing, developing, and printing is no more than a careful carrying on of the image seen on the ground glass. No after consideration such as enlarging portions, nor changing values—and of course no retouching—can make up for a negative exposed without a complete realization at the time of the exposure.

Photography is too honest a medium, direct and uncompromising, to allow of subterfuge. One notes in a flash a posed gesture or assumed expression in portraiture—or in landscape, a clear day made into a foggy one by use of a diffused lens, or an underexposed sunset labeled "Moonlight"!

The direct approach to photography is the difficult one, because one must be a technical master as well as master of one's mind. Clear thinking and quick decisions are necessary: technique must be a part of one, as automatic as breathing, and such technique is difficult. I can, and have taught a child of seven to expose, develop, and print creditably in a few weeks, thanks to the great manufacturers who have so simplified and made fool-proof the various steps in picture making: which accounts for the flood of bad photography by those who think it an easy way to "express" themselves. But it is not easy! —not easy to see on the ground glass the finished print, to mentally carry that image on through the various processes of finishing to a final result, and with reasonable surety that the result will be exactly what one originally saw and felt. I say mentally carry the image to stress the point that no manual interference is allowed, nor desired in my way of working. Photography so considered becomes a medium requiring the greatest accuracy, and surest judgment. The painter can, if he wishes, change his original conception as he works, at least every detail is not conceived beforehand, but the photographer must see the veriest detail which can never be changed. Often a moment or a second or the fraction of a second of time must be captured without hesitancy. What a fine training in seeing, in accuracy, for anyone—for a child especially. I have started two of my own boys in photography and expect to with the other two: not wanting nor even hoping that they will become photographers, but to give them a valuable aid in whatever line of work they may choose to follow.

I may be writing for a very few persons, maybe only one, no more is to be expected. To the few, or the one, I would finally say, learn to think photographically and not in terms of other media, then you will have something to say which has not been already said. Realize the limitations as well as possibilities of photography. The artist unrestrained by a form, within which he must confine his original emotion, could not create. The photographer must work out his problem, restricted by the size of his camera, the focal length of his lens, the certain grade of dry plate or film, and the printing process he is using: within these limitations enough can be said, more than has been so far—for photography is young.

Actually I am not arguing for my way. An argument indicates a set frame of mind by those who participate, and to remain fluid, ready to change, indeed eager to, is the only way to grow. Personal growth is all that counts. Not, am I greater than another, but am I greater than I was last year or yesterday. Each of us is in a certain stage of development and it would be a drab world if we all thought alike.

Some there are who will remember my work of fifteen years ago, or less, and some will like my past better than my present. To the latter I have not much to say; they are still in a world where lovely poetic impressions are more important than the aesthetic beauty of the thing itself.

A CONTEMPORARY MEANS TO CREATIVE EXPRESSION   1932
The Art of Edward Weston, edited by Merle Armitage, New York, E. Weyhe, pp. 7-8.

Man is the actual medium of expression—not the tool he elects to use as a means. Results alone should be appraised; the way in which these are achieved is of importance only to the maker. To the extent that the completed work realizes depth of understanding, uniqueness of viewpoint, and vitality of presentation, will the spectator respond and participate in the original experience. This premise, restricting too personal and therefore prejudiced interpretation, leads to revelation—the fusion of an inner and outer reality derived from the wholeness of life—sublimating things seen into things known. Explanatory statements are usually incongruous, since each expression with exclusive qualities and defined objective generates a special morale, and only exists by reason of the fact that it is incommunicable in any other way.

Due to misconceptions and to the difficulty of acquiring a technique adequate to the consummation of intention, there have been few historically important photographers; yet in authentic examples —for instance the photographs of Stieglitz, Sheeler, and Strand—a correlation between meaning and expression is attained, more vital than that released in much contemporary work presented as art. In fact, real photography has augmented knowledge, extended horizons, manifestly influenced other creative forms of the day. When understood, the inherent limitations and exclusive potentialities of any means to expression become equally important in conditioning the expression, predetermining its objective. The present status of photography, recognized as a unique, untraditional form and valued for exactly what it is, could not have been achieved without the very qualities, once depreciated, seen as a bar to "self-expression."

But self-expression is an illusion in which the artist imagines that he can conceive of and create non-existent forms. On the contrary, the most "abstract" art is derived from forms in nature; these, when "interpreted" with biased opinion, conclude in meaningless distortion, under or overstatement. A photograph may approximate reality, but cannot attain unqualified realism. By contrast, extreme departure from factual recording is possible and relevant to "straight" photography. The camera does not reproduce nature, not exactly as seen with our eyes, which are but a means to see through as impersonal as the lens and must be directed by the same intelligence that in turn guides the camera or any tool.

I make but one reservation in determining the objective of photography: that it should not be used to create a work in which it is apparent that a clearer communication might have been established in other ways. Excepting this, I have no theories which condition my work; theories follow practice, are never a part of the creative process. Logic implies repetition, the dullness of stability; while life is fluid, ever changing. Understanding is not reached through vicariously acquired information, but in living and working, fully.

SEEING PHOTOGRAPHICALLY   1943
The Complete Photographer, Vol. 9, No. 49, pp. 3200-3206.

Each medium of expression imposes its own limitations on the artist —limitations inherent in the tools, materials, or processes he employs. In the older art forms these natural confines are so well established they are taken for granted. We select music or dancing, sculpture or writing because we feel that within the *frame* of that particular medium we can best express whatever it is we have to say.

THE PHOTO-PAINTING STANDARD

Photography, although it has passed its hundredth birthday, has yet to attain such familiarization. In order to understand why this is so, we must examine briefly the historical background of this youngest of the graphic arts. Because the early photographers who sought to produce creative work had no tradition to guide them, they soon began to borrow a ready-made one from the painters. The conviction grew that photography was just a new kind of painting, and its exponents attempted by every means possible to make the camera produce painter-like results. This misconception was responsible for a great many horrors perpetrated in the name of art, from allegorical costume pieces to dizzying out of focus blurs.

But these alone would not have sufficed to set back the photographic clock. The real harm lay in the fact that the false standard became firmly established, so that the goal of artistic endeavor became photo-painting rather than photography. The approach adopted was so at variance with the real nature of the medium employed that each basic improvement in the process became just one more obstacle for the photo-painters to overcome. Thus the influence of the painters' tradition delayed recognition of the real creative field photography had provided. Those who should have been most concerned with discovering and exploiting the new pictorial resources were ignoring them entirely, and in their preoccupation with producing pseudo-paintings, departing more and more radically from all photographic values.

As a consequence, when we attempt to assemble the best work of the past, we most often choose examples from the work of those who were not primarily concerned with aesthetics. It is in commercial portraits from the daguerreotype era, records of the Civil War, documents of the American frontier, the work of amateurs and professionals who practiced photography for its own sake without troubling over whether or not it was art, that we find photographs that will still stand with the best of contemporary work.

But in spite of such evidence that can now be appraised with a calm, historical eye, the approach to creative work in photography today is frequently just as muddled as it was eighty years ago, and the painters' tradition still persists, as witness the use of texture screens, handwork on negatives, and ready-made rules of composition. People who wouldn't think of taking a sieve to the well to draw water fail to see the folly in taking a camera to make a painting.

Behind the photo-painter's approach lay the fixed idea that a straight photograph was purely the product of a machine and therefore not art. He developed special techniques to combat the mechanical nature of his process. In his system the negative was taken as a point of departure—a first rough impression to be "improved" by hand until the last traces of its unartistic origin had disappeared.

Perhaps if singers banded together in sufficient numbers, they could convince musicians that the sounds they produced through *their machines* could not be art because of the essentially mechanical nature of their instruments. Then the musician, profiting by the example of the photo-painter, would have his playing recorded on special discs so that he could unscramble and rescramble the sounds until he had transformed the product of a good musical instrument into a poor imitation of the human voice!

To understand why such an approach is incompatible with the logic of the medium, we must recognize the two basic factors in the photographic process that set it apart from the other graphic arts: the nature of the recording process and the nature of the image.

NATURE OF THE RECORDING PROCESS

Among all the arts photography is unique by reason of its instantaneous recording process. The sculptor, the architect, the composer all have the possibility of making changes in, or additions to, their original plans while their work is in the process of execution. A composer may build up a symphony over a long period of time; a painter may spend a lifetime working on one picture and still not consider it finished. But the photographer's recording process cannot be drawn out. Within its brief duration, no stopping or changing or reconsidering is possible. When he uncovers his lens every detail within its field of vision is registered in far less time than it takes for his own eyes to transmit a similar copy of the scene to his brain.

NATURE OF THE IMAGE

The image that is thus swiftly recorded possesses certain qualities that at once distinguish it as photographic. First there is the amazing precision of definition, especially in the recording of fine detail; and second, there is the unbroken sequence of infinitely subtle gradations from black to white. These two characteristics constitute the trademark of the photograph; they pertain to the mechanics of the process and cannot be duplicated by any work of the human hand.

The photographic image partakes more of the nature of a mosaic than of a drawing or painting. It contains no *lines* in the painter's sense, but is entirely made up of tiny particles. The extreme fineness of these particles gives a special tension to the image, and when that tension is destroyed—by the intrusion of handwork, by too great enlargement, by printing on a rough surface, etc.—the integrity of the photograph is destroyed.

Finally, the image is characterized by lucidity and brilliance of tone, qualities which cannot be retained if prints are made on dull-surface papers. Only a smooth, light-giving surface can reproduce satisfactorily the brilliant clarity of the photographic image.

RECORDING THE IMAGE

It is these two properties that determine the basic procedure in the photographer's approach. Since the recording process is instantaneous, and the nature of the image such that it cannot survive corrective handwork, it is obvious that *the finished print must be created in full before the film is exposed.* Until the photographer has learned to visualize his final result in advance, and to predetermine the procedures necessary to carry out that visualization, his finished work (if it be photography at all) will represent a series of lucky—or unlucky—mechanical accidents.

Hence the photographer's most important and likewise most difficult task is not learning to manage his camera, or to develop, or to print. It is learning to *see photographically*—that is, learning to see his subject matter in terms of the capacities of his tools and processes, so that he can instantaneously translate the elements and values in a scene before him into the photograph he wants to make. The photopainters used to contend that photography could never be an art because there was in the process no means for controlling the result. Actually, the problem of learning to see photographically would be simplified if there were fewer means of control than there are.

By varying the position of his camera, his camera angle, or the focal length of his lens, the photographer can achieve an infinite number of varied compositions with a single, stationary subject. By changing the light on the subject, or by using a color filter, any or all of the values in the subject can be altered. By varying the length of exposure, the kind of emulsion, the method of developing, the photographer can vary the registering of relative values in the negative. And the relative values as registered in the negative can be further modified by allowing more or less light to affect certain parts of the image in printing. Thus, within the limits of his medium, without resorting to any method of control that is not photographic (i.e., of an optical or chemical nature), the photographer can depart from literal recording to whatever extent he chooses.

This very richness of control facilities often acts as a barrier to creative work. The fact is that relatively few photographers ever master their medium. Instead they allow the medium to master them and go on an endless squirrel cage chase from new lens to new paper to new developer to new gadget, never staying with one piece of equipment long enough to learn its full capacities, becoming lost in a maze of technical information that is of little or no use since they don't know what to do with it.

Only long experience will enable the photographer to subordinate technical considerations to pictorial aims, but the task can be made immeasurably easier by selecting the simplest possible equipment and procedures and staying with them. Learning to see in terms of the field of one lens, the scale of one film and one paper, will accomplish a good deal more than gathering a smattering of knowledge about several different sets of tools.

The photographer must learn from the outset to regard his process as a whole. He should not be concerned with the "right exposure," the "perfect negative," etc. Such notions are mere products of advertising mythology. Rather he must learn the kind of negative necessary to produce a given kind of print, and then the kind of exposure and development necessary to produce that negative. When he knows how these needs are fulfilled for one kind of print, he must learn how to vary the process to produce other kinds of prints. Further he must learn to translate colors into their monochrome values, and learn to judge the strength and quality of light. With practice this kind of knowledge becomes intuitive; the photographer learns to see a scene or object in terms of his finished print without having to give conscious thought to the steps that will be necessary to carry it out.

SUBJECT MATTER AND COMPOSITION

So far we have been considering the mechanics of photographic seeing. Now let us see how this camera-vision applies to the fields of subject matter and composition. No sharp line can be drawn between the subject matter appropriate to photography and that more suitable to the other graphic arts. However, it is possible, on the basis of an examination of past work and our knowledge of the special properties of the medium, to suggest certain fields of endeavor that will most reward the photographer, and to indicate others that he will do well to avoid.

Even if produced with the finest photographic technique, the work of the photo-painters referred to could not have been successful. Photography is basically too honest a medium for recording superficial aspects of a subject. It searches out the actor behind the make-up and exposes the contrived, the trivial, the artificial, for what they really are. But the camera's innate honesty can hardly be considered a limitation of the medium, since it bars only that kind of subject matter that properly belongs to the painter. On the other hand it provides the photographer with a means of looking deeply into the nature of things, and presenting his subjects in terms of their basic reality. It enables him to reveal the essence of what lies before his lens with such clear insight that the beholder may find the recreated image more real and comprehensible than the actual object.

It is unfortunate, to say the least, that the tremendous capacity photography has for revealing new things in new ways should be overlooked or ignored by the majority of its exponents—but such is the case. Today the waning influence of the painter's tradition, has been replaced by what we may call *Salon Psychology,* a force that is exercising the same restraint over photographic progress by establishing false standards and discouraging any symptoms of original creative vision.

Today's photographer need not necessarily make his picture resemble a wash drawing in order to have it admitted as art, but he must abide by "the rules of composition." That is the contemporary nostrum. Now to consult rules of composition before making a picture is a little like consulting the law of gravitation before going for a walk. Such rules and laws are deduced from the accomplished fact; they are the products of reflection and after-examination, and are in no way a part of the creative impetus. When subject matter is forced to fit into preconceived patterns, there can be no freshness of vision. Following rules of composition can only lead to a tedious repetition of pictorial clichés.

Good composition is only the strongest way of seeing the subject. It cannot be taught because, like all creative effort, it is a matter of personal growth. In common with other artists the photographer wants his finished print to convey to others his own response to his subject. In the fulfillment of this aim, his greatest asset is the directness of the process he employs. But this advantage can only be retained if he simplifies his equipment and technique to the minimum necessary, and keeps his approach free from all formula, art-dogma, rules, and taboos. Only then can he be free to put his photographic sight to use in discovering and revealing the nature of the world he lives in.

MINOR WHITE (1908-) . . . *innocence of eye has a quality of its own. It means to see as a child sees, with freshness and acknowledgment of the wonder; it also means to see as an adult sees who has gone full circle and once again sees as a child—with freshness and an even deeper sense of wonder.* LYRICAL & ACCURATE, *Image, Vol. 5, No. 8, 1956, p. 176.*

THE CAMERA MIND AND EYE   1952
Magazine of Art, Vol. 45, No. 1, pp. 16-19.

If we had no words perhaps we could understand one another better. The burden is ours, however. So in using the word "creative" to refer to a state of mind in photographers, I expect to be fully misunderstood.

It is no longer news that a cameraman is faced with a very different situation from that of a painter starting a new canvas. The latter has a bare surface to support an invented image, or a blank space in which to spin invented volumes or, as probably some artists feel, a free space in which to live, dance, think—leaving marks where a thought passed or a tactile muscle felt a color. And as he is inventive, he is creative—or so it is popularly thought.

The photographer starts from an image already whole. Superficially it looks as whole as a finished painting, although it is rarely completed. The photographer completes the whole or total image by analyzing a variety of whole images. So the photographer invents nothing; everything is there and visible from the start. Here I should, I suppose, be worried to find that I have written that a photographer invents nothing, since in the recurrent discussions over the creative possibilities of the camera medium, the fact that the photographer invents little if anything is a point the cons labor and the pros fumble trying to circumvent. (Not that it is necessary, of course; the photographs of Stieglitz and Weston provide all the evidence needed.) However, still other evidence has accumulated—the work of the great documentary photographers, for instance—which shows very well that our continual linking of the word "inventive" with "creativeness" has kept us from remembering that creativeness is expressed in many ways. It is time that we in aesthetic fields remembered that analysis in scientific fields is often as inspired or creative as a work of art. We should also remember that the camera is a definite link between science and art, or, if not a link, that it partakes of both. It is time we recalled that "man seen" or "man found" is just as expressive of creativeness as "man made." It is time to remember (the period of discovery is long past) that the camera lures, then compels, a man to create through seeing. It demands that he learn to make the realm of his responses to the world the raw material of his creative activity. Creative understanding is more camera-like than invention.

A young man looking at a photograph of mine—in the midst of experiencing and before he could weigh his words, said, "This is like a painting." Since this did not sound very much like what he had in mind he tried again. "It is obviously a photograph. But the placement—looks—as if a man—as if a man had invented them—things are where a man would put—them—it looks man-made—not like nature—not found."

Yet it had been found, "seen," and merely recorded by the camera. (Because a man trains himself to see like a camera, it is only more appropriate that he uses a camera to record his seeing.) That this picture causes a reaction in a young painter that he can talk about only in terms of painting does not mean that an "aesthetic reaction" is taking place. Perhaps it began with little more than an impact of recognition of something *like* a painting. We must remember, however, that recognition is frequently the start of the "aesthetic" chain reaction.

If he was only surprised at the likeness, consider where he found the likeness: in the perceptive realm of man, not in the camera's imitation of some aspect of painting surfaces. His reaction is important because it shows that we are so conditioned to painting as the criterion of the visual aesthetic experience that the possibility of a photograph's being another path to aesthetic experience, like a piece of sculpture or a poem, has been overlooked or not realized—if not actually denied or pushed out of the realm of possibilities.

Yet to "see," to "find," is a human activity linked to human creativeness. The fact that this particular young man related a "found" picture to his experience of the "made" object is a simple demonstration of how human the "seeing" of photographers is. And, if one would stretch the demonstration slightly, of how inventive "seeing camerawise" is.

The state of mind of the photographer while creating is a blank. I might add that this condition exists only at special times, namely when looking for pictures. (Something keeps him from falling off curbs, down open manholes or into the bumpers of skidding trucks while he is in this condition but goes off duty at all other times.) For those who would equate "blank" with a kind of static emptiness, I must explain that this is a special kind of blank. It is a very active state of mind really, a very receptive state of mind, ready at an instant to grasp an image, yet with no image pre-formed in it at any time. We should note that the lack of a pre-formed pattern or preconceived idea of how anything ought to look is essential to this blank condition. Such a state of mind is not unlike a sheet of film itself—seemingly inert, yet so sensitive that a fraction of a second's exposure conceives a life in it. (Not just life, but *a* life.)

In a way the blank state of mind is a little like the blank canvas of the painter—that is, if we must have an analogy and insist that art must have a point of departure from nothing. (If a blank sheet of paper can be called nothing.) Poets buy a ream of paper and wonder what obscurity will darken the sheets or what revelation will illuminate the mind reading his black marks. But the paper's blankness has little to do with his creative action. Or to the sculptor feeling somehow the form lying in a block of stone, the stone is not a blank so much as a wrapping that only he can unwind.

The photographer is probably more akin to the sculptor in wood or stone than to painters, as far as his mental creative state goes. The whole visual world, the whole world of events are wraps and coverings he feels and believes to be underneath. Often he passes a corner, saying to himself, "There is a picture here"; and if he cannot find it, considers himself the insensitive one. He can look day after day—

and one day the picture is visible! Nothing has changed except himself; although, to be fair, sometimes he had to wait till the light performed the magic.

A mind specially blank—how can we describe it to one who has not experienced it? "Sensitive" is one word. "Sensitized" is better, because there is not only a sensitive mind at work but there is effort on the part of the photographer to reach such a condition. "Sympathetic" is fair, if we mean by it an openness of mind which in turn leads to comprehending, understanding everything seen. The photographer projects himself into everything he sees, identifying himself with everything in order to know it and feel it better. To reach such a blank state of mind requires effort, perhaps discipline. Out of such a state of mind he loves much, hates much and is aware of the areas of his indifference. He photographs what he loves because he loves it, what he hates out of protest; the indifferent he can pass over or photograph with whatever craftsmanship of technique and composition he commands.

If he were to walk a block in a state of sensitized sympathy to everything to be seen, he would be exhausted before the block was up and out of film long before that.

Perhaps the blank state of mind can be likened to a pot of water almost at the boiling point. A little more heat—an image seen—and the surface breaks into turbulence.

Possibly the creative work of the photographer consists in part of putting himself into this state of mind. Reaching it, at any rate, is not automatic. It can be aided by always using one's camera for serious work so that the association of the camera in one's hands always leads to taking pictures. But certainly once the mood is reached, that which happens can get out of control, as it seems it should. We have heard of inspired singing, of inspired poetry, of inspired painting—of production during moments of intensity or lucidity when one feels as if one is an instrument of transmission like a narrow channel between two oceans. (Do telephones feel this way?) The feeling is akin to the mystic and to ecstasy; why deny it? And in this condition the question of whether photography is or is not art is laughable. One feels, one sees on the ground glass into a world beyond surfaces. The square of glass becomes like the words of a prayer or a poem, like fingers or rockets into two infinities—one into the subconscious and the other into the visual-tactile universe.

Afterwards one can look at the photographs and try to find in them something by which to explain what happened. In the illustration titled 51-248, I can point out that light seems to come from inside the photograph, which is certainly not at all like the condition which my reason tells me prevailed at the time, though exactly like what I saw in a moment of highly charged vision. I can also say this symbolizes the emotion felt while making it, and know only how little of this vision the picture must cause in others. Feeling and photographing what causes feeling is no assurance that others will feel. But after once discovering what one wants to arouse in other people, the knowledge that one may frequently fumble in trying is only a challenge.

The picture mentioned above climaxed an afternoon's work in which I started out by saying to myself, "What shall I be given today?" It progressed by stages of a growing awareness of absorption into the place. Exposure after exposure were sketches leading—in no very conscious way—towards this final one. The same shapes, forms, designs recurred with a growing tension. When this was seen on the ground glass, anything separating man and place had been dissolved.

This is no isolated experience, occurring only with nature; I can parallel it with many experiences in photographing people. The duration of a session is one of growing *rapport,* of a deepening friendship. The camera is hardly more than a recording device for an experience between two people. They create in one another—only the photographer is conditioned to see like a camera, so the end result is a photograph.

This is not so much a scholarly discussion of the photographer's creative state of mind as it is a first-hand report. The scientist using the camera as an instrument will probably not have much idea of what I am talking about; however, photographers using the camera as a deeply expressive medium or those using it to document human situations will have experienced the sensation of the camera dissolving in an accord between subject and photographer. And what impresses me now is that I no longer care to prove that some photographs can do the same thing for people that paintings do. (They call it "art.") I merely want to cause in others some degree of experience: shall we call it spirituality? identification? by using photographs as the excitant. The photographs, may I add, *not* the objects photographed. While the photographer cannot eliminate the object (nor does he want to destroy the experience of the visual world transforming into an unconscious world, the very source of his excitement), he still wants the photograph to be the main source of the spectator's feeling. While he cannot erase from the viewer's mind the implications of the subject, he prefers to depend for his effect on the visual relations that are present in the print itself.

"Blank" as the creative photographer's state of mind is, uncritical as it is while photographing, as sensitized, as prepared for anything to happen, afterwards with the prints safely in hand he needs to practice the most conscious criticism. Is what he saw present in the photograph? If not, does the photograph open his eyes to something he could not see by himself? If so, will he take the responsibility for the accident and show it as his own, or will he consider it as a sketch for his subconscious to digest? He needs to study further the reactions of the viewers: do they match his own? come close? or depart in amazing directions? In a sense, this is the activity that brings the creative state of mind near the boiling point: conscious criticism of new prints, digestion of what the prints do, as compared to what he wanted them to do. Without this siege of analytical work, the state of sympathetic sensitivity, the "blank" state of mind will not recur.

EQUIVALENCE: THE PERENNIAL TREND 1963
PSA Journal, Vol. 29, No. 7, pp. 17-21.

When we speak of trends, we concern ourselves with changes, with shifts in style from here to there and back again. Trends are peripheral, yet we can lose ourselves in too blind a concern for them. Central to the changes is something else. If we have to give a name to this centrality, and I guess we do, one name is "Spirit." Every fashion, every trend, every style may function as a gateway to the central significance of the aesthetic experience if the individual persists. That is, though we follow trends or get on bandwagons we can always get off and head towards the eternal significance, Spirit. At best styles and trends and fashions are but clothes for the *raison d'etre* of any art. At the worst, fashions, styles and trends function as traps for the unwary. I will treat here of a tradition, a concept and a discipline, namely the concept or theory called "Equivalence," by which any style, fashion or trend may be worked *through* to something beyond the conformism of competition.

Probably the most mature idea ever presented to picture-making photography was the concept of Equivalence which Alfred Stieglitz named early in the 1920's and practiced the rest of his life. The idea has been continued by a few others, notably at the Institute of Design in Chicago under Aaron Siskind and Harry Callahan, and at the former California School of Fine Arts in San Francisco under the efforts of the present author. As a consequence the theory is in practice now by an ever increasing number of devoted and serious photographers, both amateurs and professionals. The concept and discipline of Equivalence *in practice* is simply the backbone and core of photography as a medium of expression-creation.

Equivalence is a pregnant discipline. Hence the photography that grows out of its practice is bound to develop and change with the photographers and writers on photographic criticism who become mature enough to understand the nature of the theory or approach. The Equivalent is one of those ideas that in practice grows by the efforts and accomplishments of the people who explore it.

To outline this theory (we hardly have space to discuss it), we will refer to "levels" of Equivalence. The term covers too much ground for a linear definition. At one level, the graphic level, the word "Equivalence" pertains to the photograph itself, the visible foundations of any potential visual experience with the photograph itself. Oddly enough, this does not mean that a photograph which functions as an Equivalent has a certain appearance, or style, or trend, or fashion. Equivalence is a function, an experience, not a thing. Any photograph, regardless of source, might function as an Equivalent to someone, sometime, someplace. If the individual viewer realizes that for him what he sees in a picture corresponds to something within himself—that is, the photograph mirrors something in himself—then his experience is some degree of Equivalence. (At least such is a small part of our present definition.)

While we are reluctant to disappoint the reader by not giving some rules or signposts by which one can spot an Equivalent twenty feet away, we would rather be true to the facts of the situation than distort them. So at this graphic level of Equivalence no specifications will be listed.

At the next level the word "Equivalence" relates to what goes on in the viewer's mind as he looks at a photograph that arouses in him a special sense of correspondence to something that he knows about himself. At a third level the word "Equivalence" refers to the inner experience a person has while he is remembering his mental image after the photograph in question is not in sight. The remembered image also pertains to Equivalence only when a certain feeling of correspondence is present. We remember images that we want to remember. The reason why we want to remember an image varies: because we simply "love it," or dislike it so intensely that it becomes compulsive, or because it has made us realize something about ourselves, or has brought about some slight change in us. Perhaps the reader can recall some image, after the seeing of which, he has never been quite the same.

Let us return for a moment to the graphic level of the photographic equivalent. While we cannot describe its appearance, we can define its function. When any photograph functions for a given person as an Equivalent we can say that at that moment and for that person the photograph acts as a symbol or plays the role of a metaphor for something that is beyond the subject photographed. We can say this in another way; when a photograph functions as an Equivalent, the photograph is at once a record of something in front of the camera and simultaneously a spontaneous symbol. (A "spontaneous symbol" is one which develops automatically to fill the need of the moment. A photograph of the bark of a tree, for example, may suddenly touch off a corresponding feeling of roughness of character within an individual.)

When a photographer presents us with what to him is an Equivalent, he is telling us in effect, "I had a feeling about something and here is my metaphor of that feeling." The significant difference here is that what he had a feeling about was not for the subject he photographed, but for something else. He may show us a picture of a cloud, the forms of which expressively correspond to his feelings about a certain person. As he saw the clouds he was somehow reminded of the person, and probably he hopes that we will catch, in the expressive quality of the cloud forms, the same feeling that he experienced. If we do and our feelings are similar to his, he has aroused in us what was to him a known feeling. This is not exactly an easy distinction to make so maybe we can repeat. When the photographer shows us what he considers to be an Equivalent, he is showing us an expression of a feeling, but this feeling is not the feeling he had for the object that he photographed. What really happened is that he *recognized* an object or series of forms that, when photographed, would yield an image with specific suggestive powers that can direct the viewer into a specific and known feeling, state or place within himself. With constantly metamorphizing material such as water, or clouds or ice, or light on cellophane and similar materials, the infinity of forms and shapes, reflections and colors suggest all sorts and manners of emotions and tactile encounters and intellectual speculations that are supported by and formed by the material but which maintain an independent identity from which the photographer can choose what he wishes to express.

The power of the equivalent, so far as the expressive-creative photographer is concerned, lies in the fact that he can convey and evoke feelings about things and situations and events which for some reason or other are not or can not be photographed. The secret, the catch and the power lies in being able to use the forms and shapes of objects in front of the camera for their expressive-evocative qualities. Or to say this in another way, in practice Equivalency is the ability to use the visual world as the plastic material for the photographer's expressive purposes. He may wish to employ the recording power of the medium, it is strong in photography, and document. Or he may wish to emphasize its transforming power, which is equally strong, and cause the subject to stand for something else too. If he uses Equivalency consciously and knowingly, aware of what he is doing, and accepts the responsibility for his images, he has as much freedom of expression as any of the arts.

To be concrete, and leave off theory for a moment, we can return to the photograph of a cloud mentioned above. If we question the photographer, he may tell us that it stands for a certain quality that he finds in a specific woman, namely her femininity. The photograph exhibits softness, delicacy, roundness, fluffiness and so corresponds to at least one feeling or emotion that he has about her. If we ask why he does not photograph the woman herself directly, he may answer that she is hardly photogenic, or that he wishes to establish a certain aesthetic distance between his direct feeling and his outward manifestation of it via the photograph. And this is pleasant—as we all know, too intimate a photograph of a person frequently gets in the way of the viewer's enjoyment.

This photograph of the cloud at one level is simply a record, but at another level it may function to arouse certain planned sensations and emotions. The factual side properly belongs to the photograph; the arousable implications are possible only when someone is looking at it sympathetically. So another aspect of Equivalency is this: Equivalency, while it depends entirely on the photograph itself for the source of stimulation functions in the mind of a viewer. Equivalency functions on the assumption that the following equation is factual:

Photograph + Person Looking ↔ Mental Image

As we can see from the equation, Equivalence is a two-way reaction. Also we can see that only in the mental image held is there any possibility of a metaphorical function occurring.

The mechanisms by which a photograph functions as an Equivalent in a viewer's psyche are the familiar ones which the psychologists call "projection" and "empathy." In the art world the corresponding phenomenon is referred to as "expressive forms and shapes." In the world of photography the vast majority of viewers remain so subject-identification bound that they stay ignorant of the "expressive" qualities of shapes and forms or are unable to overcome their fear of letting themselves go and responding to "expressive" shapes or colors, that is, the design side of the pictorial experience. Yet fortunately, or unfortunately, as the case may be, the contemporary viewer of photographs nearly always responds subconsciously to the design embedded in photographs. This he can hardly help, as the world of advertising exploits constantly and expertly. The reader no doubt has heard of "hidden persuaders." If advertisers can use the subliminal effect of design in photography to help sell a product, a knowledgeable photographer can use the same aspect of design for more enlightened aesthetic purposes.

At a deeper level of Equivalence, the term refers to the specific effect of a photograph intended to function as an Equivalent. So far in this article it would seem that any awareness of mirroring on the part of the viewer looking at a photograph is related to Equivalence. Now we can revamp the definition somewhat to indicate that the feeling of Equivalence is specific. In literature this specific feeling associated with Equivalence is called "poetic," using this word in a very broad and universal sense. Not having an exact equivalent for the word "poetic" in photography we will suggest the word "vision," meaning not only sight, but insight. The effect that seems to be associated with Equivalence may be worded thus: When both subject matter and manner of rendering are transcended, by whatever means, that which seems to be matter becomes what seems to be spirit.

A third level of Equivalence was mentioned earlier. This level revolves around the "remembered image." What a man remembers of vision, is always peculiarly his own because various distortions occur and change his recall image after the original stimulation has gone. These alterations from the original can only come from the individual himself. If a viewer happens to study in his mind a remembered image, who knows what degree or trajectory of Equivalence he might reach, or how far he might walk into his remembered image? The moment when a photograph transforms into a mirror that can be walked into, either when one is looking at it, or remembering it, must always remain secret because the experience is entirely within the individual. It is personal, his own private experience, ineffable, and untranslatable. People who report on this experience tell of literal transformations before their eyes, for example a picture that they know to be of peeled paint turns into something else.

To select this moment for which to make photographs hardly seems a likely area for productive camerawork, yet secret as this moment is, a few photographers are working today who deliberately try to start from their own known feeling states to make photographs which will arouse or reach similar feeling states in others. They consciously make photographs to function as Equivalents. We can add the names of a few—Frederick Sommer in Arizona, Paul Caponigro in Massachusetts, Walter Chappell in New York, Gerald Robinson in Oregon, Arnold Gassan in Colorado; there are others.

To work in such a manner, the photographers must be able to get their work before those persons in the world who are sensitized intellectually, emotionally, and kinesthetically—not a numerous audience to be sure, even if widespread. Universality, that quality always thought to be desirable in photographs and pictures, is not denied to such photographers. It is their efforts that matter, to communicate-evoke with individuals who are in tune with the central core of universality common to both man and spirit.

EQUIVALENCE, MIRROR OF THE PSYCHE

The perennial trend, as old as man in art, seems to have appeared in photography at the beginning of this century. At first it was rather vague in the work and writings of the Photo-Secession group around Stieglitz and Edward Steichen in New York; then it was named, as was said, by Stieglitz in the early twenties. The perennial trend is still not generally understood by photographers or their critics.

There seems to be growing frequency on the part of contemporary thinkers about photography to point out that people see themselves in photographs in spite of themselves. Nathan Lyons, Assistant Director of Eastman House, asks the members of his private classes whether they see what they believe, or believe what they see. And most of us see what we wish to see in a photograph, or anything else—not what is actually present. Cameras are far more impartial than their owners and employers. In other words projection and empathy, natural attributes in man, lead us to see something of ourselves almost automatically in anything that we look at long enough to be aware of it. So we can say that the photograph invariably functions as a mirror of at least some part of the viewer. From extensive researches in audience responses to photographs done at the Rochester Institute of Technology, it is evident that many persons looking as a photograph see something of themselves first, and the photographer behind the camera second, if at all. To the innocent, well meaning young photographer, audience response to his photographs is a disheartening experience. They see what they wish to see, and not what he thinks that he is showing them.

Some degree of mirroring happens with any photograph, but it is especially strong with photographs rendered in a stylized or non-literal way. Mirroring is also strong in photographs in which the presence of design is equal to or supersedes the sense of the presence of the subject in front of the camera. This is the usual appearance of the "pictorial" photograph which includes design and its expressive effect as well as the recording of an aesthetic object. When the subject matter is rendered in such a way that it is obscure, ambiguous, or impossible to identify, the response to the image takes on a completely different aspect. Since most of us have no experience of similar images except what we see in abstract or non-objective painting, we will tend to react to such photographs as if they were paintings and look for the same qualities or value relationships and all the rest of the attributes of design long familiar to us from the world of painting and sculpture. When we cannot identify the subject, we forget that the image before us may be a document of some part of the world that we have never seen. Sometimes art and nature meet in such photographs. We call them "abstractions" frequently because they remind us of similar paintings. Actually they are "extractions" or "isolations" from the world of appearances, often literal. This puts a different bearing on the ambiguous or unidentifiable subject in a photograph. And we are faced with a different encounter with the world of appearances than when we confront the painted "abstraction." Nevertheless, our usual tendency, if we make the attempt to engage, rather than reject, the ambiguous rendering of a subject in a photograph, *is to invent a subject for it.* What we invent is out of the stuff and substance of ourselves. When we invent a subject we turn the photograph into a mirror of some part of ourselves.

Editors such as Ralph Hattersley of *Infinity Magazine,* or myself of *Aperture,* who point out that people see themselves in photographs in spite of their protests to the contrary, are long familiar with the letters and articles of persons who insist that they do not want to solve picture puzzles. We wonder if such persons have the emotional-intellectual equipment to solve anything. Or the letters of those who insist that they are upright, honest men or women and so do not want to, or have no need, to indulge in self-searching. "Morbid" is the word most frequently applied to a knowing study of a photograph for what it might reveal of the true nature of the viewer. It would seem that any soul searching, or attempt to discover what Plato meant by "Know Thyself" is considered sickness of some sort by many contemporary Americans. In spite of protests, our own psychology finds a way to see what it wants to see in the world of appearances. This is a difficult and sore point; consequently I and many of my students have observed people's responses to photographs, and attempted to evaluate and investigate the nature of things behind the responses of many kinds of people to many types of photographs. And we observe that all too often the persons who cry "Sick, Sick, Sick" have no imagination. Or, for reasons obscure to them, they deliberately blind themselves to visual experiences that might disturb their basic insecurity. Consequently the full range of photographic possibilities of communication-evocation is a closed world to them.

Sometimes the complaint against ambiguous photographs is stated, "Art must never be a glorified Rorschach test!" Suggestibility is part of the foundations of human nature. Most of our lives depend on suggestibility, the arts especially. The documentarian in photography may communicate considerable information with his camera; the pictorialist conscious of design and its power of suggestion depends heavily on that quality in us that makes the Rorschach blot useful in therapy. The theory of Equivalence is a way for the photographer to deal with human suggestibility in a conscious and responsible way. It seems to me that to think of painting or photography as some degree of glorified Rorschach blots is not detrimental to either medium because suggestibility is the very gate to the perennial trend in art. We must observe, of course, that a gate is not quite the same as a garden.

Some contemporary photographers, such as those already named, willingly acknowledge the fact that photographs mirror some state of feeling within the viewer. They include themselves here as viewers of their own photographs and viewers of the subjects they select. They accept the truth that photographs act as a catalyst, and consequently are a step in process, not an end product. They can remember that the mental image in a viewer's mind is more important than the photograph itself.

That the photograph is a function instead of a thing is a most interesting development in the idea of the Equivalent; if indeed this is a development and not a belated understanding of what Stieglitz meant by the word. It is interesting because it reflects a certain potential change in the Freudian, Jungian and Adlerian effect on the popular ideas about psychology. Probably many a lay person still thinks psychology is dirty, has associated the dirty sides of himself with that word. True enough the inner workings of man are both dirty and clean—as are his outer relations to other men. Art traditionally claims a concern with man's pure impulses and clean motives, yet many a contemporary psychologist thinks that all this is pure hokum. So do some photographers. And in protest and in truth, in soul searching and awareness of our self-destroying age, many people in contemporary art, notably Frederick Sommer in contemporary photography, present images which are intended in such a particular way that if the viewer engages the images at all, then the viewer will see something of himself. If what he sees is unpleasant, that there may be some truth in that some part of himself is unpleasant—if dirty, morbid and so on. . . . If he is struck with terror, perhaps he has met something worthy of his fear. If he finds something magnificent, it is because something beautiful in him has been magnified.

Four photographs are presented here by the author. Of them it may be said that what you get from them is yours. The author presents them also as showing something of himself. In other words, these photographs originate in a known feeling state. They are not self-expressive, or self-searching; they are self-found. Communication is of no importance, evocation of little significance, competition nonexistent. They are shown as an event out of which Equivalence might occur. The possibility of the reader's being confronted with something of himself is their only reason for being reproduced. They will function as mirrors of the viewer, whether he admits it or not. It will not be pointed out which of the images knows happiness, the one that knows anger, or the one that knows sadness because viewers of photographs need the opportunity to learn faith in their own feelings.

With the theory of Equivalence, photographers everywhere are given a way of learning to use the camera in relation to the mind, heart, viscera and spirit of human beings. The perennial trend has barely been started in photography.

BERENICE ABBOTT, born Springfield, Ohio, 1898. Studied, Ohio State Univ., 1918-21; studied sculpture and painting in New York City. To Paris and Berlin, continued studies, 1921-23. Began photography as assistant to Man Ray (portraiture), 1924. Recognized value of work of Eugène Atget, 1925; after his death in 1927, acquired collection of his negatives and prints. Instrumental in publication of monograph in 1930, *Atget Photographe de Paris*. First exhibition, Paris, (introduction by Jean Cocteau) 1926. Returned to United States, 1929; hired by *Fortune* to make series of portraits of American businessmen, after which was commissioned by *Life* to make series of scientific subjects; began document of New York; photographs in Deutsche Werkbund exhibition "Film und Foto," Stuttgart. Worked on U.S. Government Federal Art Project, "The Changing New York Program." Publication of *Changing New York*, 1939, derived from this project. 1938, began over 20 years of teaching at New School for Social Research. Exhibition at Federal Art Gallery, 1939. Associated with Physical Science Study Committee of Educational Services, Inc., 1958-61; in conjunction with Committee and Smithsonian Institution produced "The Image of Physics," exhibition circulated throughout the country. Author of, *The World of Atget*, 1964.

BOOKS & CATALOGUES: *Changing New York* (text by Elizabeth McCausland), 1939; *The View Camera Made Simple*, Chicago, 1948; *Greenwich Village Today and Yesterday* (text by Henry W. Lanier), 1949; *New Guide to Better Photography*, 1953; *20 Photographs by Eugène Atget* (portfolio of modern prints made by Abbott from Atget's negatives, with introduction), 1956; *Physics*, Boston, 1960; *Magnet* (text by E. Valens), Cleveland, 1964.

ARTICLES BY: "Photographer as Artist," *Art Front*, Vol. 16, (1936); "Photography 1839-1937," *Art Front*, Vol. 17, (1937); "Eugène Atget," *The Complete Photographer*, No. 6 (1941; reprinted in *Encyclopedia of Photography*, Vol. 2, 1963); "Documenting the City," *The Complete Photographer*, No. 22 (1942; reprinted in *Encyclopedia of Photography*, Vol. 7, 1963); "Nadar: Master Portraitist," *The Complete Photographer*, No. 51 (1943); "View Cameras," *The Complete Photographer*, No. 53 (1943; reprinted in *Encyclopedia of Photography*, Vol. 20, 1963); "From a Student's Notebook," *Popular Photography*, 21:6 (1947); "What the Camera and I See," *Art News*, 50:5 (1951); "The Image of Science," *Art in America*, 47:4 (1959).

ARTICLES ABOUT: Elizabeth McCausland, "The Photography of Berenice Abbott," *Trend*, 3:1 (1935); Rosa Reilly, "Berenice Abbott Records Changing New York," *Popular Photography*, 3:3 (1938); "Something New Under the Sun," *Minicam Photography*, 7:5 (1944); Elizabeth McCausland, "Berenice Abbott—Realist," *Photo Arts*, 2:1 (Spring 1948); "Abbott's Non-Abstract Abstracts," *Infinity*, 11:1 (1962).

ANSEL ADAMS, born San Francisco, Cal., 1902. Trained as concert pianist. Visited Yosemite Valley, Cal., 1916, returning often to photograph. First portfolio, *Parmelian Prints of the High Sierras*, for Sierra Club, beginning long association, 1928. Decided to become full-time photographer, 1930; one-man exhibition, M. H. de Young Memorial Museum, San Francisco. With Willard Van Dyke, founded "Group ƒ64," dedicated to exploring potentials of straight photography, 1932. First technical book, *Making a Photograph*, 1935. One-man exhibition, An American Place, 1936. Directed exhibition, "A Pageant of Photography," Golden Gate Exposition, 1940. Helped establish Dept. of Photography, Museum of Modern Art, 1940; served as its Vice-Chairman. Photographed Japanese-Americans at Manzanar relocation camp, 1943; published as *Born Free and Equal*, 1944. Founded the first Dept. of Photography at California School of Fine Arts, 1946. Guggenheim Fellowship 1946, (renewed 1948), 1958. Began Basic Photo Book Series, 1948. Consultant to Polaroid Corp., since 1949. Produced *Portfolio One* and *Portfolio Two*, 1948-50. Since 1955, annual workshops in Yosemite Valley. Collaborated with Nancy Newhall on exhibition "This is the American Earth," 1955, and "The Eloquent Light," 1963; "A Nation of Nations," for United States Information Agency, 1957. Awarded honorary degree of DFA by Univ. of Cal., 1961.

BOOKS & CATALOGUES: *Taos Pueblo*, (12 original prints; text by Mary Austin) San Francisco, 1930; *Sierra Nevada: The John Muir Trail*, Berkeley, 1938; *My Camera in Yosemite Valley*, Yosemite, 1949; *My Camera in the National Parks*, Yosemite Nat. Park, 1950; *Death Valley*, (text by Nancy Newhall) San Francisco, 1954; *Mission San Xavier del Bac*, (text by Nancy Newhall) San Francisco, 1954; *Yosemite Valley*, (edited by Nancy Newhall) San Francisco, 1959; *This is the American Earth*, (with Nancy Newhall) San Francisco, 1960; *The Eloquent Light, Volume I*, (by Nancy Newhall) San Francisco, 1963.

ARTICLES BY: "The New Photography," *Modern Photography Annual*, (1934-35); "A Decade of Photographic Art," *Popular Photography*, 22:6 (1948); "Some Thoughts on Color Photography," *Photo Notes*, (Spring 1950); "Contemporary American Photography," *Universal Photo Almanac* (1951); "Creative Photography," *Art in America*, 45:4 (1957); "Some Definitions," *Image*, 8:1 (1959); "The Idea of the Workshop in Photography," *Aperture*, 9:4 (1961); "Edward Weston," *Infinity*, 13:2 (1964).

ARTICLES ABOUT: Daniel Masclet, "Ansel Adams," *Le Photographe*, 47:880 (1957); Joe Munroe, "For Adams, Always Tomorrow," *Infinity*, 13:2 (1964).

FRANCIS BRUGUIÈRE, born San Francisco, Cal., 1880. Studied painting in Europe. To New York, 1905. Met Alfred Stieglitz at "291"; became member of Photo-Secession; studied photography with photographer/painter, Frank Eugene. To San Francisco early 1900's; photographs exhibited "International Exhibition of Pictorial Photography," Albright Art Gallery, Buffalo, 1910. Began experiments with multiple exposure, 1912. First book published, *San Francisco*, 1918. Returned to New York, 1919; opened studio; became renowned for photographs of Theatre Guild Productions using stage lighting to photograph scenes of plays as audience experienced them. Worked in association with Lee Simonson and Robert Edmund Jones in production of stage settings in which light played important role in the drama. Worked in collaboration with Norman Bel Geddes on his book of stage design for Dante's Divine Comedy (foreword by Max Reinhardt), 1924. Produced and photographed film, "The Way," featuring Rosalinde Fuller and Sebastian Droste; film unfinished because of death of Droste, 1925. Began light abstractions, 1926. Exhibition of photographs and paintings, Art Center, N. Y., 1927, followed by exhibitions in Europe. To London; Der Sturm Galleries, Berlin, exhibited his photographs along with paintings; following exhibition, became honorary member, German Secession Group, 1928. Photographs in Deutsche Werkbund exhibition, "Film und Foto," Stuttgart, 1929. Film, "Light Rhythms" in collaboration with Oswell Blakeston (released in 1930) designed photographically using forms created by light. To London; worked in advertising with E. McKnight Kauffer; designed settings for Strindberg's plays, 1930. Visited New York, winter of 1932; produced series, often multiple exposures, of skyscrapers, while writing a "Pseudomorphic Film" of his impressions

of Manhattan under Depression and Prohibition for publication in *Close Up*. Produced photographic murals for British Pavilion at Paris Exhibition, 1937. Concentrated mainly on painting and sculpture until his death, 1945. The Focal Press of London produced large memorial exhibition of photographs, 1949; later shown at American Embassy. Retrospective exhibition "A Quest for Light" produced by George Eastman House, 1959.

BOOKS & CATALOGUES: *San Francisco*, San Francisco, 1918; *Photographs and Paintings by Francis Bruguière*, (Catalogue), 1927; *Beyond This Point* (by Lance Sieveking), London, 1929; *Few Are Chosen* (by Oswell Blakeston), London, 1932.

ARTICLE BY: "What 291 Means to Me," *Camera Work*, No. 47, (1914).

ARTICLES ABOUT: "Bruguière as Artist in Lights," *Boston Evening Transcript* (Apr 9, 1927); Oswell Blakeston, "Five Minutes with Francis Bruguière," *Close-Up*, 4:4 (1929); Harry A. Potamkin, "Francis Bruguière," *Transition* (Nov 1929); Harry A. Potamkin, "New Ideas for Animation," *Movie Makers* (Dec 1929); Oswell Blakeston, "Pseudomorphic Film," *Close-Up*, 10:1 (1933); "The Work of Kauffer and Bruguière," *Commercial Art and Industry* (Feb 1934); Walter Chappell, "Francis Bruguière," *Art in America*, 47:3 (1959).

WYNN BULLOCK, born Chicago, Illinois, 1902. To California at age five. Pursued musical education in Berlin, Milan, and Paris after attending Columbia University and University of West Virginia. In Europe became interested in the visual arts, particularly photography. Returned to United States, 1929; went into real estate business. In 1937 decided on photography as career; studied at Art Center School, Los Angeles, with Edward Kaminski. First one-man exhibition, Los Angeles County Museum of photographs using partial-reversal technique, 1941; work in this field led to basic patents in United States, Canada and Great Britain. During war produced illustrated instruction manuals for Armed Forces. Since 1949 principal interest has been serious creative photography, inspired by work of Moholy-Nagy, Alfred Stieglitz, and Edward Weston. Has published numerous articles for scientific journals. Became Head of Photography Department, San Francisco State College, 1959. Conducts workshops and photographic seminars.

BOOKS & CATALOGUES: *The Photograph as Poetry*, Pasadena, 1960; *Three Photograph-*

ers, Kalamazoo Art Center Bulletin No. 2, 1961; *Encyclopedia of Photography* ("Wynn Bullock"), 1963; *The Heritage of Edward Weston* (catalogue), University of Oregon, 1965.

ARTICLES BY: "Portfolio," *Aperture*, 2:3 (1953); "Partial Reversal Line," *Photographic Journal*, Vol. 95 (1955); "Partial Reversal Line Photography," *Medical and Biological Illustration*, 7:4 (1957); "A Lyrical Journey to Big Sur" (with Eric Barker), *Carmel Pacific Spectator Journal*, 13:6 (1957); "A New Concept in Photography," *Carmel Pacific Spectator Journal*, 15:1 (1958); "Time's Vital Relationship to Photography," *Contemporary Photographer*, 1:1 (1960); "The Fourth Dimension," *Photography*, 17:9 (1962).

ARTICLES ABOUT: C. Weston Booth, "Photographic Horizon," *U.S. Camera*, Vol. 9 (1946); Lew Parrella, "Wynn Bullock," *U.S. Camera Annual* (1956); George Baker, "Wynn Bullock and the Camera Eye," *The Argonaut Monthly* (June 1958); George Bush, "Thoughts on Wynn Bullock," *International Photo Technik*, No. 1 (1961); Nat Herz, "Wynn Bullock: A Critical Appreciation," *Infinity*, 10:9 (1961); Jonathan Williams, "The Eyes of Three Phantasts: Laughlin, Sommer, Bullock," *Aperture*, 9:3 (1961); "Nature Photography," *Pacific Discovery*, 6:3 (1963); George Bush, "The Nude in Nature," *International Photo Technik*, No. 2 (1963); "Bullock," *Photography Annual* (1965).

HARRY CALLAHAN, born Detroit, Michigan, 1912. Studied engineering, Michigan State University, two years. Began photographing, 1938. Strongly impressed by Ansel Adams, whose lectures he attended, 1941, and by life and work of Alfred Stieglitz. Worked as processor, photo lab, General Motors, 1944-45. Met Moholy-Nagy; began teaching at Institute of Design of the Illinois Institute of Technology, 1946; became head of photography department, 1949. Taught, Black Mountain College, Summer 1951. One-man exhibition, Kansas City Art Institute; received Graham Foundation award, 1956. Year's leave to photograph in France, 1957. One-man exhibition, George Eastman House, 1958. Became associate professor, Rhode Island School of Design, 1961; appointed professor, 1964. Exhibition with Robert Frank, Museum of Modern Art, 1962. "Ideas in Images," Worcester Art Museum, 1962; Hallmark Gallery exhibition, New York, 1964. Monograph published, *Photographs: Harry Callahan*, 1964.

BOOKS & CATALOGUES: *On My Eyes* (poetry by Larry Eigner), Highlands, N. C., 1960; *The Multiple Image* (introduction by Jonathan Williams), Chicago, 1961; *Encyclopedia of Photography* ("Harry Callahan"), 1963.

ARTICLES BY: "Learning Photography at the Institute of Design," (with Aaron Siskind) *Aperture*, 4:4 (1956); "Pattern," *ASMP Picture Annual* (1957).

ARTICLES ABOUT: Edward Steichen, "In and Out of Focus," *U.S. Camera Annual* (1949); "One in a Thousand," *Newsweek*, 37:19 (1951); "10 Photographs by Harry Callahan," *Gentry*, No. 20 (1956); David Ebin, "Harry Callahan: Conventional Subjects Become Extraordinary Photographs," *Modern Photography*, 21:2 (1957); Robert Creeley, "Harry Callahan: A Note," *Black Mountain Review*, No. 7 (1957); Minor White, "The Photographs of Harry Callahan," *Aperture*, 6:2 (1958); Willy Rotzler, "Harry M. Callahan: 7 Farbaufnahmen," *Du*, 22:251 (1962); "Photographs by Harry Callahan," *Choice*, No. 2 (1962).

HENRI CARTIER-BRESSON, born Chanteloup, France, 1908. Early interest in cinema and photography. Studied painting with André Lhote; literature and painting at Cambridge, England, 1928. Early influences, Man Ray and Atget; began photographing seriously, 1930. With Leica camera, traveled Europe, exhibited Madrid, Mexico City (with Manuel Alvarez Bravo), New York (with Walker Evans). Returned to France, 1936; worked with Jean Renoir on films. Documentary film on medical aid, Spanish Civil War, 1937. Began reportage for periodicals and newspapers. Drafted, outbreak of Second World War; captured in 1940. Third attempt to escape from German prison camp successful. Began organizing French underground photographic units to document German occupation and retreat. Made film "Le Retour" for U.S. Office of War Information, 1945. Following one-man exhibition at Museum of Modern Art, 1946, spent year traveling and photographing in United States. With Robert Capa, George Rodger, David Seymour, founded Magnum Photos (international photographic co-operative), 1947. To Far East, 1948-50. Exhibition, Art Institute of Chicago, 1954. Retrospective exhibition, Pavillon de Marsan at Louvre, Paris, 1955, circulated throughout Europe, Japan, United States; now in permanent collection of Bibliothèque Nationale, Paris. Société Française de Photographie award, 1959. Third Overseas Press Club award for China coverage, 1960. To Cuba, 1963. Photo-essay, "Irish Time," *Horizon,* Autumn, 1965.

BOOKS & CATALOGUES: *The Photographs of Henri Cartier-Bresson* (essays by Lincoln Kirstein & Beaumont Newhall), 1947 (new edition with different selection of plates and new essays, *Photographs by Cartier-Bresson,* 1963); *Les danses a Bali* (text by Antonin Artaud, commentaries by Béryl de Zoete), Paris, 1954; *D'Une Chine a l'Antre* (preface by Jean P. Sartre), Paris, 1954 (N. Y. edition, text by Han Suyin, 1956); *The Europeans,* 1955; *The People of Moscow,* 1955; *Encyclopedia of Photography* ("Henri Cartier-Bresson," by Arthur Goldsmith), 1963; *China as Photographed by Henri Cartier-Bresson* (text by Cartier-Bresson & Barbara Brakeley Miller), 1964.

ARTICLES BY: "The Moment of Truth," *Camera,* 33:4 (1954); "The Deciding Eye," *Lilliput,* 44:3 (1959); "One Man Shows are Best," *Infinity,* 8:10 (1959).

ARTICLES ABOUT: James T. Soby, "The Art of Poetic Accident—The Photographs of Cartier-Bresson & Helen Levitt," *Minicam,* 6:7 (1943); Lincoln Kirstein, "A Great Book of Great Photographs," *Infinity,* 8:11 (1952); Daniel Masclet, "Les maitres de la caméra," *Le Photographe,* No. 783 (1953); Nancy Newhall, "Controversy and the Creative Concepts," *Aperture,* 2:2 (1953); Beaumont Newhall, "The Instant Vision of Henri Cartier-Bresson," *Camera,* 34:10 (1955); Lucien Lorelle, "Du salon national a l'exposition de Cartier-Bresson," *Le Photographe,* 5:851 (1955); Byron Dobell, "A Conversation with Henri Cartier-Bresson," *Popular Photography,* 41:3 (1957); Byron Dobell, "Magnum," *Popular Photography,* 41:3 (1957); Tom Hopkinson, "Henri Cartier-Bresson," *Photography,* (London) 12:1 (1957); "Henri Cartier-Bresson," *British Journal of Photography,* 104:5044 (1957); Judith Holden, "The Disciplines of Henri Cartier-Bresson," *Infinity,* 10:2 (1961); Dorothy Norman, "Stieglitz and Cartier-Bresson," *Saturday Review,* 45:38 (1962); Ralph Hattersley, "Photographs by Cartier-Bresson," *Infinity,* 12:8 (1963).

ALVIN LANGDON COBURN, born Boston, Mass., 1882. Introduced to photography by F. Holland Day, his cousin, 1890. First exhibited, Boston, 1898. First one-man exhibition, London Salon, 1900. Founding member Photo-Secession, 1902. Elected to "Linked Ring," 1903. Portfolio appeared in *Camera Work;* to London; met George Bernard Shaw, 1904. Illustrated edition of H. G. Wells' short stories, *Door in the Wall,*

1905. One-man exhibition, Royal Photographic Society, (catalogue introduction by George Bernard Shaw); began collaboration with Henry James, 1906. Exhibited at "International Exhibition of Pictorial Photography," Albright Gallery, Buffalo, 1910. Trip to American West, 1911. Returned to London, 1912. Met Ezra Pound, 1913. Exhibition of Vortographs, (first intentionally abstract photographs) 1917. Second one-man exhibition, Royal Photographic Society, 1924. Elected Honorary Fellow, Royal Photographic Society, 1931. Became naturalized British subject, 1932. Robert Louis Stevenson's *Edinburgh—Picturesque Notes* published, illustrated with photographs by Coburn from 1905-50. Third one-man exhibition, Royal Photographic Society, 1957. Address "Photographic Adventures," at Univ. of Reading, 1962. *A Portfolio of Sixteen Photographs by Alvin Langdon Coburn,* with text by Nancy Newhall, published by George Eastman House, 1962. Died 1966.

BOOKS & CATALOGUES: *The Novels and Tales of Henry James* (illustrated by Coburn), 1908; *London,* London, 1909; *Mark Twain* (Archibald Henderson), London, 1910; *New York* (foreword by H. G. Wells), London, 1910; *The Cloud* (P. B. Shelley), Los Angeles, 1912; *Men of Mark,* London, 1913; *Pictures by Alvin Langdon Coburn* (catalogue with statements by Coburn and W. Howe Downes), London, 1913; *London* (G. K. Chesterton), London, 1914; *Moor Park, Rickmansworth,* London, 1914; *Vortographs and Paintings by Alvin Langdon Coburn* (catalogue essay by Ezra Pound), London, 1917; *The Book of Harlech,* Harlech, 1920; *More Men of Mark,* London, 1922.

ARTICLES BY: "American Photographs in London," *Photo Era,* 6:1 (1901); "Modern Photography at the English Art Club," *Photographic News,* Vol. 51 (1907); "Astrological Portraiture," *Photographic Journal,* Vol. 63 (1923); "Photography and the Quest of Beauty," *Photographic Journal,* Vol. 64 (1924); "Bernard Shaw, Photographer, *Photoguide Magazine,* (Dec. 1950); "Frederick H. Evans," *Image,* Vol. 2 (1953); "Retrospect," *Photographic Journal,* Vol. 98 (1958); "Photographic Adventures," *Photographic Journal,* Vol. 102 (1962).

ARTICLES ABOUT: Sidney Allan, "The Exhibition of the Photo-Secession," *Photographic Times-Bulletin,* Vol. 36 (1904); Anthony Guest, "Mr. A. L. Coburn's Vortographs at the Camera Club," *Amateur Photographer,* Vol. 60 (1917); J. Dudley Johnston, "Phases in the Development of Pictorial Photography in Britain and America," *Photographic Journal*, Vol. 63 (1923); Norman Hall, "Alvin Langdon Coburn," *Photography*, 16:10 (1961).

ROBERT DEMACHY, born 1859, Paris banker, came to photography from drawing. Elected member Société Français de Photographie, 1882. Exhibitor and member of jury, 1st International Exhibition of Photography, Palais des Beaux-Arts, 1892. Participated in first Exhibition of Photographic Art, Photo-Club de Paris; began work with gum prints, 1894. Exhibition of gum prints, Photo-Club de Paris, 1895. Published with Alfred Maskell, *Photo-Aquatint or the Gum Bichromate Process*, London, 1897. First exhibition, Royal Photographic Society, 1901; member of General Committee of the Photographic Salon. Commissioned as a member of the Advisory Committee for France, Hamburg Jubilee Exhibition, 1903. One-man exhibition, Royal Photographic Society, 1904. Elected an. Honorary Member, Royal Photographic Society; elected member of "Linked Ring," 1905. First oil prints; published with C. Puyo, *Les Procédes Photographie d'Argent*, Paris, 1906. Exhibited oil prints, Royal Photographic Society, 1907. Introduced a modern transfer method for oil printing, 1911. Ceased photographic activity at outbreak of war, 1914. Retrospective exhibition of gum prints with C. Puyo, 1931. Died 1937.

ARTICLES BY: "A Few Notes on the Gum Bichromate Process," *Photographic Times*, 30:4 (1898); "Gum Bichromate Prints at the Salon," *Photographic Times*, 30:8 (1898); "What Difference is There Between a Good Photograph and an Artistic Photograph?" *Camera Notes*, 3:2 (1899); "Artistic Photography in France," *Photograms of the Year* (1899-1904); "Monsieur Demachy's Opening Address," *Photographic Journal*, N. S. 25:8 (1901); "The American New School of Photography in Paris," *Camera Notes*, 5:1 (1901-2); "The Training of the Photographer in View of Pictorial Results," *American Annual of Photography and Photographic Times Almanac for 1901;* Address in *Photographic Journal*, 47:7 (1907), "Demachy and English Photographic Art," (with commentaries by G. B. Shaw, F. H. Evans, F. M. Sutcliffe), *Camera Work*, No. 18 (1907); "Three Years' Experience with the Oil Printing Process," *Photographic Journal*, 50:7 (1910); "The Oil Transfer Process," *Photographic Journal*, 51:6 (1911).

ARTICLES ABOUT: "The Exhibition of Works of M. Demachy," *Photography*, 13:655 (1901); "Behind the Scenes," *Photography*,

15:756 (1903); Joseph Keiley, "Robert Demachy," *Camera Work*, No. 5 (1904); R. Child Bayley, "Oil Printing," *Photography*, 23:970 (1907).

PETER H. EMERSON, born Cuba, 1856, of an American father and British mother. Spent youth in Mass. To England, 1869; studied medicine. Bought photographic equipment; received instruction from E. Griffiths, 1881-82. Joined Royal Photographic Society; first photograph exhibited at Pall Mall, 1882. "Amateur Photographers At Home" competition and first medal at Bond Street Amateur Photographic exhibition, 1885. Abandoned medical career, 1886. Published *Naturalistic Photography*, defending photography as an independent art, 1889. In the midst of resultant controversy, published *The Death of Naturalistic Photography*, doubting validity of photography as an art form, 1890. Withdrew remaining copies of *Naturalistic Photography* for revision, 1890. Continued work; received Royal Photographic Society Progress Medal for work in artistic photography, 1895. Published expurgated and expanded third edition of *Naturalistic Photography*, 1899. Retrospective exhibition, Royal Photographic Society, 1900. Died Falmouth, 1936.

BOOKS & CATALOGUES: *Life and Landscape on the Norfolk Broads* (with T. F. Goodall), London, 1886; *Idyls of the Norfolk Broads* (portfolio of 12 photogravures), London, 1886; *The Centenary Edition of Isaac Walton's Complete Angler*, London, 1887; *Pictures from Life in Field and Fen* (portfolio of 20 photogravures), London, 1888; *Pictures of East Anglian Life*, London, 1888; *Wild Life on a Tidal Water* (with T. F. Goodall), London, 1890; *On English Lagoons*, London, 1893; *Birds, Beasts, and Fishes of the Norfolk Broadland*, London, 1895.

ARTICLES BY: "Photography A Pictorial Art," *Amateur Photographer*, Vol. 3 (1886); "Photography," *Amateur Photographer*, Vol. 3 (1886); "Dr. P. H. Emerson's Rejoinder," *The Photographic Art Journal*, N. S. Vol. 3 (1890); "Our English Letter— O. G. Rejlander," *American Amateur Photographer*, Vol. 2 (1890); "Dr. Emerson's Latest on Focussing," *Photographic Art Journal*, N. S. Vol. 3 (1890); "Mrs. Cameron," *Sun Artists*, No. 5 (1890); "Tone Reproduction and its Limitations," (a letter), *Photographic Art Journal*, Vol. 57 (1917).

ARTICLES ABOUT: Philip Newman, "Imagining and Imaging," *Photographic Art*

Journal, N. S. Vol. 3 (1890); "Three Important Pictures," *Photographic Art Journal*, N. S. Vol. 3 (1890); T. R. Dallmeyer, "Dr. P. H. Emerson," *Photogram*, 6:72 (1899).

ROBERT FRANK, born Zurich, Switzerland, 1924. Began photography, 1942; apprenticeship with Hermann Eidenbenz in Basel and Michael Wolgansinger in Zurich. Still photographer for motion picture company, Zurich. To United States, 1947; fashion photographs for *Harper's Bazaar;* encouraged by Alexey Brodovitch. South America for six months, late 1948; traveled in Peru and Bolivia. Photographs from trip first published, *Neuf*, 1952; later in book form with additional photographs by Werner Bischof and Pierre Verger. Free-lance reportage; photographs for *Fortune, Junior Bazaar, Life, Look, McCalls*. England, France, Spain, Wales in 1949; photographed Welsh miners, London business people and the city. Returned, New York, early 1951; free-lanced again with some advertising photographs, particularly for *The New York Times*. Met Edward Steichen, accompanied him to Europe for collection trip leading to exhibition "Post-War European Photographers," 1953. First European photographer to receive Guggenheim Fellowship, 1955. Photographed throughout United States, 1955-56; subsequent publication of this work in book, *Les Americains*. Began film making, 1958. "Pull My Daisy," co-produced and filmed with painter Alfred Leslie, narrated by Jack Kerouac, 1959, won first prize at San Francisco Film Festival; "The Sin of Jesus," story by Isaac Babel, 1960; request showing at Spoleto Film Festival. To Europe briefly, 1961. "OK End Here," based on original story by Margaret Maggid, 1963. In production, 1965-66, film based in part on Allen Ginsberg's narrative poem, "Kaddish."

BOOKS & CATALOGUES: *Les Americans*, (text by Alain Bosquet) Paris, 1958, (N. Y. edition, *The Americans*, text by Jack Kerouac, 1959); *Pull My Daisy*, (with Jack Kerouac and Alfred Leslie) 1961.

ARTICLE BY: "Ben James: Story of a Welsh Miner," (portfolio) *U.S. Camera Annual* (1955).

ARTICLES ABOUT: "Robert Frank," *Camera*, 28:12 (1949); Gotthard Schuh, "A Letter Addressed to Robert Frank," (with portfolio by Frank) *Camera*, 36:8 (1957); Walker Evans, "Robert Frank," *U.S. Camera Annual* (1958); Willy Rotzler, "Der Photograph Robert Frank," *Du*, 22:251 (1962);

"Photographs by Robert Frank," *Choice*, No. 2 (1962).

DOROTHEA LANGE, born Hoboken, N. J. 1895. Worked briefly for Arnold Genthe, ca. 1915. Studied under Clarence H. White, Columbia University, 1917-18. Opened portrait studio, San Francisco, 1919. Became member "Group *f*64," 1934. Began photographing the jobless during Depression. Made photograph, "White Angel Breadline," 1933. Met Paul Taylor, University of California economics professor, who had been engaged by State of California to report on migrant labor, 1934; became his research assistant, functioning as photographer. Joined Rural Resettlement Administration (later Farm Security Administration) as photographer under Roy Stryker, 1935. With Taylor, worked on and published *An American Exodus: A Record of Human Erosion*. Guggenheim Fellow, 1941; resigned fellowship after Pearl Harbor to photograph internment of Japanese-Americans. During war continued to photograph, working with Ansel Adams and several government agencies including Office of War Information. Covered initial United Nations Conference, San Francisco, 1945; became ill before completion of project. Health restored, 1951; began again to photograph. Produced several photo-essays including "Three Mormon Towns," 1954; "The Public Defender," 1955; "Death of a Valley," (with Pirkle Jones), 1956-57; 1958 Asian portfolio published in 1964 *Photography Annual* entitled "Remembrance of Asia." To Venezuela, 1960; Egypt, 1963. Last and one of largest essays, "The American Farm Woman" completed early in 1965, to be published by Amon Carter Museum of Western Art. Conducted seminars and workshops at San Francisco Art Institute. Died Oct. 11, 1965. Retrospective exhibition, Museum of Modern Art, January 25-March 22, 1966.

BOOKS & CATALOGUES: *Land of the Free* (by Archibald Macleish), 1938; *Encyclopedia of Photography* ("Dorothea Lange" by Willard Morgan), 1963; *A Piece of Lettuce* by George P. Elliott), 1964; *Dorothea Lange* (catalogue, essay by George P. Elliott) 1966. *The American Country Woman*, 1967.

ARTICLES BY: "Fortune's Wheel," (with Ansel Adams) *Fortune*, 31:2 (1945); "Miss Lange's Counsel: Photographer Advises Use of Picture Themes," *New York Times*, (Dec 7, 1952); "The Assignment I'll Never Forget: Migrant Mother," *Popular Photography*, 46:2 (1960); "The American Farm Woman," *Harvester World*, 51:11 (1960); Postscript on Stryker by Lange and others in "Focus on Stryker," *Popular Photography*, 51:3 (1962); "Remembrance of Asia," *Photography Annual* (1964).

ARTICLES ABOUT: Willard Van Dyke, "The Photographs of Dorothea Lange," *Camera Craft*, 41:10 (1934); "Lucretia Penny: Peapicker's Child," *Survey Graphic*, 24:7 (1935); Pare Lorentz, "Camera With a Purpose," *U.S. Camera Annual* (1941); Daniel Dixon, "Dorothea Lange," *Modern Photography* 16:12 (1952); Herm Lenz, "Interview with Three Greats," *U.S. Camera*, 18:8 (1955); Henry Holmes Smith, "Image, Obscurity & Interpretation," *Aperture*, 5:4 (1957); Nat Herz, "Dorothea Lange in Perspective," *Infinity*, 12:4 (1963); W. Eugene Smith, "One Whom I Admire, Dorothea Lange 1895-1965," *Popular Photography*, 58:2 (1966).

LÁSZLÓ MOHOLY-NAGY, born Barsebarsod, Hungary, 1895; law studies to 1915; interrupted by service in Hungarian army, 1st World War. During recovery from wounds, 1917, began drawing; joined "MA" group in Budapest; helped found review "Jelenkor." Left army and finished law studies; began painting, studied old masters, 1918. Increasingly sympathetic to work of German Expressionists and Russian avantgarde; to Vienna, then Berlin, 1920. First exhibition, 1921. First photograms, 1922. Joined Bauhaus, Weimar (later Dessau), 1923; head of metal workshop; later head of preparatory course. Collaborated with Bauhaus faculty on murals, ballet and stage design, light and color experiments, typography and layout. With Walter Gropius planned, edited, designed "Bauhaus Bücher," including two of his own books stating visual and pedagogical principles. Resigned from Bauhaus, 1928. Collaborator on Deutsche Werkbund exhibition "Film und Foto," Stuttgart, 1929. Stage designer, Berlin; continued film experiments, photograms and sound-film combinations including "Light Display, Black, White and Grey," 1931. To London after year in Paris and Amsterdam; created effects for H. G. Wells' film "Things to Come," 1935. One-man photographic exhibition, Delphic Studios, N. Y., 1931. Exhibition, Royal Photographic Society, London, 1936. Became first director of New Bauhaus, Chicago, later Institute of Design, 1937. Died 1946.

BOOKS & CATALOGUES: *Horizont*, Vienna, 1921; *Buch Neuer Künstler*, (with L. Kassak) Vienna, 1922; *Die Bühne in Bauhaus*, (with O. Schlemmer) Munich, 1925; *Malerei, Photographie, Film, Munich*, 1925; *Von Material zu Architektur*, Munich, 1928

(revised English edition, *The New Vision*, 1928, revised and enlarged, 1946); *60 Fotos*, (edited by Franz Roh) Berlin, 1930; *The Street Markets of London* (Mary Benedetta), London, 1936; "Photography" in *A Pageant of Photography*, San Francisco, 1940; "Photography" in *Encyclopedia of the Arts*, 1946; *Moholy-Nagy's Experiment in Totality* (S. Moholy-Nagy), 1950; *Vision in Motion*, Chicago, 1947 (revised 1961).

ARTICLES BY: "La Photographie ce qu'elle était ce qu'elle devra etre," *Cahiers d'Art*, 4:1 (1929); "Now Photography Revolutionizes Vision," *The Listener*, Nov. 8, 1933; "Photographers of Today," *Modern Photography Annual* (1935/36); "New Approach to Fundamentals of Design," *More Business*, 3:11 (1938); "Surrealism and the Photographer," *The Complete Photographer*, No. 52 (1943); "Space-Time and the Photographer," *American Annual of Photography* (1943); "The Coming World of Photography," *Popular Photography*, 14:2 (1944); "Photography in the Study of Design," *American Annual of Photography*, (1945); "In Defense of Abstract Art," *Journal of Aesthetics and Art Criticism*, 4:2 (1945).

ARTICLES ABOUT: Beaumont Newhall, "The Photographs of Moholy-Nagy," *Kenyon Review*, 3:3 (1941); "Reunion in Chicago: An Investigation into the Work of Moholy-Nagy," *Minicam Photography*, 8:4 (1945); "Message in a Bottle," *Time*, 47:7 (1946); Thomas B. Hess, "Moholy-Nagy," *Art News*, 46:4 (1947).

MAN RAY, born Philadelphia, Pennsylvania, 1890; settled with family in New York, 1897. Completed formal education, high school, 1909; courses in architectural drawing and engineering. Began variety of jobs in layout, lettering, typography; painting and drawing independently. Studied drawing informally, Freer Center, New York. Met Alfred Stieglitz, became frequent visitor at "291," 1910. First exhibition paintings, 1912. First one-man exhibition, paintings, Daniel Gallery, New York, 1915; met Marcel Duchamp; began work in collage, constructions. Participated in quasi-Dadaist group in New York with Duchamp, Francis Picabia and others, 1916-17. Began photography in 1920. To Paris, 1921; first "Rayograph," 1922, published 12 Rayographs, *Champs Délicieux*, preface by Tristan Tzara. Member of Paris Dadaist group. Professional photographer; fashion illustration and portraiture. First Paris exhibition of paintings and photographs, Librairie Six, 1922. Filmed: "Le Retour à la Raison,"

1923, "Emak Bakia," 1926, "L'Etoile de Mer," 1926, "Les Mysteres du Chateau de Dé," 1929. Member of Surrealist group, 1924; first exhibition Gallerie Surréaliste, 1926. Began solarization techniques, 1929. To New York, for photographic commission, 1936. Returned to United States, 1940; active as painter-photographer, exhibited and lectured, California, 1940-50. Returned to Paris. Concentrates on painting, continues personal photographic work. Exhibition, "L'Oeuvre Photographique," Bibliothèque Nationale, Paris, 1962. Group exhibition, "Pop Por Pop Corn Corny," Jean Larcade Art Contemporain, Paris, 1965.

BOOKS & CATALOGUES: Les champs délicieux (preface by Tristan Tzara), Paris, 1922; G. Ribemont-Dessaignes, Man Ray, Paris, 1924; Revolving Doors, 1916-1917, Paris, 1926; Souvenirs de Kiki, Paris, 1929; Electricite, Paris, 1931; Photographs by Man Ray, 1920-1934 (edited by James Thrall Soby), Hartford, 1934; Facile (with Paul Eluard), Paris, 1935; Les Mains libres (with Paul Eluard), Paris, 1937; La photographie n'est pas l'art (preface by André Breton), Paris, 1937; To Be Continued Unnoticed, Beverly Hills, 1948; Alphabet for Adults, Beverly Hills, 1948; Man Ray: l'oeuvre photographique (catalogue with introduction by Jean Adhémar), Paris, 1962; Portraits (introduction by L. Fritz Gruber) Gutersloh, 1963; Self Portrait, Boston, 1963; Man Ray: 12 Photographs 1921-1928, Stuttgart, 1963.

ARTICLES BY: "A l'heure de l'observatoire . . . les amoureux," Cahiers d'Art, 10:5/6 (1935); "On Photography," Commercial Art, Vol. 18 (1935); "Sur le réalisme photographique," Cahiers d'Art, 10:5/6 (1935) "Picasso, photographe," Cahiers d'Art 12: 6/7 (1937); "Is Photography Necessary?" Modern Photography, 21:11 (1957).

ARTICLES ABOUT: Robert Desnos, "The Work of Man Ray," Transition, No. 15 (1929); C. Bauer, "Photography: Man Ray and Paul Strand," Arts Weekly, (May 1932); André Thevenet, "Man Ray," Camera, 31:10 (1952); Robert Melville, "Man Ray in London," Arts, (June 1959); Morris Gordon, "Man Ray, The Fiery Elf," Infinity, 11:11 (1962); William Copley, "Man Ray: The Dada of Us All," Portfolio, No. 7 (1963); Carl Belz, "Man Ray and New York Dada" Art Journal, 23:3 (1964).

HENRY PEACH ROBINSON, born Ludlow, in Shropshire, England, 1830. First discovered photography through advertisement for Talbot's Pencil of Nature, 1844. Trained as a painter; learned daguerreotype process,

1850. Exhibited paintings at Royal Academy, 1852. Opened studio at Leamington; exhibited three photographs, "Mr. Werner as Richelieu," (first effort at pictorial photography) at Manchester Art Treasures exhibition; elected member Photographic Society of London, 1857. Advertised his business for sale; "Fading Away" made in April 1858, (from five separate negatives, first of long series of composite photographs shown at Crystal Palace; made series of photographs of story "Red Riding Hood," 1858. First photographic exhibition medal, 1860. Elected member Council of the Royal Photographic Society; first appearance of "Bringing Home the May," 1862. Sold business, 1864. Built new studio in Tunbridge Wells with Nelson K. Cherrill, 1868. Became a major spokesman for pictorial tradition with publication of Picture Making by Photography, 1884, based heavily on Burnet's Treatise on Painting and Ruskin's Modern Painters. Vice-President, Royal Photographic Society. 1887. Died 1901.

BOOKS & CATALOGUES: Warwickshire Illustrated, A History of Remarkable Places in the County of Warwick, London, 1857; Pictorial Effect in Photography, London, 1869; The Art and Practice of Silver Printing (with Capt. William Abney), London, 1881; Picture Making by Photography, 1884; Letters on Landscape Photography, London, 1888.

ARTICLES BY: "Retouching and Exhibitions," Photographic News, 16:699 (1872); "Naturalism and Photography," Philadelphia Photographer, No. 286 (1886); "Art or Accident," International Annual of Anthony's Photographic Bulletin, Vol. 1 (1888); "Fog or Focus." International Annual of Anthony's Photographic Bulletin, Vol. 2 (1889); "Impossible Photography," Photographic Quarterly, 3:9 (1891); "Musings on Some Recent Mistakes," Photography Annual (1891); "The Study of Nature," Photography, 3:113 (1891); "The Transition Period," Photographic Quarterly, 3:9 (1891); "Individuality in Photography," Anthony's Photographic Bulletin, 23:17 (1892); "The Application of Art to Photography," Anthony's Photographic Bulletin, 23:3+ (1892); "Expression in Landscape," American Annual of Photography and Photographic Times Almanac (1895); "Autobiographical Sketches," Photographic Times, 29:2+ (1897-98).

ARTICLES ABOUT: Thomas Sutton, "On Some of the Uses and Abuses of Photography," Photographic Notes, Vol. 8 (1863); George Bruce, "Retouching the Negative," (letter), *Photographic News*, 16:700 (1872); "The Late H. P. Robinson," *Photogram*, 8:88 (1901); Charles Hastings, "H. P. Robinson and His Work," *Focus*, 2:31 (1904).

ARTHUR SIEGEL, born Detroit, Mich., 1913. Began photographing, 1927. Majored in Sociology at University of Mich., and Wayne State Univ. Experimental, documentary photography in the 1930's; scholarship to the New Bauhaus. Early 1940's, Office of War Information; 3½ years in Air Force. Invited to organize four-year course and graduate photography department at New Bauhaus, 1946. Subsequent courses widely influenced photography and photographic education. Since 1950 has written, lectured, and taught; working photojournalist for many national publications; continuing work in experimental still and motion picture photography. One-man exhibition, Art Institute of Chicago, 1954; George Eastman House, 1955. Edited, *Chicago's Famous Buildings*, 1965.

CATALOGUE: *Six States Photography* (exhibition at Milwaukee Art Inst., critique by Siegel) Milwaukee, 1950.

ARTICLES BY: Statement in *U.S. Camera Annual* (1941); Statement in *U.S. Camera Annual* (1951); "Creative Color Photography," *Modern Photography*, 16:1, 2, 3 (1952); "Anonymous Art and Choice: The Photographer's World," *Aperture*, 11:2 (1964); "Basic Approaches to the Education of a Photographer," (paper presented at Symposium on the Teaching of Photography, Society for Photographic Education, Chicago 1965.)

ARTICLE ABOUT: "Experiment in Color," *American Annual of Photography* (1952).

AARON SISKIND, born New York City, 1903. Received BSS, College of the City of N. Y., 1926; began teaching English in NYC public schools. First experience with camera on trip to Bermuda, 1930. Active interest in photography; joined Film & Photo League; began work on "Tabernacle City" document, 1932. Left Photo League; "Architecture of Bucks County" document, 1935. Rejoined Photo League; organized Feature Group that produced "Harlem Document," "Dead End: the Bowery," "Portrait of a Tenement," "St. Joseph's House: the Catholic Worker Movement," 1936. Exhibited "Tabernacle City" at Photo League, 1941; left the League shortly thereafter; first exhibited at Museum of Modern Art. Summer on Martha's Vineyard; began to work on flat plane with organic objects in geometrical setting, 1943. Summer in Gloucester; subject matter as such ceased to be of primary importance, 1944. First exhibition at Egan Gallery, 1947; broadened acquaintance with N. Y. painters and their work. Visited Chicago, met Harry Callahan, 1948. Sabbatical leave from teaching, 1949; went West; spent some time with Frederick Sommer in Arizona; resigned teaching position. Taught photography at Black Mountain College with Callahan, 1951. Directed advanced students at Institute of Design, Illinois Inst. of Tech., in development of definitive study of architecture of Adler and Sullivan, 1952. Summer in Mexico, 1955. Publication of first book, *Aaron Siskind: Photographs*, New York, 1959. Appointed Head of Photography, Institute of Design; summer in Mexico, 1961. Co-editor of *Choice*, (magazine of poetry and photography) 1962. Four months in Italy, seven weeks in France; founding member of Society for Photographic Education, 1963. Member of the Board of Trustees of the Gallery of Contemporary Art, Chicago, 1964. Comprehensive exhibition (200 photographs) George Eastman House; monograph published, *Aaron Siskind Photographer*, George Eastman House, 1965. Guggenheim Fellowship, 1966.

BOOKS & CATALOGUES: *Photographs by Professors* (catalogue, notes by Lew Parella), 1960; *Spring of the Thief* (by John Logan), 1963.

ARTICLES BY: "What is Modern Photography?" *American Photography*, 45:3 (1951); Review of *The Decisive Moment* by H. Cartier-Bresson, *Saturday Review* (Dec 20, 1952); "Accidents of Time . . ." *Art Photography* (June 1954); "The Essential Photographic Act," *Art News*, 54:8 (1955); "Learning Photography at the Institute of Design," (with Harry Callahan) *Aperture*, 4:4 (1956); "Notes on the Photographic Act," *Spectrum*, 6:2 (1956); "It Makes No Difference . . ." *Modern Photography*, 22:2 (1958).

ARTICLES ABOUT: Beaumont Newhall, "Dual Focus," *Art News*, 45:4 (1946); Hilda L. Wilson, "The Camera's New Eye," *Mademoiselle* (Dec 1947); Minna Lippmann, "Chilmark Summer Visitor Expresses Abstract in his Unusual Photographs," *New Bedford Standard Times* (Sept 4, 1948); Elizabeth Timberman, "Aaron Siskind," *Photo Notes* (ca. June 1948); Hilda L. Wilson, "Aaron Siskind," (typescript introduction to 1948 exhibition, Egan Gallery, N. Y.); Elaine de Kooning, "The Photographs of Aaron Siskind," (typescript introduction to 1951 exhibition, Egan Gallery); Jacob Deschin, "Two Ways of Seeing," *Modern Photography*, 15:5 (1951); Bruce Downes, "Let's Talk Photography," *Popular Photography*, 29:1 (1951); Jacob Deschin, "Siskind's World: Strange Pictures Found on Decayed Surfaces," *New York Times* (Feb 11, 1951); Georgine Oeri, "Aaron Siskind: 'Abstract' Photography," *Graphis*, 7:3 (1951) Fritz Neugass, "Aaron Siskind," *Camera*, 32:1 (1955); Beaumont Newhall, "Photographing the Reality of the Abstract," *New Directions*, No. 15 (1955); Jonathan Williams, "Aaron Siskind/Eight Signs," *Black Mountain Review*, No. 5 (1955); Minor White, review of *Aaron Siskind: Photographs*, *Aperture*, 7:3 (1959); Walter Chappell, review of *Aaron Siskind: Photographs*, *Image*, 9:2 (1960); Bill Coss, "Aaron Siskind: Humanity in Abstraction," *Metronome*, 78:1 (1961); "Aaron Siskind," *Foto*, 28:2 (1966).

HENRY HOLMES SMITH, born Bloomington, Illinois, 1909. Attended Illinois State University, 1927-29, 1930-32; School of the Art Institute, Chicago, 1929-30; received BS degree, Ohio State Univ., 1933. Attended the New Bauhaus, Chicago; met and was strongly influenced by Moholy-Nagy; taught photography workshop with Gyorgy Kepes, 1937-38. Wrote article for *Minicam*, "Solarization Process," at suggestion of Moholy-Nagy, 1939. Offered position as associate editor, *Minicam*, 1940. Served with Air Service Groups, United States Army, 1942-45. Returned to Bloomington, Indiana, 1946; in collaboration with Nathan Lerner began experimentation with light interceptors and photographic possibilities of color synthesis without reference to natural or local color of objects, experiments which have continued to the present. To support this experimentation, took newspaper editorial position, Feb. 1947. Instructor in photography, Dept. of Fine Arts and Audio-Visual Center, Indiana University, Sept. 1947. Associate editor, *College Art Journal*, 1955-64. Founding member of Society for Photographic Education, 1963. Promoted to full professor, 1965. Has organized several workshops on interpretation of photographs and the teaching of photography.

BOOKS & CATALOGUES: *Photographer's Choice*, ("The Unseen Photographer") Bloomington, Ind., 1959; *Invitational Teaching Conference at the George Eastman House 1962* ("A Pilot Regional Workshop and Conference on Photography Instruction") Rochester, N. Y., 1962; *Aaron*

Siskind Photographer (with essays by H. H. Smith and T. B. Hess, edited with introduction by N. Lyons), Rochester, N. Y., 1965.

ARTICLES BY: "Photographs and Public," *Aperture*, 2:3 (1953); "The First Indiana University Photography Workshop," *Aperture*, 5:1 (1957); "Two for the Photojournalist," *Aperture*, 8:4 (1960); "The Photography of Jerry N. Uelsmann," *Contemporary Photographer*, 5:1 (1964).

W. EUGENE SMITH, born Wichita, Kansas, 1918. News photographer at fifteen; photographic scholarship to Notre Dame University, 1936, left early in 1937. Photographer for *Newsweek*, 1937-38. Joined Black Star Agency, did first stories for *American Magazine, Colliers, Harper's Bazaar*, and *Life*. Retainer contract with *Life*, 1939-41. War correspondent for *Popular Photography* and other Ziff-Davis publications, 1942-44; for *Life*, 1944-45. Covered thirteen invasions, made twenty-three combat air missions, was wounded at Okinawa, 1945. Returned to photojournalism, and to *Life*, 1947; produced a number of photoessays including "Country Doctor," 1948; "Spanish Village," 1951; "Man of Mercy," (Albert Schweitzer in Africa) 1954. Resigned from *Life* and joined Magnum Photos, 1955. Began photo-essay, "Pittsburgh" which was completed with assistance of two Guggenheim Fellowships, 1956 and 1957. Commissioned to photograph in color, contemporary American architecture by American Institute of Architects, 1956. Resigned from Magnum Photos; appeared with Dan Weiner on television program, "The Press and the People," produced nationally by WGBH-TV, Boston, 1959. Commissioned by Japanese industrial firm, Hitachi, Ltd., to photograph its operations, 1961; again contributed to *Life* with Hitachi photo-essay, "Colossus of the Orient," 1963.

ARTICLES BY: "W. Eugene Smith Talks About Lighting," *Popular Photography*, 39:5 (1956); "The Walk to Paradise Garden!" *Croton-Harmon News* (Mar 31, 1955; republished in *Gentry*, No. 22, 1957); Statement in "Photographs and Truth," *Infinity*, 7:4 (1958); Statement in "How They Think About the Picture Story," *Popular Photography*, 44:6 (1959); "The Photojournalist," *Infinity*, 8:5 (1959); Review of *Images of War, Infinity*, 13:7 (1964).

ARTICLES ABOUT: Peter Martin, "The Kid Who Lives Photography," *Popular Photography*, 13:1 (1943); John Whiting, "Camera on a Carrier," *Popular Photography*, 14:6 (1944); Notes on the W. E. Smith meeting at the Photo League, *Photo Notes* (Nov 1947); Jacquelyn Judge, "W. Eugene Smith's Spain," *Modern Photography*, 15:12 (1951); "A Spanish Village," (portfolio) *U.S. Camera Annual* (1952); Fritz Neugass, "W. Eugene Smith," *Camera*, 31:6/7 (1952); "W. Eugene Smith: an Exclusive Portfolio of His Unpublished Photographs," *Popular Photography*, 31:4 (1952); "W. Eugene Smith," *Camera*, 33:4 (1954); "Portfolio by W. Eugene Smith," *Popular Photography Annual* (1954); "W. Eugene Smith—A Portfolio," *Photography*, 10:6 (1955); Lew Parrella, "W. Eugene Smith," *U.S. Camera Annual* (1956); "Pittsburgh," (portfolio), *Photography Annual* (1959); Emily A. Mack, "The Myth Named Smith," *Camera 35* (Dec/Jan 1960); Bill Pierce, "W. Eugene Smith Teaches Photographic Responsibility," *Popular Photography*, 49:5 (1961); "Gene Smith in Japan," *Popular Photography*, 51:5 (1962); "W. Eugene Smith: 12 Unpublished Photographs," *Photography Annual* (1962); Jean Lattes, "W. Eugene Smith," *Techniques Graphiques*, No. 59 (1965).

EDWARD STEICHEN, born Luxembourg, 1879. Family settled in United States, 1881. Educated in Milwaukee, Wis.; studied art while apprentice to lithographic company there. First photographs, 1896. First exhibition, 2nd Philadelphia Salon, 1899. Participated in exhibition, "The New School of American Photography," Royal Photographic Society, London, 1900. Elected member of "Linked Ring," 1901. First one-man exhibition, La Maison des Artistes, Paris, 1902, included paintings as well as photographs. Founding member of Photo-Secession, 1902. Collaborated with Stieglitz in establishing "The Little Galleries of the Photo-Secession," (later known as "291") New York, 1905. Until First World War assisted in gathering work by modern European artists for exhibitions in the gallery. Joined U.S. Army, 1917; became Commander, Photographic Division, Air Service, Army Expeditionary Forces; retired with rank of Lieutenant Colonel, 1919. Gave up painting to concentrate on photography, 1920. Maintained studio, New York City, advertising and illustration; chief photographer for Condé-Nast Publications, 1923-38. Organized, with Edward Weston, American Section of Deutsche Werkbund exhibition, "Film und Foto," Stuttgart, 1929. One-man exhibition, Baltimore Museum of Art, 1938. Joined U.S. Naval Reserve, 1942; Commanding Officer,

Naval Aviation Photographic Unit; retired with rank of Captain, 1946. Directed exhibitions "Road to Victory," 1942, and "Power in the Pacific," 1945, for Museum of Modern Art. Appointed Director, Department of Photography, Museum of Modern Art, 1947. Retrospective exhibition, American Institute of Architects, 1950. Organized numerous exhibitions, notably "The Family of Man," 1955. Retrospective exhibition, Museum of Modern Art, 1961. Retired, Museum of Modern Art, 1962. Awarded Medal of Freedom by President of United States, 1963. Retrospective exhibition, Bibliothèque Nationale, Paris, 1965. Award of Commandeur de l'Ordre de Merite of Grand Duchy of Luxembourg, 1966.

BOOKS & CATALOGUES: *The Steichen Book*, 1906; *Steichen The Photographer* (Carl Sandburg), 1929; *Walden or Life in the Woods* (Henry David Thoreau), Boston, 1936; *The Blue Ghost*, 1947; *The Family of Man* (prologue by Carl Sandburg), 1955; *Steichen the Photographer* (foreword by Rene d'Harnoncourt), 1961; *A Life in Photography*, 1963.

ARTICLES BY: "British Photography from an American Point of View," *Amateur Photographer*, 32:839 (1900; reprinted in *Camera Notes*, 4:3, 1901); "Ye Fakers," *Camera Work*, No. 1 (1903); "Color Photography," *Camera Work*, No. 22 (1908); "The Fighting Photo-Secession," *Vogue*, (June 15, 1941); "The Living Joy of Pictures," *Holiday*, Vol. 19 (1956); "Photography, Witness and Recorder of Humanity," *Wisconsin Magazine of History*, (Spring 1958); "Problems of Portraiture: Photography," *Art in America*, (Winter 1958); "My Half-Century of Delphinium Breeding," *The Delphinium Society's Year Book for 1959*.

ARTICLES ABOUT: Sidney Allen, "Eduard J. Steichen, Painter-Photographer," *Camera Notes*, 6:1 (1902); Christian Brinton, "Four Portrait-Photographs by Eduard Steichen," *The Critic*, Vol. 42 (1903); Roland Rood, "Eduard J. Steichen . . ." *American Amateur Photographer*, 18:4 (1906); Charles H. Caffin, "Progress in Photography . . ." *Century Magazine*, Vol. 75 (1908); Clare Boothe Brokaw, "Edward Steichen, Photographer," *Vanity Fair*, 38:4 (1932); Matthew Josephson, "Commander With a Camera," *New Yorker*, 20: 16/17 (1944); Beaumont Newhall, "Photography as Art in America," *Perspectives USA*, No. 15 (1956); Lenore Cisney and John Reddy, "Edward Steichen: Dissatisfied Genius," *Saturday Review*, Vol. 40 (Dec 14, 1957); Gilbert Millstein, " 'De

Lawd' of Modern Photography," *New York Times Magazine,* (Mar 22, 1959).

ALFRED STIEGLITZ, born Hoboken, N. J., 1864. Family moved to New York, 1871. Enrolled at Berlin Polytechnic Inst. to study mechanical engineering, 1882. First photographs, 1883. Transferred to course in photo-chemistry with H. W. Vogel until 1886. First photographs sent to competitions, 1886. Continued scientific studies at Univ. of Berlin until 1890. First prize for photographs awarded by P. H. Emerson, *Amateur Photographer* (London) competition, 1887. Returned to New York, 1890; entered photo-engraving business, 1890-95. Joined Society of Amateur Photographers of New York, 1890; began to further cause of creative photography; first extensive use of hand camera for serious photographic work. Began editorial work, *American Amateur Photographer,* 1893-96. Summer in Europe, 1894; first American elected to "Linked Ring." Following merger of Society of Amateur Photographers with N.Y. Camera Club, founded and edited club organ, *Camera Notes,* 1897-1902. One-man exhibition, Camera Club of N. Y., 1899. Organized exhibition of pictorial photography at National Arts Club, N. Y., 1902, of group he named "The Photo-Secession." Founded, edited, and published fifty numbers of quarterly, *Camera Work,* 1903-17. Elected Honorary Fellow of Royal Photographic Society, 1905. Opened, with Edward Steichen, "The Little Galleries of the Photo Secession," (later known as "291") 1905. Showed drawings of Pamela Coleman Smith, 1907. Began to show work of modern European artists, 1908. Organized "International Exhibition of Pictorial Photography," Albright Art Gallery, Buffalo, with other members of Photo-Secession, 1910. One-man exhibition at "291," 1913. "291" closed, 1917. One-man exhibition, Anderson Galleries, 1923. First cloud photographs ("equivalents"), 1923, exhibited at Anderson Galleries, 1924. Married Georgia O'Keeffe, 1924; received Progress Medal from Royal Photographic Society. Director, Intimate Gallery, 1925-29; An American Place, 1929-46. One-man exhibition, An American Place, 1934. Last photographs, 1937. Died New York, 1946.

BOOKS & CATALOGUES: *Picturesque Bits of New York and Other Studies* (portfolio of twelve photogravures, introduction by Walter Woodbury), 1897; *The Camera Club* (catalogue of retrospective exhibition), 1899; *Photography As a Fine Art,* Charles H. Caffin, 1901; *Exhibition of American*

Pictorial Photography at the National Arts Club, (arranged by the Photo-Secession), 1902; *Photo-Secessionism and Its Opponents,* 1910; Anderson Galleries, N.Y. (catalogues of four exhibitions with statements, 1921, 1923, 1924, 1925); Intimate Gallery, N. Y. (catalogues, 1925-1929); *America and Alfred Stieglitz, A Collective Portrait,* (edited by Waldo Frank, *et al.*) 1934; *Alfred Stieglitz: Photographer* (Doris Bry), Washington, D. C., 1958; *The American Earthquake* (Edmund Wilson), 1958; *Alfred Stieglitz* (Dorothy Norman), 1960; *Pioneers of Modern Art in America, The Decade of the Armory Show, 1910-1920* (Lloyd Goodrich), 1963; *Alms for Oblivion* (Edward Dahlberg), Minneapolis, 1964; *Alfred Stieglitz: Photographer* (Doris Bry), Boston, 1965.

ARTICLES BY: "A Natural Background for Out-of-Door Portraiture," and "Night Photography with the Introduction of Life," *American Annual of Photography and Photographic Times Almanac,* (1898); "The Photo-Secession—Its Objects," *Camera Craft,* (Aug 1903); "The Fiasco at St. Louis," *Photographer,* (Aug 1904); "Simplicity in Composition," *The Modern Way in Picture Making,* Rochester, (1905).

ARTICLES ABOUT: Clarence Moore, "Leading Amateurs in Photography," *Cosmopolitan,* (Feb 1892); Theodore Dreiser, "A Master of Photography . . ." *Success,* (June 10, 1899); Sadakichi Hartmann, "Gessler's Hat," *The Camera,* (Nov 1904); "Camera Club Ousts Alfred Stieglitz," *New York Times,* (Feb 14, 1908); "Alfred Stieglitz, Artist, and his Search for the Human Soul," *New York Herald,* (Mar 8, 1908); Djuna Barnes, "Giving Advice on Life and Pictures . . ." *Morning Telegraph,* (Feb 25, 1917); Guido Bruno, "The Passing of '291'," *Pearsons Magazine,* (Mar 1918); Ananda Coomaraswamy, "A Gift from Mr. Alfred Stieglitz," *Museum of Fine Arts Bulletin,* Boston, (April 1924); Elizabeth McCausland, "Stieglitz's 50-Year Fight for Photography Triumphant," *Springfield Sunday Union and Republican,* Springfield, (May 14, 1933); Lewis Mumford, "A Camera and Alfred Stieglitz," *New Yorker,* (Dec 22, 1934); Edward Alden Jewell, "Alfred Stieglitz," *New York Times,* (July 14, 1946); Georgia Englehard, "The Face of Alfred Stieglitz," *Popular Photography,* 19:3 (1946); Georgia O'Keeffe, "Stieglitz: His Pictures Collected Him," *New York Times Magazine,* (Dec 11, 1949); Doris Bry, "The Stieglitz Archive at Yale University," *Yale University Library Gazette,* (April 1951).

PAUL STRAND, born New York City, 1890. Began photography, 1907. Studied under Lewis W. Hine at Ethical Culture School. Through Hine met Alfred Stieglitz, who first encouraged him to consider photography seriously, later gave him his first one-man exhibition at "291," 1916. First abstract photographs, 1915; published in *Camera Work*, 1915-16. First close-up photographs of machine forms, 1917. X-ray technician with U.S. Army, 1918-19. To Nova Scotia, made first landscapes, 1919. Cameraman with group making medical films; made film "Manahatta" with Charles Sheeler (text from Walt Whitman), 1921. Stieglitz exhibited work again, Intimate Gallery, 1929. Photographed architecture, landscapes, portraits in New Mexico, 1930-32. One-man exhibition, An American Place, 1932. Appointed Chief of Photography and Cinematography, Dept. of Fine Arts, Secretariat of Education, Mexico, 1933-34; photographed and supervised production of film "Redes," released in U.S. as "The Wave." Trip to Moscow; met Eisenstein and Dovzhenko, 1935. On return to U.S., associate cameraman, U.S. documentary film "The Plow that Broke the Plains" (directed by Pare Lorentz), 1935; "Heart of Spain," 1937. President of Frontier Films, 1937-42. Co-directed "Native Land" with Leo Hurwitz, 1942. Returned to still photography, 1943-44. One-man exhibition, Museum of Modern Art, 1945. To France to reside, began work on book subsequently published as *La France de Profil*, 1950-51; this project and all future projects made with the help of Hazel Kingsbury Strand. Continued work in Italy, 1952-53; Outer Hebrides, 1954; Egypt, 1959; Roumania, 1960; Morocco, 1962; Ghana, 1963-64.

BOOKS & CATALOGUES: *America and Alfred Stieglitz* (edited by Waldo Frank, et al.), 1934; *Paul Strand: Photographs, 1915-1945* (with Nancy Newhall), 1945; *Mexico* (foreword by Leo Hurwitz, portfolio of 20 gravures), 1940; *Time in New England* (with Nancy Newhall), 1950; *La France de Profil* (text by Claude Roy), Lausanne, 1952; *Un Paese* (text by Cesare Zavattini), Milan, 1955; *Paul Strand* (Frantisek Vrba), Bratislava, 1961; *Tir A' Mhurain: Outer Hebrides* (text by Basil Davidson), London, 1962.

ARTICLES BY: "Photography," *Seven Arts*, (Aug 1917); "Steichen and Commercial Art," *New Republic*, (Feb 1930); "Dorothea Lange and Paul Taylor *An American Exodus*," *Photo Notes*, (Mar/Apr 1940); "Photography to Me," *Minicam Photography*, 8:8 (1945); "Stieglitz: an Appraisal," *Popular Photography*, 21:1 (1947); "Address by Paul Strand," *Photo Notes*, (Jan 1948); "Paul Strand Writes to a Young Photographer," *Photo Notes*, (Fall 1948); "A Platform for Artists," *Photo Notes*, (Fall 1948); "Report of International Congress of Cinema, Perugia, Sept 24-27, 1949," *Photo Notes*, (Spring 1950); "Letters from France and Italy," *Aperture*, 2:2 (1953); "Painting and Photography," (letter), *Photographic Journal*, 103:7 (1963).

ARTICLES ABOUT: Alfred Stieglitz, "Photographs by Paul Strand," *Camera Work*, No. 48 (1916); Harold Clurman, "Photographs by Paul Strand," *Creative Art*, 5:4 (1929); Lola Ridge, "Paul Strand," *Creative Art*, 9:4 (1931); C. Bauer, "Photography: Man Ray and Paul Strand," *Arts Weekly*, (May 7, 1932); Elizabeth McCausland, "Paul Strand," *U.S. Camera*, 1:8 (1940); Walter Rosenblum, "Paul Strand," *American Annual of Photography*, (1952); Nancy Newhall, "Paul Strand," *Modern Photography*, 17:9 (1953); James Thrall Soby, "Two Contemporary Photographers," *Saturday Review*, (Nov 5, 1955); Beaumont Newhall, "Paul Strand, Traveling Photographer," *Art In America*, 50:4 (1962); Milton Brown, "Paul Strand Portfolio," *Photography Year Book* (1963).

EDWARD WESTON, born Highland Park, Illinois, 1886. Made first photographs, 1902. To Tropico, Cal., 1906. Attended Illinois College of Photography, 1908. Opened portrait studio, Tropico, Cal., 1911. Soft focus pictorial photographs receive awards and honors, many one-man exhibitions, 1914-17. Around 1920 re-examined prior work, experimented with semi-abstractions. First used 8 x 10 view camera; met Stieglitz, Strand, Sheeler in N. Y. To Mexico, opened portrait studio with Tina Modotti; met Rivera, Siqueiros, Orozco, Charlot, 1923. Opened studio with son, Brett, San Francisco, 1928. Contributed foreword, and with Steichen, organized American section of Deutsche Werkbund exhibition "Film und Foto," Stuttgart, 1929. Member "Group f64," 1932. First photographer awarded Guggenheim Fellowship, 1937; extended, 1938; traveled throughout California and Western states making some 1500 negatives. Trip through Southern and Eastern states, to photograph for special edition of Whitman's *Leaves of Grass*, terminated by war; returned to Carmel. Major retrospective exhibition, Museum of Modern Art, with monograph *The Photographs of Edward Weston* by Nancy Newhall, 1946. "The Photographer," film photographed and directed by Willard Van Dyke, 1948. Stricken with Parkinson's Disease, 1948; made last photographs at Point Lobos. Retrospective exhibition, Paris, 1950. With aid of Brett, issued *Fiftieth Anniversary Portfolio*, 1952. Died on New Year's Day, 1958, Wildcat Hill, Carmel, Cal. *Daybooks of Edward Weston, Volume I, Mexico*, edited by Nancy Newhall, published by George Eastman House, 1961.

BOOKS & CATALOGUES: *Edward Weston*, (edited by Merle Armitage), 1932; *Photography* (pamphlet), Pasadena, 1934; *Making a Photograph* (by Ansel Adams, preface by Weston), London, 1935; *California and the West* (with Charis Wilson Weston), 1940; *The Cats of Wildcat Hill* (with Charis Wilson Weston), 1947; *Edward Weston: Fifty Photographs* (edited by Merle Armitage), 1947; *My Camera on Point Lobos*, Yosemite, 1950; *The Heritage of Edward Weston* (catalogue), Eugene, Oregon, 1965; *The Day Books of Edward Weston, Vol. II, California*, George Eastman House, 1966.

ARTICLES BY: Statement in *Experimental Cinema*, 1:3 (1931); "What is a Purist?" *Camera Craft*, 46:1 (1939); "Light vs. Lighting," *Camera Craft*, 46:5 (1939); "What is Photographic Beauty?" *Camera Craft*, 46:6 (1939); "Photographic Art," *Encyclopedia Britannica*, Vol. 17 (1941); "A Letter by Edward Weston," *U.S. Camera*, 1:14 (1941); "Portrait Photography," *The Complete Photographer*, 8:45 (1942).

ARTICLES AND FILMS ABOUT: "An Artist Photographer," *The Camera*, (June 1916); Diego Rivera, "Edward Weston y Tina Modotti," *Mexican Folkways*, Vol. 2 (1926); Arthur Miller, "Some Photographs by Edward Weston," *Los Angeles Sunday Times*, (Jan 2, 1927); Ira Martin, "What are the Moderns Thinking About?" *Light and Shade*, (June 1931); Beaumont Newhall, "Edward Weston in Retrospect," *Popular Photography*, 18:3 (1946); Louis Stoumen, "The Naked Eye," (film featuring Weston's work, 1957); Ansel Adams, "Edward Weston," *Infinity*, 13:2 (1964); "Edward Weston, Photographer," *Aperture*, 12:1/2 (1965).

MINOR WHITE, born Minneapolis, Minn., 1908. Graduated, Univ. of Minn., 1933; major in botany, minor in English. Began graduate work in botany; did not complete studies, turned instead to odd jobs and writing poetry. Developed initial understanding of photography making microscope slides in college. To Portland, Oregon; WPA Project photographer, 1938. Ap-

pointed director, La Grande Art Center; began teaching photography, 1940. Drafted 1941; served in South Pacific. Discharged; attended Columbia Univ., courses in art history, 1945. Thesis under Meyer Schapiro on application of Wolfflin's aesthetic concepts to photographs. Served as trainee under Beaumont Newhall at Museum of Modern Art; met Harry Callahan, Alfred Stieglitz, Paul Strand, Edward and Brett Weston. Began teaching at California School of Fine Arts; first of several extended visits with Edward Weston at Point Lobos, 1946. Began to produce series of original print portfolios entitled, "sequences," 1947. Editor and publisher of *Aperture* magazine, 1952-65; currently editor. To Rochester, N. Y.; became assistant to curator, George Eastman House and editor of *Image*, 1953-57. Appointed lecturer, Rochester Inst. of Tech., 1955-64. Teaching activity also includes private and group workshops conducted throughout United States. Retrospective exhibition, "Sequence 13: Return to the Bud," George Eastman House, 1959. Founding member, Society for Photographic Education, 1963. Began teaching photography at Mass. Inst. of Tech., 1965.

BOOKS & CATALOGUES: *Exposure with the Zone System*, 1956; (revised: *Zone System Manual*, 1963); *The Encyclopedia of Photography*, ("Pictorial Photography"), 1964.

ARTICLES BY: "Photography is an Art," *Design*, 49:4 (1947); "Photography in an Art School," *U.S. Camera*, 12:7 (1949); "What is Photography?" *Photo Notes* (Spring 1950); Statement in *U.S. Camera Annual* (1950); "The Right Instant," *American Annual of Photography* (1951); "Your Concepts are Showing," *American Photography*, 45:5 (1951); "How to Find Your Own Approach to Photography," *American Photography*, 45:7 (1951); "How Concepts Differ for Two Cameras," *American Photography*, 45:9 (1951); "Are Your Prints Transparent?" *American Photography*, 45:11 (1951); "Analysis of Five Prints," *Universal Photo Almanac* (1951); "The Use of Space in Designing Pictures," *American Annual of Photography* (1952); "Towards Camera," *Photography* 10:10 (1955); "Happenstance and How It Involves the Photographer," *Photography* 11:10 (1956); "Ansel Adams: Musician to Photographer," *Image*, 6:2 (1957); "On the Strength of a Mirage," *Art in America*, 46:1 (1958); "The Craftsmanship of Feeling," *Infinity*, 9:2 (1960); "Call for Critics," *Infinity*, 9:9 (1960).

ARTICLE ABOUT: "Minor White," *Camera*, 38:8 (1959).